Conversations with
Joe R. Lansdale

Literary Conversations Series
Monika Gehlawat
General Editor

Conversations with Joe R. Lansdale

Edited by Andrew J. Rausch and Mark Slade

University Press of Mississippi / Jackson

The University Press of Mississippi is the scholarly publishing agency of the Mississippi Institutions of Higher Learning: Alcorn State University, Delta State University, Jackson State University, Mississippi State University, Mississippi University for Women, Mississippi Valley State University, University of Mississippi, and University of Southern Mississippi.

www.upress.state.ms.us

The University Press of Mississippi is a member of the Association of University Presses.

First printing 2022
∞

Library of Congress Cataloging-in-Publication Data

Names: Rausch, Andrew J., editor. | Slade, Mark, 1970– editor.
Title: Conversations with Joe R. Lansdale / edited by Andrew J. Rausch and Mark Slade.
Other titles: Literary conversations series.
Description: Jackson : University Press of Mississippi, 2022. |
   Series: Literary conversations series | Includes bibliographical references and index.
Identifiers: LCCN 2022034835 (print) | LCCN 2022034836 (ebook) |
   ISBN 9781496842282 (hardback) | ISBN 9781496842299 (trade paperback) |
   ISBN 9781496842305 (epub) | ISBN 9781496842312 (epub) |
   ISBN 9781496842329 (pdf) | ISBN 9781496842336 (pdf)
Subjects: LCSH: Lansdale, Joe R., 1951—Interviews. | Authors, American—Interviews.
Classification: LCC PS3562.A557 Z46 2022 (print) | LCC PS3562.A557 (ebook) |
   DDC 813/.54—dc23/eng/20220830
LC record available at https://lccn.loc.gov/2022034835
LC ebook record available at https://lccn.loc.gov/2022034836

British Library Cataloging-in-Publication Data available

Books by Joe R. Lansdale

Act of Love, Forest Hill: Zebra Books, 1981.

With Brad Foster, as Mark Simmons, *Molly's Sexual Follies*, New York: Carlyle Communications, 1982.

As Ray Slater. *Texas Night Riders*, New York: Liesure Books, 1983.

As Jack Buchanan, *M.I.A. Hunter: Hanoi Deathgrip*, New York: Jove Books, 1985.

As Jack Buchanan, *M.I.A. Hunter: Mountain Massacre*, New York: Jove Books, 1985.

Best of the West, New York: Doubleday, 1986.

Dead in the West, New York: Space & Time, 1986.

The Magic Wagon, New York: Doubleday, 1986.

The Nightrunners, Arlington Heights: Dark Harvest Books, 1987.

As Jack Buchanan, *M.I.A. Hunter: Saigon Slaughter*, New York: Jove Books, 1987.

The Drive-In, New York: Bantam Spectra, 1988.

Cold in July, New York: Bantam Books, 1989.

On the Far Side of the Cadillac Desert with Dead Folks, Rantoul: Avatar Press, 1989.

With Pat LoBrutto, *Razored Saddles*, Chicago: Dark Harvest, 1989.

By Bizarre Hands, Willimantic: Mark V. Ziesing, 1989.

The Drive-In 2 (Not Just One of Them Sequels), New York: Bantam Spectra, 1989.

The New Frontier, New York: Doubleday, 1989.

With Richard Klaw, *Weird Business*, Austin: Mojo Press, 1989.

Savage Season, Willimantic: Mark V. Ziesing, 1990.

Batman: Captured by the Engines, New York: Warner Books, 1991.

With Karen Lansdale, *Dark at Heart*, Arlington Heights: Dark Harvest Books, 1991.

Stories by Mama Lansdale's Youngest Boy, Eugene: Pulphouse Publishing, 1991.

The Steel Valentine, Eugene: Pulphouse Publishing, 1991.

Batman: Terror on the High Skies, New York: Little, Brown and Company, 1992.

God of the Razor, Hertford: Crossroads Press, 1992.

Steppin' Out, Summer '68, Eugene: Pulphouse Publishing, 1992.

Bestsellers Guaranteed, New York: Ace Books, 1993.

Mister Weed-Eater, Viejo: James Cahill, 1993.

With Thomas W. Knowles, *The West That Was*, New York: Wings Books, 1993.

With Timothy Truman and Rick Magyar, *Lone Ranger & Tonto*, New York: Topps Comics, 1993.

Mucho Mojo, New York: Mysterious Press, 1994.
Electric Gumbo: A Lansdale Reader, New York: Quality Paperback Book Club, 1994.
With Thomas W. Knowles, *Wild West Show!*, New York: Random House Publishing, 1994.
Writer of the Purple Rage, Forest Hill: Cemetery Dance Publications, 1994.
With Timothy Truman, *Jonah Hex: Two-Gun Mojo*, New York: Vertigo/DC Comics, 1994.
With Edgar Rice Burroughs, *Tarzan: The Lost Adventure*, Milwaukie, Dark Horse
    Comics, 1995.
My Dead Dog Bobby, Auburn: Cobblestone Books, 1995.
The Two-Bear Mambo, New York, Mysterious Press, 1995.
The Good, the Bad, and the Indifferent, Burton: Subterranean Press, 1996.
A Fistful of Stories, Burton: Subterranean Press, 1996.
Bad Chili, Austin: Mojo Press, 1997.
The Drive-In: A Double Feature Omnibus, New York: Carroll & Graf, 1997.
Tight Little Stitches in a Dead Man's Back, Eugene: Pulphouse Publishing, 1998.
With Lewis Shiner, *Private Eye Action, As You Like It*, Hertford: Crossroads Press, 1998.
Rumble Tumble, Burton, Subterranean Press, 1998.
My Dead Dog Bobby, Sacramento: Cobblestone Books, 1998.
The Boar, Burton: Subterranean Press, 1998.
Freezer Burn, Hertford, Crossroads Press, 1999.
With Sam Glanzman, *Red Range*, Austin: Mojo Press, 1999.
The Long Ones: Nuthin' But Novellas, Sanford: Necro Publications, 1999.
Something Lumber This Way Comes, Burton: Subterranean Press, 1999.
Triple Feature, Burton: Suberranean Press, 1999.
Waltz of Shadows, Burton: Subterranean Press, 1999.
With Andrew Vachss, *Veil's Visit: A Tale of Hap and Leonard*, Burton, Subterranean
    Press, 1999.
High Cotton: Selected Stories of Joe R. Lansdale, Urbana: Golden Gryphon Press, 2000.
The Big Blow, Burton: Subterranean Press, 2000.
Blood Dance, Burton: Subterranean Press, 2000.
The Bottoms, Burton: Subterranean Press, 2000.
Captains Outrageous, Burton: Subterranean Press, 2001.
Zeppelins West, Burton: Subterranean Press, 2001.
A Fine Dark Line, Burton: Subterranean Press, 2002.
For a Few Stories More, Burton: Subterranean Press, 2002.
Bubba Ho-Tep, San Francisco: Night Shade Book, 2003.
A Little Green Book of Monster Stories, Benson: Borderlands Press, 2003.
Bumper Crop, Urbana: Golden Gryphon Press, 2004.
Mad Dog Summer and Other Stories, Burton: Subterranean Press, 2004.

The Horror Hall of Fame: The Stoker Winners, Forest Hill: Cemetery Dance
Publications, 2004.

Sunset and Sawdust, New York: Knopf Publishing, 2004.

The Drive-In: The Bus Tour, Burton: Subterranean Press, 2005.

Duck Footed, Burton: Subterranean Press, 2005.

The King and Other Stories, Burton: Subterranean Press, 2005.

Night They Missed the Horror Show, Benson: Borderlands Press, 2005.

Flaming London, Burton: Subterranean Press, 2005.

With Scott A. Cupp, Cross Plains Universe: Texans Celebrate Robert E. Howard, Austin:
MonkeyBrain Books, 2006.

Retro Pulp Tales, Burton: Subterranean Press, 2006.

Lost Echoes, Burton: Subterranean Press, 2007.

The God of the Razor, Burton: Subterranean Press, 2007.

The Shadows, Kith and Kin, Burton: Subterranean Press, 2007.

Leather Maiden, New York: Knopf Publishing, 2008.

With Robert E. Howard and Nathan Fox, *Pigeons from Hell*, Milwaukie: Dark Horse
Comics, 2008.

Vanilla Ride, New York: Knopf Publishing, 2009.

Sanctified and Fried Chicken, Austin: University of Texas Press, 2009.

With Keith Lansdale, *Son of Retro Pulp Tales*, Burton: Subterranean Press, 2009.

Unchained and Unhinged, Burton: Subterranean Press, 2009.

With Michael Moorcock, *Under the Warrior Star*, Redmond: Paizo Publishing, 2010.

Christmas with the Dead, Hornsea: PS Publishing, 2010.

The Complete Drive-In, Portland: Underland Press, 2010.

The Best of Joe R. Lansdale, San Francisco: Tachyon Publications, 2010.

Flaming Zeppelins: The Adventures of Ned the Seal, San Francisco: Tachyon
Publications, 2010.

Dread Island, San Diego: IDW Publishing, 2010.

Deadman's Road, Burton: Subterranean Press, 2010.

By Bizarre Hands Rides Again, Modesto: Bloodletting Press, 2010.

The Cases of Dana Roberts, Burton, Subterranean Press, 2011.

With Sam Keith, *30 Days of Night: Night Again*, San Diego: IDW Publishing, 2011.

Devil Red, New York: Knopf Publishing, 2011.

With Peter S. Beagle, *The Urban Fantasy Anthology*, San Francisco: Tachyon
Publications, 2011.

Hyenas: A Hap and Leonard Novella, Burton: Subterranean Press, 2011.

Crucified Dreams, San Francisco: Tachyon Publications, 2011.

All the Earth, Thrown to the Sky, New York: Delacorte Press, 2011.

Edge of Dark Water, New York: Mullholland Books, 2012.

The Horror Hall of Fame: The Bram Stoker Winners, Forest Hill: Cemetery Dance Publications, 2012.

Trapped in the Saturday Matinee, Hornsea: PS Publishing, 2012.

Shadows West, Burton: Subterranean Press, 2012.

With Karen and Keith Lansdale. *In Waders from Mars*, Burton: Subterranean Press, 2012.

Written with a Razor, Hertford: Crossroads Press, 2012.

Dead Aim, Burton: Subterranean Press, 2013.

The Thicket, New York: Mulholland Books, 2013.

With Keith Lansdale and Brian Denham, *Crawling Sky*, San Antonio: Antarctic Press, 2013.

Hot in December, Portland: Dark Regions Press, 2013.

Bleeding Shadows, Burton: Subterranean Press, 2013.

The Ape Man's Brother, Burton: Subterranean Press, 2014.

Black Hat Jack, Burton: Subterranean Press, 2014.

Prisoner 489, Portland: Dark Regions Press, 2014.

With Tim Truman and Sam Glanzman, *Jonah Hex: Shadows West*, New York: DC/Vertigo, 2014.

With Neal Barrett Jr., *A Pair of Aces*, Hertford: Crossroads Press, 2014.

With Daniele Sera, *I Tell You It's Love*, Birmingham: Scary Tales Publications, 2014.

Fender Lizards, Burton: Subterranean Press, 2015.

Paradise Sky, New York: Mulholland Books, 2015.

Christmas Monkeys, Hornsea: PS Publishing, 2015.

Briar Patch Boogie: A Hap and Leonard Novelette, Portland, Gere Donovan Press, 2015.

With Kasey Lansdale, *The Case of the Bleeding Wall*, Burton, Subterranean Press, 2015.

The Tall Grass and Other Stories, Vancouver: Gere Donovan Press, 2015.

With Stephen Mertz, *M.I.A. Hunter Omnibus*, Burton: Subterranean Press, 2015.

With John Lansdale. *Hell's Bounty*, Burton: Subterranean Press, 2016.

Honky Tonk Samurai, New York: Mulholland Books, 2016.

Miracles Ain't What They Used to Be, Oakland: PM Press, 2016.

Dead on the Bones: Pulp on Fire, Burton: Subterranean Press, 2016.

Hap and Leonard, San Francisco: Tachyon Publications, 2016.

Hap and Leonard Ride Again, San Francisco: Tachyon Publications, 2016.

Hoodoo Harry, New York: The Mysterious Book Shop, 2016.

With Mark Allen Miller, *The Steam Man*, Milwaukie: Dark Horse Books, 2016.

Bubba and the Cosmic Blood-Suckers, Burton: Subterranean Press, 2017.

Coco Butternut: A Hap and Leonard Novella, Burton: Subterranean Press, 2017.

Rusty Puppy, New York: Mulholland Books, 2017.

Hap and Leonard: Blood and Lemonade, San Francisco: Tachyon Publications, 2017.

Cold Cotton: A Hap and Leonard Novella, Hertford: Crossroads Press, 2017.

The Big Book of Hap and Leonard, San Francisco: Tachyon, 2018.

Jackrabbit Smile, New York: Mulholland Books, 2018.

With Kasey Lansdale, *Terror Is Our Business: Dana Roberts' Casebook of Horrors*, Herndon: Cutting Block Books, 2018.

Driving to Geronimo's Grave and Other Stories, Burton: Subterranean Books, 2018.

Cosmic Interruptions, Birmingham: Scary Tales Publications, 2018.

With Delilah S. Dawson and Keith Lansdale. *X-Files: Case Files*, San Diego: IDW Publishing, 2018.

The Elephant of Surprise, New York, Mulholland Books, 2019.

Blood in the Gears, Birmingham: Scary Tales Publications, 2019.

The Sky Done Ripped, Burton: Subterranean Press, 2019.

Of Mice and Minestrone: Hap and Leonard: The Early Years, San Francisco: Tachyon Publications, 2020.

Jane Goes North, Burton: Subterranean Press, 2020.

More Better Deals, New York: Mulholland Books, 2020.

Fishing for Dinosaurs and Other Stories, Burton: Subterranean Press, 2020.

With Keith Lansdale, *Big Lizard*, Birmingham: SST Publications, 2020.

Wet Juju, Birmingham: SST Publications, 2020.

Apache Witch, Trieste: Independent Legions Publishing, 2021.

The Hungry Snow, Houston; Death's Head Press, 2021.

In the Ditch, Burton: Subterranean Press, 2021.

Moon Lake, New York: Mulholland Books, 2021.

Radiant Apples, Burton: Subterranean Press, 2021.

Born for Trouble: The Further Adventures of Hap and Leonard, San Francisco: Tachyon Publications, 2021.

Contents

Introduction

No matter what your opinion on Joe R. Lansdale and his work may be, his originality cannot be disputed (nor overstated). We state this not only in regards to the stories he writes, but also in the way he fashions them and the way he has achieved all that he has at this point in his career. Like Frank Sinatra, he did it (and continues to do it) his way. In the documentary *All Hail the Popcorn King* (Hansi Oppenheimer, 2019) Andrew J. Rausch asserts that Lansdale is a genre unto himself. This statement is absolutely correct, and Lansdale himself is well aware of the fact. In his introduction to the collection *Fishing for Dinosaurs and Other Stories*, he writes, "It's no secret that I like to write a variety of stories in a variety of genres, and my favorite of those is the Lansdale genre" (7).

Lansdale's statement is significant for multiple reasons. It is important because he, like most published authors, was advised by countless agents and publishers to confine himself to a single literary genre. The thinking behind this stock advice is that potential readers will come to recognize the type of book they are seeing simply by reading the author's name on the cover. In the publishing industry, authors are packaged and presented as brand names for the genres in which they work. For instance, readers know immediately that a book with Nicholas Sparks's name on the cover will most likely be a romance. This is the same with Dean Koontz (horror), Stephen King (horror), J. K. Rowling (fantasy), and John Grisham (legal thriller) in their respective genres. (Most of those authors have worked outside the single genre, but they each published enough work within that genre to become forever linked with it.) Despite the insistence of others that he pick a single genre, Lansdale refused, choosing to work in whatever genre tickled his fancy at any given point in time.

As he explained on a September 7, 2020, episode of *The Movie Crypt* podcast:

> I want to be a writer who's doing [things that are] why I became a writer in the first place, and that doing being having fun. Because when I was a kid I wanted

to tell stories. I loved stories. I wanted to be excited. I wanted to feel that energy that went through me from reading a good story or seeing a good film or reading a good novel or a great comic book. Comic books were the original inspiration for me, but all of that stuff, I wanna maintain it. I've also been inspired by a lot of literary writers, literary novels, and things of that nature. I want all of it to come together to be something I'm excited about doing, or else why the hell do this? I could have had a career in something else; banking or something. But I chose this because it was fun and I don't wanna turn it into a misery, even though I have turned it into a job. It's how I make a living, I make a good living at it, but if I'm going to do that every day—I'm sixty-nine this year—I wanna have the same enthusiasm I had when I started. And I still do, and I hope to maintain that.

Maintaining his love and enthusiasm for the craft by alternating genres and only writing things he's passionate about, Lansdale's infectious sense of fun and joy spills out on to the pages. It also keeps him from falling into the trap of repetition that so many authors ultimately fall victim to.

Beyond the freshness he's maintained in his work, it should be noted that Lansdale's ignoring cautionary advice and the unspoken literary rules makes his success even more impressive. Despite having always possessed the necessary talent for success, he subjected himself to more hurdles than many of his contemporaries faced. Because he chose to leap from genre to genre like a frog maneuvering from one lily pad to the next, he's had to build his fan base little by little, picking up readers from each genre he's worked in. Although Lansdale has published steadily since his first novel, *Act of Love* debuted in 1981, and despite the fact that his work has continuously been qualitative and has received critical acclaim, he is still not a household name on par with Grisham, King, or Rowling. Through decades of perseverance and consistency, Lansdale has developed a sizable following and is highly respected in the field. One aspect of his fan base that is impressive and fairly unique is the height of their loyalty. As such, a great many of them will eagerly follow him into any genre in which he chooses to write. This explains the number of readers who have read Lansdale works as varied as his self-proclaimed "weird Westerns" like *Dead in the West*, horror such as *The Nightrunners*, hardboiled crime novels such as *Cold in July*, the comedic road novel *Jane Goes North*, the literary *To Kill a Mockingbird* homage *The Bottoms*, the bizarro (for lack of a better term as none fits snugly) novel *The Drive-In*, historical fiction such as *Paradise Sky*, and the outlandish "Ned the Seal" series. And these examples are only the tip of the iceberg of the broad landscape of the Lansdale *oeuvre*.

So what, exactly, is the "Lansdale genre"? One of the more apparent elements is his daring, unflinching cross-pollination of genres. The introduction to Lansdale's 2010 collection *Dead Man's Road* is telling. There he writes about his lifelong passion for comics, movies, novels, and storytelling. This is noteworthy for a number of reasons. First, Lansdale is, above all else, a storyteller in the purest sense of the word. He is akin to the mischievous old man who sits in the same seat in the local barber shop each day spinning outlandish yarns with the greatest of ease, utilizing the precise panache, creativity, and timing required to consistently entertain his audience. (Hearing Lansdale address a public audience at a book reading or as part of a literary panel is as great a treat as reading one of his books because he is every bit as talented and entertaining an orator as he is a scribe.)

The second key aspect of Lansdale's *Dead Man's Road* confession is his unabashed love of comics. He writes, "I was especially enraptured by comics because they didn't bother with genre at all. They could be about anything, and they had no problem mixing Westerns and science fiction, fantasy and horror, and even romance." While Lansdale's work reflects elements of all the different mediums he mentions, it is the cross pollination of genres he had first encountered through comics (particularly in his earlier work) that immediately set him apart from more conventional authors. Obviously talent plays an enormous role in this as well, and Lansdale is a truly gifted writer. But many of his most beloved works, such as *The Drive-In, Dead in the West, Bubba Ho-Tep,* and *The Nightrunners* (just to name a few) are blatant mashups of seemingly different genres. Despite these wild combinations, his stories always feel genuine and organic; they are not forced marriages of mismatched concepts, themes, and tones.

While the combination of genres and influences is a significant aspect of the "Lansdale genre," it is not the single most important aspect. The key attribute to Lansdale's work is his distinct authorial voice, which is the primary reason readers return to his works again and again, no matter the genre. Like Kurt Vonnegut or Mark Twain, Lansdale's work is equal parts laugh-out-loud humor and biting social commentary. And like Vonnegut and Twain, Lansdale delivers it without pretension. While Lansdale, like any writer, would like his writings to be enjoyed and appreciated, this is not his primary concern. Lansdale's most famous and oft-repeated piece of writing advice is to "write like everyone you know is dead," and this is precisely what he does; he creates works that make him happy as an artist without regard for what may or may not please readers, editors, and publishers. It should also be noted that one element that stands out as a distinctive characteristic of

Lansdale's work and authorial voice is his continuous display of East Texas representation, from story locale to regional colloquialisms and dialect.

In terms of social commentary, one easily identifiable theme present in much of his work is his preoccupation with racial and sexual politics and his firm and unabashed belief in equality. A great many of his stories address these themes, and his personal views on these subjects is immediately apparent. While it is a given that literary characters are simply that—*characters*, and as such should not be seen as representations of their authors, Lansdale is quick to identify Hap Collins, one of the titular characters from his wildly popular Hap and Leonard series, as being modeled after himself. Thus, Hap's outspoken liberal views on (and actions regarding) race and sexual politics mirror those voiced by Lansdale in interviews and in his nonfiction pieces.

Lansdale's Hap and Leonard novels are a point of focus in the discussion of his writings on racial and sexual politics as his character Leonard Pine is both homosexual and Black. In a 2019 interview, Lansdale tells filmmaker/journalist Hansi Oppenheimer: "[N]inety-nine percent of my response [to Hap and Leonard] was positive right from the first. People loved them. I've had people actually tell me 'I've changed my views on gays' or 'I've changed my views on race.' " And I'm like, really? I feel like it's such a minor thing, and for it to have a major impact means a lot."[1] This section of the interview is further significant because it goes well beyond Lansdale's tackling of racism and homophobia. He continues:

> I get things from people—not just on the Hap and Leonard books, but books in general—and it's what makes you realize that it's worth doing for a lot of reasons. I can't tell you how many people have told me, "You know, I was going through such a bad time and I found this series and I just fell in love with these characters. They helped me get through my hospital time or my parents being ill or fighting cancer . . . ." You know, things that you would never think about when you're writing the novels. I had one guy that said, "I had gone to prison. I had made a fool out of myself. And I picked up this book of yours—this wasn't even a Hap and Leonard, it was one of the others—" and it just sort of rejuvenated me." And to think that fiction can do that. To think that it can have that impact. That's kind of humbling.[2]

Lansdale is fond of sharing these reader experiences, but he doesn't brag about it. His sharing them does not come from ego. In fact, one almost gets the feeling that he's more shocked by these reader reactions than anyone else is. Their reactions are a point of pride for him. They are a large part of why he writes (although one gets the distinct feeling that Lansdale is a writer who writes because he feels he *has* to and could not imagine himself ever not writing).

In attempting to document Lansdale's awards and award nominations for this volume—a duty we could not fully accomplish—we learned something telling about him; he has so little concern for awards and honors that he's not completely sure exactly what awards he's won, what books or stories he's received them for, or even where many of the physical awards themselves are currently located. With his boundless talent and countless accomplishments, Lansdale is a man one might expect to carry a healthy amount of ego, and yet he seemingly has none (or very little). He is a writer who takes far more pride in a job well done—be that his writing, martial arts, or raising his children with his wife, Karen—than he does trophies, plaques, or platitudes. Lansdale's proud astonishment was recently on display at the Austin, Texas, unveiling of the documentary *All Hail the Popcorn King.* He seemed genuinely surprised that anyone might be interested in making or watching a documentary about his life and work. He is a man who appears absolutely gobsmacked by all the praise and glory heaped upon him. He is fond of quoting his friend, the late actor Bill Paxton, as saying all he ever wanted was a seat at the table. Now that he has secured that seat, Lansdale seems genuinely humbled and appreciative to be there and perhaps even slightly distrusting of it.

A great many authors look up to him as the de facto Patron Saint of Writers, as he has consistently gone above and beyond to advocate for others. He is mindful of a time when he himself was a young writer struggling to find his way in the industry, and as such he has helped and advised many young writers. In 1985, he and his wife Karen, along with authors Dean Koontz and Robert McCammon established the organization known today as the Horror Writers Association. This is a nonprofit organization created to promote the interests of horror and dark fantasy authors.

Lansdale's work has paved the road for the writers who have read and followed him. By channeling the genre-bending comics discussed previously, he has helped normalize the mixing of literary genres. Through his own writing, Lansdale has proven that such works can be successful, making publishing houses less leery of publishing such works. Lansdale has also set an example for a new generation of writers who might wish to set the rules for their own careers. In addition, he has repeatedly pulled off the impressive feat of straddling the line between works that would be considered highbrow literature and those that would be considered lowbrow; he writes stories and novels that arguably fall into each of these categories, as well as works that some-how fit into both simultaneously.

His work has been adapted to film and television, and he has found suc-cess in nearly every medium. He has published more than one hundred books, which doesn't include individual issues of the many comic books he's writ-ten. (The only comics included in this volume's bibliography are graphic novels and trade paperback collections.) Lansdale has penned short stories, children's books, young adult novels, very adult novels (one of his earliest full-length writing gigs was the erotic novel *Molly's Sexual Follies* under the pseudonym Mark Simmons), novelettes, novellas, chapbooks, comics, graphic novels, screenplays, teleplays, collections, and others. Not one to rest on his laurels, Lansdale's professional aspirations do not stop there; in an interview included in this collection ("Champion Joe on Screen: Joe R. Lansdale Dis-cusses *Love, Death & Robots, Creepshow, Hap and Leonard,* and the Possibility He'll Direct"), he discusses his hopes to direct a motion picture one day soon. Even though he has only just begun to truly reach the level of popularity his work has always deserved, he is an author we felt was truly deserving of inclu-sion in the University Press of Mississippi's "Conversations" series.

Per the guidelines of the Conversations with Authors series, the interviews in this collection are unedited from their original publications and ordered chronologically. Although there is naturally some repetition due to the nature of the collection, there are enough nuances within these instances to vali-date the appearance of every piece reprinted here.

When we first embarked on this endeavor, it was our belief that compil-ing this book would be an easy task. We quickly realized we were wrong. Locating quality interviews from each period of Lansdale's career that cov-ered the most prominent topics needing addressed was difficult. Then, when we would locate the appropriate interviews, we would often find difficulty in tracking down the authors, or, even worse, we would learn that they were dead. Once appropriate interviews were discovered and we had the permis-sions to reprint them, they would (in most cases) have to be retyped. As a result of all this, the book became a labor of love that took two full years to complete.

It should be noted that there are interviews regarding Lansdale's atheism and his martial arts studies included here. Although they are not specifically about his writing, they help paint a fuller picture of him and are aspects of his life that play a significant role in his work.

This book could not have been completed without the help of Joe R. Lans-dale himself. He was invaluable in pointing us towards certain interviews and providing background information for the book's chronology and bibliography. Katie Salzmann, Stephanie J. Forsythe, and Steve Davis at the Alkek Library at Texas State University were also invaluable in assisting us in locating the *Gladewater Mirror* and *Daily Sentinel* articles from the Joe Lansdale papers housed in the library's Wittliff Collections. Many other individuals played substantial roles in the completion of this book, including our editors, Katie Keene and Mary Heath. Stanley Wiater provided a good deal of help during the completion of this book. Author James Grady also went above and beyond (at the behest of Mr. Lansdale himself) in conducting a special interview about Lansdale's martial arts studies expressly for this book. We'd also like to thank Mick Garris for allowing us to print the transcript of his wonderful interview with Lansdale and director Don Coscarelli from his *Post Mortem* podcast. Thank you to Nancy Bueller for transcribing one of the interviews. Beyond that, we'd like to thank every writer and publication who allowed us to reprint their interviews and articles in this collection.

AJR
MS

Notes

1. Oppenheimer, Hansi, "Squee Presents! A Conversation with Joe R. Lansdale," 2019 (YouTube).
2. Hansi, "Squee Presents!"

Chronology

1951 Joe Richard Lansdale, the youngest child of Alcebee "Buddy" Lansdale, a mechanic, and O'Reta Wood Lansdale, is born on 28 October in Gladewater, Texas. He has one older brother, John Leonard Lansdale.

1956 The Lansdale family leaves Gladewater and moves to Mount Enterprise.

1959 His father begins teaching him boxing, wrestling, and self-defense moves.

1961 Lansdale moves back to Gladewater during fifth grade school year.

1965 He begins to study Judo.

1969 Lansdale graduates from Gladewater High School.

1970 He marries Cassie Ellis in the summer (date unknown). Lansdale enrolls at Tyler Community College in Tyler, Texas, and brings a class action suit (Lansdale, et al., v. Tyler Junior College) for the college's rule prohibiting male students from having long hair or beards. United States District Judge William Wayne Justice declared that the rule was unconstitutional. The college then appealed, contending that long-haired students were prone to violence. The 5th US Circuit Court of Appeals would ultimately affirm Judge Justice's ruling two years later.

1971 Lansdale leaves Tyler Community College.

1972 He divorces Cassie Ellis. He is drafted to go to Vietnam but refuses induction and is ultimately deemed unfit for duty; he enrolls at Stephen F. Austin State University in Nacogdoches, Texas. He attends various courses on and off there through 1977, ending up with approximately sixty hours.

1973 Lansdale co-writes an agricultural article with his mother (and credited to his mother, O'Reta Lansdale), which becomes his first published writing. It is accepted by *Farm Journal* but will not appear in print until the following year. He meets Karen Morton and then marries her on 25 August.

1978	His first piece of published fiction, "The Full Count," appears in the June issue of *Mike Shayne Mystery Magazine*.
1981	Zebra Books publishes Lansdale's first novel, *Act of Love*.
1982	His first child, a son, Keith Jordan Lansdale is born 28 April. Using the pseudonym Mark Simmons, Lansdale writes and publishes an erotic novel with Brad Foster titled *Molly's Sexual Follies*.
1983	A Western novel, *Texas Night Riders*, written under the pseudonym Ray Slater is published.
1985	Lansdale assists his wife, Karen, and writers Robert McCammon and Dean Koontz, in establishing HOWL (Horror/Occult Writers League) with the mission of encouraging public interest in and fostering an appreciation of quality horror and dark fantasy literature. The group will be formally incorporated two years later, changing its name to the Horror Writers Association (HWA). *Hanoi Deathgrip* and *Mountain Massacre*, two entries in the men's adventure series M.I.A. Hunter (written under the pseudonym Jack Buchanan) are published.
1986	A second child, a daughter, Kasey JoAnn Lansdale, is born 24 June. Lansdale is nominated for a World Fantasy Award for "Tight Little Stitches in a Dead Man's Back" (from the anthology *Nukes* edited by John Maclay. He returns to the Western genre three times, publishing two novels, *Dead in the West* and *The Magic Wagon*, and editing an anthology of short stories titled *Best of the West*.
1987	The noir/horror hybrid novel, *The Nightrunners* is published. *Saigon Slaughter*, a third M.I.A. Hunter novel (again under the pseudonym Jack Buchanan) is published. Lansdale is nominated for World Fantasy Convention Award for Short Fiction for "Tight Little Stitches in a Dead Man's Back."
1988	The horror/fantasy novel, *The Drive-In* is published. The short story "Night They Missed the Horror Show" is first published in the anthology *Silver Scream* (edited by David J. Schow). Lansdale wins Bram Stoker Award for Short Fiction for "Night They Missed the Horror Show," and he is also nominated for Novel for *The Drive-In*. *The Drive-In* is nominated in the category of Novel by the World Fantasy Awards.
1989	The crime novel *Cold in July* is published. *The Drive-In 2 (Not Just One of Them Sequels)* is published. The short story collection *By Bizarre Hands* is published. Two Lansdale-edited anthologies,

The New Frontier and *Razored Saddles* (coedited by Pat LoBrutto) are published. The short story "Subway Jack" is published in *The Further Adventures of Batman* (edited by Martin H. Greenberg). The short story "The Joker's Trick or Treat" is published in *The Further Adventures of The Joker* (edited by Martin H. Greenberg). The graphic novel *Weird Business*, coedited with Richard Klaw is published. The short story "On the Far Side of the Cadillac Desert with Dead Folks" is first published in the anthology *Book of the Dead* (edited by John Skipp). It is then released as a standalone chapbook. Lansdale wins the Bram Stoker Award for Long Fiction for "On the Far Side of the Cadillac Desert with Dead Folks." He is nominated for Fiction Collection for *By Bizarre Hands*. He is nominated for World Fantasy Convention Award for Novel for *The Drive-In* and Short Fiction for "Night They Missed the Horror Show." "Night They Missed the Horror Show" is also nominated for a British Fantasy Award in the category Short Fiction.

1990   The first Hap and Leonard novel, *Savage Season* is published. Lansdale wins the Bram Stoker Award for Long Fiction for *On the Far Side of the Cadillac Desert with Dead Folks*. He receives a second Bram Stoker nomination in the category of Novel for *Savage Season*. Lansdale wins the British Fantasy Award for Best Short Story for *On the Far Side of the Cadillac Desert with Dead Folks*. He is nominated for World Fantasy Convention Award for Novella for *On the Far Side of the Cadillac Desert with Dead Folks*. He is also nominated for Anthology (with Pat LoBrutto) for *Razored Saddles* and Collection for *By Bizarre Hands*. Lansdale wins the American Horror Award for *On the Far Side of the Cadillac Desert with Dead Folks* for Novelette.

1991   A Batman novel, *Captured by the Engines*, is published. A short story collection, *Stories by Mama Lansdale's Youngest Boy* is published. The Lansdale-edited (with wife, Karen Lansdale) anthology *Dark at Heart* is published. The chapbook *The Steel Valentine* is published. Lansdale is nominated for the Bram Stoker Award for Short Fiction for "Love Doll: A Fable."

1992   A young adult Batman novel, *Terror on the High Skies* is published. Two chapbooks, *God of the Razor* and *Steppin' Out, Summer '68* are published. "Perchance to Dream," an episode of *Batman: The Animated Series* written by Lansdale, airs. He wins the Bram Stoker

Award for Long Fiction for *The Events Concerning a Nude Fold-Out Found in a Harlequin Romance* (shares the award with Steve Bissette's *Aliens: Tribes*).

1993   The collection of short stories *Bestsellers Guaranteed* is published. The Lansdale-edited book (coedited by Thomas H. Knowles) *The West That Was: A Lively and Authoritative Story and Picture Album* is published. The comic book series and trade paperback, *Lone Ranger & Tonto*, featuring artwork by Tim Truman and Rick Magyar is published. The five-issue comic series and trade paperback *Jonah Hex: Two Gun Mojo*, featuring artwork by Tim Truman is published. Lansdale adapts Andrew Vachss's short story "Drive-By" for issue number five of the comic *Andrew Vachss: Hard Looks*. "Read My Lips," an episode of *Batman: The Animated Series* written by Lansdale, airs. The novella *Dead in the West* is adapted by Neal Barrett Jr. for a graphic novel of the same title. Lansdale wins the Bram Stoker Award for Other Media for *Jonah Hex: Two-Gun Mojo*.

1994   The second Hap and Leonard novel *Mucho Mojo* is published and is named a *New York Times* Notable Book of the Year. Two short story collections, *Electric Gumbo: A Lansdale Reader* and *Writer of the Purple Rage*, are published. The Lansdale-edited book (coedited by Thomas W. Knowles) *Wild West Show!* is published. The novella *Bubba Ho-Tep* is first published in the anthology *The King Is Dead: Tales of Elvis Post-Mortem* (edited by Paul M. Sammon). The five-issue comic series *Jonah Hex: Riders of the Worm and Such*, featuring artwork by Tim Truman is published. Lansdale adapts his story "Grease Trap" for the anthology comic *Creature Features*. Several stories are adapted by Neal Barrett Jr. and Jerry Prosser for the three-issue comic series *By Bizarre Hands*. He is nominated for the Bram Stoker Award for Long Fiction for *Bubba Ho-Tep* and Fiction Collection for *Writer of the Purple Rage*. He wins International Horror Guild Award in the category Graphic Novel for *Jonah Hex: Two-Gun Mojo*.

1995   *Tarzan: The Lost Adventure*, based on an incomplete fragment of a Tarzan novel written by Edgar Rice Burroughs, is published. The third Hap and Leonard novel, *The Two-Bear Mambo*, is published. "Showdown," a Lansdale-written episode of *Batman: The Animated Series*, airs.

1996   A collection of early previously unpublished stories titled *The Good, the Bad, and the Indifferent* is published. The short story collection *A Fistful of Stories* is published. The four-issue comic series *Blood and Shadows*, featuring art by Mark A. Nelson, is published. He cowrites "Shootout at Ice Flats" (with Neal Barrett Jr.) for *Supergirl Annual* number one. Several stories are adapted by a variety of writers for the one-shot comic *Atomic Chili: The Illustrated Joe R. Lansdale*. The project is immediately nominated by the International Horror Guild Awards in the category Grapic Story. He establishes the self-defense system Shen Chuan Martial Science.

1997   The fourth Hap and Leonard novel *Bad Chili* is published. A limited-edition collection containing three short stories titled *Triple Feature* is published. The novella *The Big Blow* is first published in the anthology *Revelations* (edited by Douglas E. Winter). "Identity Crisis," a Lansdale-conceived episode of *Superman: The Animated Series*, airs. Lansdale writes "The Elopement" for issue number two of the comic *Weird War Tales*. He wins the Bram Stoker Award for Long Fiction for *The Big Blow*.

1998   The short story "The Companion" (cowritten by his children, Keith and Kasey Lansdale) is published in the anthology *Great Writers and Kids Write Spooky Stories* (edited by Martin H. Greenberg). The fifth Hap and Leonard novel, *Rumble Tumble* is published. The novel *The Boar* is published. A collection of crime stories co-written with Lewis Shiner titled *Private Eye Action, As You Like It* is published. Two chapbooks with Pulphouse Press, *Tight Little Stiches in a Dead Man's Back* and *My Dead Dog Bobby* are published. The faux children's story chapbook *My Dead Dog Bobby* featuring artwork by Joe Vigil is published. He writes issue number eight of the comic book *The Spirit: The New Adventures*, featuring artwork by John Lucas. He adapts (with his son Keith Lansdale) his own story "Dog, Cat, and Baby" for issue number one of the comic *Crowquill*. He cowrites "The Initiation" (with Rick Klaw) for issue number four of the comic *Gangland*. "Critters," a Lansdale-written episode of *The New Batman Adventures*, airs.

1999   The novel *Freezer Burn* is published. The Western-themed graphic novel *Red Range*, featuring artwork by Sam Glanzman, is published. *Red Range* is then nominated by the International Horror Guild Awards in the category Graphic Novel. The novella collection *The Long Ones: Nuthin' But Novellas* is published. The novel *Waltz of Shadows*, which is the first volume in the "Lost Lansdale" series, is published. The children's book titled *Something Lumber*

This Way Comes, which is the second volume in the "Lost Lansdale" series, is published. A collection of Hap and Leonard short stories titled *Veil's Visit*, which features the titular story cowritten by Andrew Vachss, is published. The three-issue comic series *Jonah Hex: Shadows West*, featuring artwork by Tim Truman, is published. Writes "Betrothed" for issue number five of the comic series *Flinch*. He wins the Bram Stoker Award for Long Fiction for *Mad Dog Summer* (and shares the award with Brian A. Hopkins for *Five Days in April*). Also, he is nominated for Works for Young Readers for *Something Lumber This Way Comes* and Illustrated Narrative for *Jonah Hex: Shadows West* #1.

2000   The novel *The Bottoms* is published. It receives the Mystery Writers of America's Edgar Award for Best Novel and is also named a *New York Times* Notable Book of the Year. It receives the Herodotus Award for Best Historical Novel. It is nominated for a Dashiell Hammett Award for Best Novel and the Mystery Readers International's Macavity Awards' Best Mystery Novel. The short story collection *High Cotton: Selected Stories of Joe R. Lansdale* is published. *The Big Blow* is published as a standalone book for the first time. The novella *Blood Dance*, which is the third volume in the "Lost Lansdale" series, is published. He is nominated for two Bram Stoker Awards for Illustrated Narrative for "Red Romance" and *Jonah Hex: Shadows West* #1. Writes "The Split" for issue number three of the comic series *Strange Adventures*. Lansdale writes "Red Romance" for issue number eleven and "Brer Hoodoo" for issue number thirteen of the comic series *Flinch*. "Red Romance" is nominated for the Bram Stoker Award for Illustrated Narrative.

2001   The sixth Hap and Leonard novel, *Captains Outrageous* is published. The first "Ned the Seal" novella *Zeppelins West* is published. He writes "Devil's Sombrero" for issue number two of *Weird Western Tales*. The story "Bob the Dinosaur Goes to Disneyland" is adapted by Rick Klaw for a graphic novel of the same title. *The Bottoms* wins the Edgar Award for Mystery Novel.

2002   The novel *A Fine Dark Line* is published. The short story collection *For a Few Stories More*, which is the fourth volume in the "Lost Lansdale" series, is published. *Bubba Ho-Tep*, the Don Coscarelli scripted and directed adaptation of Lansdale's novella, is released.

2003   The short story collection *A Little Green Book of Monster Stories* is published as part of Borderlands Press's "Little Book" series. He adapts his own story "On the Far Side of the Cadillac Desert with Dead Folks" for the three-issue comic *Lansdale & Truman's Dead Folks*. The novella *The Drive-In* is adapted by Christopher Golden for four-issue comic series of the same title.

2004   The novel *Sunset and Sawdust* is published. *Bubba Ho-Tep* is published as a standalone book for the first time. Two short story collections, *Bumper Crop* and *Mad Dog Summer and Other Stories*, are published. Lansdale writes the three-issue comic series and trade paperback *On the Far Side with Dead Folks*. The Lansdale-edited collection *The Horror Hall of Fame: The Stoker Winners* is published.

2005   The first episode of Showtime's Masters of Horror series debuts. It is an adaptation of Lansdale's "Incident On and Off a Mountain Road" and is scripted and directed by Don Coscarelli. Lansdale writes four issues of the *Masters of Horror* comic book series. The story "Incident On and Off a Mountain Road" is adapted by Chris Ryall for the series as well. The four-issue graphic novel series and trade paperback of *The Drive-In* are published. The second "Ned the Seal" novella, *Flaming London*, is published. The third book in the "Drive-In" series, *The Drive-In: The Bus Tour*, is published. The short story collection *The King and Other Stories* is published. The chapbook *Duck Footed* is published. *Mad Dog Summer and Other Stories* is nominated for a World Fantasy Award in the Collection category.

2006   The Lansdale-edited the anthology *Cross Plains Universe: Texans Celebrate Robert E. Howard* (coedited by Scott A. Cupp) is published. Lansdale writes the five-issue comic series *Conan and the Songs of the Dead*, featuring artwork by Tim Truman. He writes "Steam Rider: The Steam-Powered Heart" for issue number twenty of the comic book series *Amazing Fantasy*. Lansdale writes "Mice and Money" for issue number five of the comic series *Marvel Romance Redux*. He writes "Gunhawk: Midnight Gun" for the one-shot comic *Strange Westerns Starring the Black Rider*. The Lansdale-edited anthology *Retro Pulp Tales* is published. Bill Sheehan and William Schafer coedit an anthology titled Joe R. Lansdale's *Lords of the Razor*, which features stories about Lansdale's character "The God of the Razor." The collection features Lansdale's short story "The God of the Razor" and a Lansdale novella titled *King of Shadows*. *The Drive-In 2* is adapted by Neal Barrett Jr. for four-issue comic series of the same title. Lansdale wins the Bram Stoker Award for Edited Anthology for *Retro Pulp Tales* (and shares the award with John Skipp for *Mondo Zombie*).

2007   The novel *Lost Echoes* is published. A collection of short stories titled *The God of the Razor* is published. A collection of short stories titled *The Shadows, Kith and Kin* is published and is nominated for the World Fantasy Award for Collection. He receives two World Fantasy Award nominations in the category of Anthology, one with Scott A. Cupp for *Cross Plains Universe: Texans Celebrate Robert E. Howard* and a second for *Retro Pulp Tales*. He receives the World Horror Convention Grand Master Award.

2008   The novel *Leather Maiden* is published. Lansdale adapts Robert E. Howard's short story "Pigeons from Hell" into a four-issue comic book of the same title featuring artwork by Nathan Fox and Dave Stewart. He writes "The War at Home" for issues one through three of the comic series *Zombie Tales*. He writes or co-writes three stories for issues six, seven, and eight of the comic series *Tales from the Crypt*. These are "A Ripping Good Time" (co-written with brother, John Lansdale), "Moonlight Sonata," and "Virtual Hoodoo" (again cowritten with John Lansdale). He writes issue number thirty-two of the comic *Marvel Adventures: Fantastic Four*.

2009   The seventh Hap and Leonard novel, *Vanilla Ride* is published. The short story collection *Sanctified and Fried Chicken* is published. A collection of short fiction and essays titled *Unchained and Unhinged* (featuring artwork by Glenn Chadbourne) is released. The Lansdale-edited (with son, Keith Lansdale) anthology *Son of Retro Pulp Tales* is published.

2010   The Western-themed collection *Deadman's Road* is published. The third installment in the "Ned the Seal" series, *Flaming Zeppelins: The Adventures of Ned the Seal*, is published. The short story collections *The Best of Joe R. Lansdale* and *By Bizarre Hands Rides Again* are published. *Dread Island* is published as part of IDW's "Classics Mutilated" series. The Michael Moorcock cowritten "double feature" novella collection *Sojan the Swordsman/Under the Warrior Star* is published. The chapbook *Christmas with the Dead* is published. The Lansdale cowritten five-episode series *Jonah Hex: Motion Comics* airs. Writes the three-issue comic series (with brother, John Lansdale) *Yours Truly, Jack the Ripper* (based on the story by Robert Bloch), featuring artwork by Kevin Colden. He wins the Bram Stoker Award for Short Fiction for "The Folding Man."

2011   The eighth Hap and Leonard novel, *Devil Red*, is published. *Hyenas: A Hap and Leonard Novella* is published. The Young Adult novel *All the Earth, Thrown to the Sky* is published. The Lansdale-edited (coedited by Peter S. Beagle) anthology *The Urban Fantasy Anthology* is published. The short story collection *Crucified Dreams* is published. Lansdale writes the four-issue comic book sequel to Steve Niles' *30 Days of Night* titled *30 Days of Night: Night, Again*, which features artwork by Sam Kieth. He writes the three-issue comic book series *That Hell-Bound Train* (based on the story by Robert Bloch), featuring artwork by Dave Wachter. Lansdale writes the four-issue comic book series *H. P. Lovecraft's The Dunwich Horror*, featuring artwork by Peter Bergting. The chapbook *The Cases of Dana Roberts* is published. He wins the Rick Hautala Bram Stoker Award for Lifetime Achievement. Receives the SUGARPRIZE at the Sugar Pop Festival for his body of work. He receives the Grinzane Cavour Prize for Literature for his body of work and is inducted into the United States Martial Arts Hall of Fame.

2012   The novel *Edge of Dark Water* is published and listed as Booklist Editor's Choice for Adult Books for Young Adults. The 52-page children's book (cowritten by his wife and son, Karen and Keith Lansdale) *In Waders from Mars* is published. The chapbook *The Ape Man's Brother*, featuring artwork by Ken Laager, is published. The Lansdale-edited anthology *The Horror Hall of Fame: The Bram Stoker Winners* is published. The short story collection *Trapped in the Saturday Matinee*, which features twenty-one stories from earlier in his career, is published. The short story collection *Shadows West* (cowritten by his brother, John Lansdale) is published. Terrill Lee Lankford directs Lansdale and son Keith Lansdale's screenplay adaptation for the straight-to-DVD film *Christmas with the Dead*. Lansdale is inducted into the Texas Literary Hall of Fame on 19 October.

2013   The novel *The Thicket* is published and is voted one of the best historical novels by *Library Journal*. The Hap and Leonard novella *Dead Aim* is published. The graphic novel *Crawling Sky* (cowritten by his son, Keith Lansdale) is published. Featuring artwork by

Brian Denham. The 488-page collection *Bleeding Shadows*, which includes short stories, poems, and novellas, is published.

2014   The novella *Black Hat Jack* is published. The novella *Prisoner 489*, featuring artwork by Santiago Caruso, is published. The collection of novellas and screenplays (cowritten by Neal Barrett, Jr.) titled *A Pair of Aces* is published. The comic anthology *Jonah Hex: Shadows West*, featuring artwork by Sam Glanzman and Tim Truman, is published. The graphic novel *I Tell You It's Love*, featuring artwork by Daniele Sera, is published and receives a Bram Stoker Award nomination in the Collection category. Nic Damici and Jim Mickle's film version of *Cold in July* is released. The Lansdale-scripted animated film *Son of Batman* is released. An anthology film cowritten by Lansdale titled *Creepers* is released. He wins the Bram Stoker Award for Long Fiction for *Fishing for Dinosaurs*. He is also nominated for Graphic Novel for *I Tell You It's Love*.

2015   The Western novel *Paradise Sky* is published and receives the Western Writers Association's Western Spur Award for Historical Fiction. *Briar Patch Boogie: A Hap and Leonard Novelette* is published. The novella (cowritten with daughter Kasey Lansdale) *The Case of the Bleeding Wall* is published. The chapbook *The Christmas Monkeys*, featuring artwork by Pete VonSholly, is published. Subterranean Press publishes the three "M.I.A. Hunter" books (cowritten by Stephen Mertz) together in a collection titled *M.I.A. Hunter Ominibus*. This marks the first time these works have appeared under Lansdale's own name. The short story collection *The Tall Grass and Other Stories* is released as a Kindle exclusive. He receives the Raymond Chandler award for lifetime achievement.

2016   The graphic novel (cowritten with Mark Allen Miller) *The Steam Man*, featuring artwork by Piotr Kowalski, is published. It is nominated for the Bram Stoker Award for Graphic Novel. A collection of memoirs and essays titled *Miracles Ain't What They Used to Be* is published as part of PM Press' "Outspoken Authors" series. The ninth Hap and Leonard novel, *Honky Tonk Samurai* is published. Two Hap and Leonard story collections, *Hap and Leonard* and *Hap and Leonard Ride Again* are published. The Hap and Leonard novella *Hoodoo Harry* is published. The horror novella (cowritten with brother, John Lansdale) *Hell's Bounty* is published. The short story collection *Dead on the Bones: Pulp on Fire*, featuring artwork by Tim Truman, is published. The television series *Hap and*

Leonard, based on Lansdale's book series, debuts on Sundance TV. It airs for three seasons.

2017   The tenth Hap and Leonard novel, *Rusty Puppy* is published. Two Hap and Leonard novellas, *Coco Butternut* and *Cold Cotton* are published. *Bubba and the Cosmic Blood-Suckers*, the sequel to *Bubba Ho-Tep*, is published. The Hap and Leonard mosaic novel, *Hap and Leonard: Blood and Lemonade* is published. Lansdale adapts his own story, "The Boy Who Turned Invisible," for the graphic anthology *Outside*.

2018   The eleventh novel in the Hap and Leonard series, *Jackrabbit Smile*, is published. Two short story collections, *Driving to Geronimo's Grave and Other Stories* and *Cosmic Interruptions*, are published. A collection of novellas (cowritten with daughter Kasey Lansdale), *Terror Is Our Business: Dana Roberts' Casebook of Horrors*, is published. He cowrites (with son Keith Lansdale and Delilah S. Dawson) the graphic novel *X-Files: Case Files*.

2019   The twelfth Hap and Leonard novel, *The Elephant of Surprise* is published. The fourth entry in the "Ned the Seal" series, *The Sky Done Ripped* is published. *The Big Book of Hap and Leonard*, which includes short stories, one novella (*Dead Aim*), a comic book script, and several essays, is published. The short story collection *Blood in the Gears* is published. The graphic novel adaptation (cowritten with Joshua Jabcuba) of *Bubba and the Cosmic Blood-Suckers*, which features artwork by Tadd Galusha, is published. The Lansdale documentary (directed by Hansi Oppenheimer) *All Hail the Popcorn King* is completed and begins screening. Season one of the Netflix series *Love, Death & Robots* airs, featuring two episodes based on Lansdale stories. These are "Fish Night" and "The Dump." An episode of the Shudder television series *Creepshow* based on "The Companion" (a story written by Lansdale with his children, Keith and Kasey Lansdale) airs.

2020   The novels *Jane Goes North, More Better Deals*, and *Big Lizard* (cowritten with son, Keith Lansdale) are published. The Hap and Leonard short story collection *Of Mice and Minestrone: Hap and Leonard: The Early Years* is published. The collection also includes recipes by his daughter Kasey Lansdale, which play important roles in the tales. The novella collection *Fishing for Dinosaurs and Other Stories* is published. The short story collection *Wet Juju* is published.

2021   The novel *Moon Lake* is published. Lansdale's first poetry collection, *Apache Witch*, is published. Death's Head Press publishes the chapbook *The Hungry Snow*. The Nat Love novella *Radiant Apples* is published. The ebook-only short story collection *In the Ditch* is published by Subterranean Press. The first book about Lansdale, Fred Isajenko's *The World Lansdalean: The Authorized Joe R. Lansdale Bibliography*, is published. Lansdale executive produces the motion picture, *The Pale Door*, directed by Aaron B. Koontz.

2022   The collection of previously uncollected stories, *Born for Trouble: The Further Adventures of Hap and Leonard*, is published.

**Conversations with
Joe R. Lansdale**

12 Acres and a Mule . . . Why Not?

Cherie Hopkins / 1975

Published in *The Gladewater Mirror*, February 2, 1975. Reprinted by permission of *The Gladewater Mirror*.

Forty years ago, and before, it wasn't unusual in this country to find a family living on a 40-acre subsistence farm, raising everything they needed. If they were lucky, they made a cash crop to buy a few things they wanted. Mostly they worked like dogs from daylight to dark hoping someday to be able to get off that farm.

Joe Lansdale of Gladewater figures that they didn't know when they were well off. Joe and his wife, Karen, like many other young people around the country today, have chosen lifestyle that harkens back to those days of simplicity, self-reliance, and hard work.

On a twelve-acre piece of land near the Starrville community, Joe and Karen are beginning a new life together that disdains the Puritan ethic, the American dream, and the striving of the materialistic rat race.

Success for the Lansdales means having wood for the cookstove, kerosene for the lamps, and the ability to provide the basic necessities of life for themselves.

Complete self-sufficiency.

The couple's first crop yielded abundantly. For six months they lived off turnip greens; they had everything from turnip green soup to turnip green sandwiches.

"Once we got past the turnip greens," Joe laughed, "I knew we had it beat."

That was almost two years ago, and the couple is still gardening, but even more extensively than when they began as Stephen F. Austin State University students.

And they're digging into more than the garden path now; they're homesteading in the fullest sense of the word.

By May they hope to be living in the cabin they will build on their new farm. For the past eighteen months they've experimented with organic gardening, hog butchering, soap making, canning, goat raising, hide tanning and a little bit of everything else that will enable them to become self-sufficient.

On average they spend $5 a week at the grocery store, with the money going for staples, food supplements, and things they have "uncontrollable cravings" for.

They have other expenses, of course, like gasoline for the two pickups they drive. Karen holds down a full-time job at Southland in Tyler, and Joe has a four-day-a-week, jack-of-all-trades job. Their earnings are earmarked for payments on the farm that they consider their "rightful piece of land." Last winter they even opted for farm payments rather than butane for heating the farmhouse they now occupy.

"When it got cold, we just wore more clothes," Joe explained, adding that their being outdoors so much helped accustom them to the chill. They are softies this year, heating their home with butane.

Learning the Hard Way

They have learned a lot since they began their back-to-nature project, some of it the hard way. Joe is the son of Mr. and Mrs. A. B. Lansdale of Gladewater and was a farm boy. But Karen is a Pasadena product who spent her spare hours on the racetrack with her father. (Even yet she's the mechanic and Joe's the cook in their household.)

The Lansdales' knowledge has come from hard knocks and written information from sources such as "Country Side," "Mother Earth News," "Farm journal," and other magazines and literature.

Inspiration for the undertaking is founded on Thoreau's "Walden."

"We read an article about butchering a hog in 'Mother Earth News,'" Joe said, "and then we did our first butchering."

He admitted that slaughtering the animal made him ill and he retreated into the house. By the time he recovered, Karen had the hog strung up in the tree and had begun butchering.

The sources from which they get their knowledge also provide a market for the homesteading type material Joe writes. He's to have a feature on cooking on a wood stove (like the one they will use in the cabin) to be published in February's "Country Side."

"Don't believe what people tell you," farmer Joe warned. "They told me I couldn't grow watermelons because I didn't have enough space. But I trellised the vines and they grew fine."

Organic upgrading of his three garden sites has priority. His last garden stocked their cupboard with canned vegetables, filled his deep freeze, and provided saleable and giveaway products. Peas and beans were dried.

Want a Blind Hog?

Joe and Karen can laugh now about their first livestock ventures. They bought a hog that was blind and a goat that was stunted. At one time they overstocked the goat herd and had almost as much goat mills as they once had turnip greens.

"I'm not trying to build House Beautiful," Joe frankly admitted. He had budgeted $100 for the entire cabin project, which he says will be a "miscellaneous" cabin. Salvage lumber, slabs bought for $1 a load, wood he will cut himself, and mud chinking will form the structure.

The frame farmhouse they now occupy is almost twice as large as the cabin will be and it has electricity and running water (albeit cranky). Despite their frugality, the Lansdales have comforts including a seldom watched television and carpeting. But a treadle sewing machine and kerosene lamps are ready, waiting for their cabin home.

They will build nothing on their new farm that they cannot provide their own energy for. A wind generator will be the most likely form of power supply. Solar and methane energizers are also under consideration by the former architecture student who says with quiet confidence that, with instructions, he can build the energizers.

But at first the couple will be roughing it at their new home. Bathing will be in the pond, cooking will be on the wood stove, and lighting will be with kerosene. A well will provide water and it will be back to the outhouse for restroom facilities.

Karen said her worst experience through the whole farm scene came the day a snake challenged her for use of the outhouse. The snake won.

"It was just a chicken snake," Joe teased his wife.

"Yeah, but it was big!" she protested.

At a small desk facing a front window, Joe turns author. He's finished one novel and is working on his second. They, along with his shorter works, are science fiction, a literary form which fascinates him.

"I write science fiction," he explains. "Hard science fiction deals with machinery and science. Soft is adventure and romance on other planets."

During spring and summer, Joe is more often in the garden than at the typewriter. But winter schedules are easier and he spends more than the average of a couple of hours each day writing.

Karen is a severe critic. So far, Joe says, she's liked only three of the things he's written, and those are the ones he has sold.

The anthropology major explained that he didn't enjoy himself in school, even though he made good grades and earned four scholarships. He graduated in 1970, president of his senior class from Gladewater High School, and attended Tyler Junior College, the University of Texas, and SFASU.

"I've written all my life and sold my first things while I was still in school. I even wrote Boy Scout news for the Mirror once," he said.

Scoutmaster Top Advisor

(The Boy Scout recollection turns him on. He credits Jayson Heath, a former scoutmaster, for having done more than any other man to teach him things that have been useful to him.)

"It's masochistic to write," Joe says. "You write and write and they (editors) say they don't want it. They say it stinks."

He considers his most recent rejection a success. He admires the style of science fiction written from the 1930s through 1950s. He wrote a story using this style, submitted it to an editor, and received a rejection. The editor noted that the style had been out of date since the 1950s.

"It made me feel good. I did it. That was what I was trying to say," he grinned, holding the returned packet on his lap.

"I'd rather write than anything else."

Karen is his severest critic, admitting that she's not interested in his literature. But, she explains, it is the style she dislikes, not the author. She's not a science fiction fan, of her husband or anyone else.

This semester she has discontinued her college work, but plans to resume it in Tyler next term, working toward a degree in criminology.

"Karen's okay," her husband says. He married her almost two years ago on the front steps of their farmhouse. "She's extremely quiet and shy. I wouldn't trade her for nothing!"

Off the cuff, Joe can't explain why the homesteading idea appeals to him so strongly that he's devoted his future to it. He will say that he doesn't like to be subject to prices and availabilities set by people in the market. He calls his lifestyle a form of security.

As a kid he enjoyed *Robinson Crusoe* and *Swiss Family Robinson.*

"It always appealed to me to be able to live by your own wit. I don't feel secure about the rising prices."

Acknowledging that his is not a common philosophy, Joe admits that he has always been an individualist. He began wearing long hair in high school, went four years without a haircut (until it was within four inches of his waist), and instigated the court case at Tyler Junior College that set state precedents barring school hair codes.

But when that hair began causing him trouble in getting jobs and became a bother in his outdoor work, he cut it.

"I'm a realist," he said. "People didn't like my long hair and I needed a job."

He sees his life becoming more and more stabilized as he and Karen move to the new acreage.

Plans for the farm stretch into twenty years, Joe says, and he feels that it will take that long to do all the things they want to do. This weekend he cleared the cabin site.

"It was kind of scary at first," he admits, "but it (moving to the farm) is the most intelligent thing I ever did.

"Once we got past the turnip greens, I knew we had it beat."

He enjoys experimenting: corn was spaced six inches rather than the recommended one-to-three-feet apart. Black compost drew the sun into the compact planting area and the corn flourished. He once used a mirror to reflect sunlight into a shaded garden patch. That worked, too.

Planting by moon signs has produced no noticeable difference in his garden, one way or the other.

Men who have spent their lives farming have been an invaluable help to the green hand.

"I've learned more from them than I ever learned in school," he said.

Initial turning with a mechanical tiller gives way for plowing the old way, behind a mule. Joe believes in disturbing the soil as little as possible.

The Lansdales' cultivated diet is supplemented with wild foods such as polk salad and sassafras. Joe has no conscientious objections to hunting squirrels and rabbits to fill the pot.

As if in tune with the whole project, the couple's animals all earned their keep. Chickens provide eggs; sheep are butchered and their hides salvaged; rabbits are eaten; goats are milked; and Butch the watchdog earns his keep ferociously.

Meet Joe the Mystery Writer

Dianne Webb / 1978

Published in the *Daily Sentinel*, July 26, 1978. Reprinted by permission of the *Daily Sentinel*.

A mystery writer is living in Nacogdoches. In fact, he really is a mystery writer—Joe R. Lansdale writes detective stories and is working on his first novel.

Although Joe is not too well known in the writing field, he is on his way to becoming what he has wanted to be for some time—a detective and science fiction writer.

Joe recently had his first detective story accepted by *Mike Shayne Mystery Magazine*, and the story was published in the magazine's June 1978 issue.

The writer was unaware that his story had been published until he received the following note from another detective writer—Bill Pronzini of San Francisco:

Dear Joe:

Just got back from vacation to find your note of the 6th. Your story didn't appear in the July "MSMM," but it was in the June issue. I meant to drop you a note to tell you that I enjoyed it and that I hope to read more stories and Slater (Raymond Slater—Joe's character) in the near future (he's a strong character). If you missed the June issue and don't have a copy, I'll be glad to ship mine to you: the idea of a writer not having a copy of the magazine in which his first story appears is depressing. You might also write to Sam Merwin (editor of "MSMM") to get additional copies.
Best, Bill

Joe never doubted that his story had been accepted by *MSMM*; he just wasn't sure when it would be published. He knew he had already cashed the check from the magazine!

Actually the story, titled "The Full Count" and set in and around a town Joe calls "Gulf City"—a place with many similarities to Pasadena, Texas—is not the first story sold by the aspiring mystery writer.

The first writing Joe sold was an article, written in collaboration with his mother, Oreta Lansdale, for *The Farm Journal* magazine.

The article was what Joe refers to as "a filler" and was about the therapeutic value of digging holes and planting flowers.

The flower planting article won a prize for Joe and his mother—it was selected as the best article in the "farm life" category of the magazine.

Probably it has occurred to the reader that an author does not make enough money to support himself when he is first beginning to have stories and articles accepted for publication. So, what does Joe do to support himself, his wife, Karen, and his writing habit?

Joe replied good humoredly that he works primarily at odd jobs so he can have the time to write. He is presently employed as a janitorial supervisor at Stephen F. Austin State University.

Also he has been a karate instructor, farmed for two years, and has done a lot of writing, too.

Even Joe was a little surprised when he and his mother sold that first article to *Farm Journal*, because he had been told writers could rely on receiving a number of publishers' rejection slips before they ever had a story accepted for publication.

Joe tries to write at least four or five hours a day—preferably between 8:30 a.m. and noon.

"There was a time when I wasn't that disciplined," said the writer, who also emphasized, "You have to be disciplined and stay with it [the writing]."

In discussing his writing, Joe said he remembered reading somewhere that the way to be a writer is to get a chair, sit down, and write at the typewriter; and when you get up ten years later, you're a writer! He is hopeful that it won't take him that long to be considered a writer.

"In fact," said Joe, "I'm out to make a buck and have fun doing it!"

The writer said he feels that guts are sometimes more important than talent in the writing field. "I've got the drive," said Joe.

The writer has received encouragement from his parents, and he credits his sister-in-law, Mary Louise Lansdale, and Jeff Banks, an English professor at SFASU, with encouraging him to continue writing.

He feels that the acceptance of "The Full Count," based on the boxing term, is a major step in the right direction—becoming what he wants to be: a detective and science fiction writer.

Joe refers to himself as more of a detective writer than a mystery writer and explains that there is a fine line between the two types of stories.

In a detective story, the writer is usually more interested in character development; whereas in a mystery story, the writer enjoys the puzzle of the crime.

"I like the characters better than the puzzle," said Joe. He has studied the writings of detective writers Raymond Chandler and Dashiell Hammett, with his own opinion being that Chandler has a much better wit than Hammett.

Chandler wrote *The Big Sleep* and *Farewell My Lovely*, and Hammett wrote *The Thin Man*, *The Dain Curse*, and *The Maltese Falcon*; and the latter is studied in English courses at SFA as an example of excellent and worthwhile writing.

In Joe's estimation, Chandler is a more stylistic writer and has made the "American" language more interesting.

"I read for style and the approach if it's a good mystery in my estimation," said the writer. Joe makes frequent references to both Chandler and Hammett in his conversations, and one gets the impression that these two writers have influenced Joe's writing and his desire to achieve success as a detective fiction writer. The writer verified the preceding observation.

Joe explained that there are really only three mystery fiction magazines on the market—*Mike Shane Mystery Magazine*, *Ellery Queen*, and *Alfred Hitchcock*. He submitted "The Full Count" to both *MSMM* and *Ellery Queen*. The story was accepted by *MSMM*.

When Joe first submitted the story to *MSMM*, however, Sam Merwin Jr., said to Joe, "It's a good story, well-written, but it's too much Humphrey Bogart and Raymond Chandler." Merwin wanted Joe to rework the story and send it back to him.

Joe reworked the story all right—all he did was change the first person "I" to the third person "he." Then the writer mailed the story back to *MSMM*'s editor, and the story was accepted immediately—so much for reworking the story!

Joe said he objected to changing his story from the first person to the third person, but he also stressed that, in the beginning, a writer doesn't quarrel with a publisher.

If the magazine wants the story and suggests a few changes, then Joe willingly complies, because he thinks it is more important for him to get his name before the public at this time.

When he is better-known professionally, he can write the story exactly the way he wants it written; and if his recent successes are any indicator, Joe R. Lansdale will not have to change many stories in the future.

Joe R. Lansdale

William J. Grabowski / 1987

Published in *The Horror Show*, January 1987. Reprinted by permission of the author.

A man slips into a bizarre realm where cows round up humans for slaughter . . . an old wandering bag lady discovers a set of dentures that possess an insatiable, ravenous appetite of their own . . . Frankenstein's monster, tired of being persecuted, visits a psychiatrist only to be set afire . . .

Who, one asks, is the creator of these ingenious—and on occasion, nasty—yarns?

The answer, of course, is Joe R. Lansdale, who seems to have cornered the market in his own literary genre, even though some might label his irreverent short-short stories "absurdist"—a somewhat accurate but nevertheless limiting term. For short-short stories are not all Lansdale writes; those brief, often hilarious excursions are a small clearing in his labyrinthine literary landscape, as he has produced many different forms of writing appearing in numerous publications as disparate as *Twilight Zone* and *Mississippi Arts & Letters*, plus anthologies and his own novels. And as you will read in this interview, the journey was anything but easy.

Joe R. Lansdale resides in Nacogdoches, Texas, with his wife Karen (also a writer) and two children.

THE HORROR SHOW: Tell me something of your background; are you a native Texan?

JOE R. LANSDALE: Yes, I'm a native Texan and proud of it. I was born in Gladewater, Texas, in 1951, moved to a town of about three hundred called Mt. Enterprise, then about fifth grade moved back to Gladewater. Gladewater had a population of about five thousand, and it was a pretty rough town. There was always something unusual happening there, but it was seldom pleasant.

THS: Like what?

LANSDALE: A huge number of the kids I went to school with ended up in prison, committed suicide, were killed, or had rather bizarre things happen to them. Not all, mind you, but an uncomfortable number.

Many of my stories take place in a town called Mud Creek, and though it is not Gladewater, it is inspired by Gladewater and a number of other small towns I've lived in or known.

THS: How long have you been writing?

LANSDALE: I've been writing since I was nine. I began sending things out when I was twenty-one, all nonfiction. The first thing I wrote—a collaboration with my mother—sold to *Farm Journal*. It was a brief letter article, and it was later picked as the best article and won a prize of twenty-five dollars. The second, third, and fourth things I wrote sold, and I thought I was in hog heaven.

But I didn't start trying to write seriously until I was about twenty-five. Just didn't sit down to do it. I was busy making a living truck cropping, teaching martial arts, and later working at Goodwill Industries, not to mention a lot of work in the rose fields and some hay hauling. Just before I quit truck cropping, due to a very bad year, I took three months off to do nothing but write. I wrote a short story a day for about three months, sent them out and had them all rejected, three and four times, nearly all of which I heard from within three months.

THS: I once did the same thing—same results, too!

LANSDALE: That's how fast editors were just eight or nine years ago. So, roughly speaking, I got about one thousand rejects for three months of work. But turning out a story a day was great practice, helped me whittle down the clichés, and first quantity makes quality . . . the more you write the better you get. It's like lifting weights; the more you do it, he easier it gets, the bigger the muscles become. Inspiration is like that. The more you sit in front of the typewriter and try to produce, the easier it is to turn on inspiration . . . also, the imagination grows instead of shrinks with age. Use it or lose it.

Anyway, I wrote off and on for about a year and a half, sent out a few things, then we moved to Nacogdoches and I got serious. In 1978, I sold my first fiction, a novelette, to *Mike Shayne Mystery Magazine*. Been at it ever since and have been a full-time writer for about five years.

THS: Who are some of the writers that helped shape your career?

LANSDALE: Personally, I never met a writer until I was published. The first writer I remember meeting was Garland Roark, author of *Wake of the Red Witch*. He lived here in Nacogdoches. Died a year or so ago. But at the time I met him, he was basically retired. The next writer I met was Ardath Mayhar [author of *Khi to Freedom, Golden Dreams, World Ends at Hickory Hollow* and others], but at that time she was primarily a poet, though she had published a few short stories, the best of them being "Crawfish," which was in an Alfred Hitchcock anthology. It's a story I had read before I met her, and it was one I greatly admired—still admire. Ardath and I sort of got our feet wet together. She sold her first book before I did, but in many ways we've been writing and producing and learning right along with each other.

Other than the two mentioned, Neal Barrett, Jr. [author of *Stress Pattern, Aldair, Master of Ships* and others], a very underrated science fiction and fantasy writer—though he's lately, to my estimation, branched out into being wonderfully unclassifiable—gave me words of encouragement. Also, Bill Pronzini, who bought stories of mine for anthologies was a lot of help. I didn't meet him until he had bought the stories from me, but we had kept up a lengthy correspondence by mail for some time, talked on the phone now and then. After I was in the business, Jeff Wallman, who has written well over two hundred books, a lot of them under other names, gave me good, solid professional advice on dealing with editors, publishers, agents, that sort of thing. That's been a big help.

But primarily, the works of other writers have been more of an influence than words of wisdom. Writers I admire are Ray Bradbury, Robert Bloch, Harlan Ellison, Flannery O'Connor, Dorothy Johnson, Gerald Kersh—the short work; I've not read a novel—some of F. Scott Fitzgerald's work, primarily *The Diamond as Big as the Ritz* and a practically unknown fantasy/ horror tale of his called "A Short Trip Home." Also Philip Jose Farmer, who'll try anything.

William Goldman, Stephen King, Harry Crews, Raymond Chandler— God, I love Raymond Chandler; Dashiell Hammett, T. V. Olsen for good solid Westerns, Elmore Leonard—especially the Western stuff. Brian Garfield, early and middle period. Dean Koontz, damn near everything he's written. Don't think I realized just how much he's influenced me until lately. I'm impressed with Richard Christian Matheson's work and feel he and I have a lot in common storywise. I admire his lean style. Can't forget his dad, Richard Matheson, who influenced both of us. I like all of his short story collections and most of the novels. William F. Nolan has also been a great influence. Evan Hunter for dialogue and a certain method of attack. I love to read his stuff, although I admit, storywise it doesn't stay with me that well. All the 87th Precinct runs together to me, but he's still entertaining. And man, what a stylist.

Glendon Swarthout, Pete Hamil—primarily for *Flesh and Blood* and *The Gift*, Rudyard Kipling—the short stories mainly, H. G. Wells, and Edgar Rice Burroughs—personally, the most important writer I read. The man captivated me and tossed me into a magical realm, and I've never come out. He, more than any other writer, made me want to be a writer. At his best, Burroughs was a whole hell of a lot better than the critics thought, and he could damn sure tell a story. What he lacked in rounded characterization, he made up in swift pace, color, invention . . . and for that matter, I remember Tarzan, John Carter of Mars, and David Innes a lot better than characters from many novels well thought of by the critics. His people may not have been real in the strictest sense, but they were like Max Brand's characters, bigger than life and memorable. A case might even be made for *The Mucker* or *Tarzan of the Apes* as mainstream novels, if one were so inclined. I could care less about defining him. He was magic, and that is enough.

I adore lots of Jules Verne, John Wyndham, Theodore Sturgeon (didn't care much for his science fiction, but his fantasy and horror were unique), Roald Dahl, Robert E. Howard, Jack London, Jack Finney, Charles Beaumont, John Collier, Harlan Ellison, again, though lately his work doesn't seem to have that hammer-and-tongs fiery magic it once had. But maybe he's just gone off in a direction I don't appreciate.

Better quit now.

THS: That just about answers my next question, which is: name some books that might be found on Joe R. Lansdale's preferred reading list . . . .

LANSDALE: On my preferred reading list would be a lot of short story collections as well as novels by all of the writers just mentioned. *Tom Mix Died for Your Sins* by Darryl Poniscan; *In the Heat of the Night* by John Ball; *A Trace of Memory* by Keith Laumer; *'Salem's Lot, The Shining, The Stand, The Dead Zone*, by Stephen King; *The Shootist* by Glendon Swarthout; *A Feast of Snakes* by Harry Crews; *Wise Blood* and *A Good Man is Hard to Find* by Flannery O'Connor; *Fahrenheit 451* and *Something Wicked This Way Comes* by Ray Bradbury. All of Charles Beaumont's work. Complete works of: Jack London, Twain, Kipling, Lewis Carroll; Stoker's *Dracula*; all of John D. McDonald, especially the non-Travis McGee novels. All of Chandler's work. *Honkytonk Man* by Clancy Carlisle; *The Great Gatsby* by Fitzgerald; *The Marathon Man, Your Turn to Curtsy, My Turn to Bow, No Way to Treat a Lady, Magic*, and *Control* by William Goldman. *The Maltese Falcon* by Hammett; *The Natural* by Bernard Malamud—only book I could read by the man, and it's wonderful. *Semi-Tough* and *Baja Oklahoma* by Dan Jenkins; *Pride of the Bimbos* and *Union Dues* by John Sayles, as well as

WILLIAM GRABOWSKI / 1987 **15**

his short story collection, *The Anarchist Convention* (which isn't really on my bookshelf, as I can't find a copy! I read it out of the library); *The Spirit* and *The Man Who Would Not Die* by Thomas Page. The best works by Robert B. Parker, though he's gotten kind of silly in his later books. Ones to have are: *Mortal Stakes* (the best one), *God Save the Child, Promised Land, Valediction* (the best of the later ones), probably *The Godwulf Manuscript*, though it's before he refined his style. James Crumley's *The Last Good Kiss* and *Dancing Bear*, the first being the best private-eye novel written since Chandler's work.

Good grief, that's a mixed bag, isn't it?

Also, *Riverworld and Other Stories* and *The Book of Philip Jose Farmer*.

THS: A very mixed bag—but I like complete responses. What do you think of the small-press publications?

LANSDALE: The small-press scene seems healthier than ever to me. And the quality of the material seems even better. Also, it's not only attracting semipro writers; it's attracting pros. With the clumsy New York system flushing itself down the drain, more and more small-press houses will come along, and not only survive, but thrive. In fact, many of them are thriving now.

The Horror Show gets better and better with each issue. It will most likely be the *Whispers* and *Weirdbook* of the eighties if it can survive. Of course, it has its own personality, quite unlike the aforementioned magazines.

THS: For people who might be reading this magazine for the first time, tell us a little about the column you've been writing for *The Horror Show*, Joe.

LANSDALE: The column is informal, general comments on the horror scene. Books, movies, comics, anything related to the field. It's been fun, and a couple of columns have generated some letters. Also, since we're talking about nonfiction, that gives me a lead to say this year [1986] I won the Small Press Writers and Artists Organization's award for best nonfiction writer of the year. I'm proud of that. I didn't even know I was in the running. For that matter, I'm not even sure if I won for a specific article or for my work in *The Horror Show* column, which is called, by the way, "The Lansdale House of Horror." Tacky title, but it fits the fun mood of what I'm doing.

THS: Let's talk about your novel *Act of Love*. It's one of the most excruciatingly graphic presentations of a homicidal maniac I've ever read. How did you come to create it? Was the killer—the Houston Hacker—drawn from actual case histories?

LANSDALE: It was based on a number of true-life murders and a lot of reading in the area of psychotic killers. Jack the Ripper was a big influence, but so were a number of modern-day killers. In fact, though I didn't know it, there were a series of hacker-type murders going on in Houston even as I was writing the book. It was kept low-profile in the newspapers, but a friend of mine in Houston heard the police talking about it over their radios. She had a scanner and picked up a lot of weird things about the killer. When she told me about them it was pretty creepy. It was sort of like I'd picked up on the killer's wavelength and it had come out during the writing of the book.

Act of Love was the first intense writing experience of my life. I'm a much better writer now, but the book remains powerful and important to me. It actually taught me how to write.

THS: Are those short-short stories you're famous for dashed off quickly at the typewriter, or do you take some time honing them?

LANSDALE: Basically, I'm a fast writer, but the short-shorts were nearly always written in fifteen to thirty minutes, once through the typewriter. Longer stories generally take three to four days. I've written a lot of stories, and a lot of different kinds of stories—different types of fantasy/horror, but those fantasy shorts in *The Twilight Zone* [magazine] seem to be the thing I'm known for if anything. Guess they just reach more readers.

THS: Have you a novel in the works?

LANSDALE: Novels have been my downfall. I've sold several, but only one under my name, and the others were pennamed or ghosted. And for very little money. They were, for the most part, written in about the time it would have taken me to write one ambitious short story or half a dozen shorts—and I'd have to say the money was about the same too. Just worth it.

However, I realize that if I'm ever going to make any money in this business—and get my name around to readers—I'm going to have to write more novels. I put it off for so long because I always needed money to continue writing, and though the short stories didn't make much, they could be written quickly, and I could get, relatively speaking, a fast response on them. Keep enough money rolling in to allow me my dream factory. But as the responsibilities grow, I'm doing novels with my name on them. I hope I'm out of ghost work for good, because, as I said, for me it's been about as profitable as writing short stories, and that isn't going to cut it. I have a four-year-old son and a new daughter. I also have a book collection that has outgrown my study and my house. So I need money for the kids and to buy a larger house, plus I'm just acquiring a number of good old middle-class desires. I like my VCR and I want more movies, and I like my books, and I want more of them. I want to be able to pay my bills without sweating it day-to-day. So far we've never missed a payment and our checks don't bounce, but we sweat all the time. If my wife didn't work full-time and make quite a bit more money than I do, we'd be out there pecking shit with the chickens.

This year, however, *Dead in the West*, which is also being serialized in a considerably different form in Eldritch Tales, is coming out from Space and Time Books, a new small-press publisher. The money, again, isn't much better than a couple of short stories, but it's a start in the right direction—a book I wanted to do with my name on it. It's a tribute to the pulps, *Weird Tales*–type especially, and the "B" horror movies, the handful of offbeat horror Westerns in particular.

In October, *The Magic Wagon* is coming out from Doubleday. About two years ago I remember talking to you about this as nothing more than an idea I hoped would jell. Well, it did. It's an offbeat novel that takes place in East Texas in 1909 and involves a wrestling chimpanzee, a corpse in a box that might be that of Wild Bill Hickok, and a medicine show wagon constructed of wood possessed by Indian spirits. And a lot more.

You can't honestly say it's a fantasy novel, or for that matter that it's a Western, though that's how it's going to be marketed.

Next year Dark Harvest is doing *Night of the Goblins*, a novel I wrote back in 1982 and have never been able to sell because it is too grim, too upsetting. Even my rejects on this were terrific, but no one wanted to touch it. It wasn't for the New York houses—at least at that time. I'm glad Dark Harvest has the courage to do it, and I hope it does well for them. Parts of it have appeared in out-of-the-way publications like *Mississippi Arts & Letters* and *Hardboiled*, and the latter magazine had one reader cancel he was so offended by that piece, which was called "Boys Will Be Boys."

Also, I've sold on proposal, *The Drive-In*, a horror novel, to Doubleday and that will come out in either '87 or '88, depending on when I finish.

As for other things in the works, I have an anthology of offbeat Western stories I edited, and it's coming out from Doubleday. It's all new stuff, and damn good, I think. But the authors get credit for that, not me. Bantam will publish yet another anthology of mine this year, a nonfiction Western anthology that will be something like a Western version of *Murderer's Ink* and *The Book of Lists* and The Time-Life Western series all rolled up into one. It's been a bitch, and I'm not out of the woods on it yet.

Finally, on the short stories, a collection of my work is forthcoming from The Strange Company sometime this year. It has an introduction by William F. Nolan, a preface by me and some intro material by me on all the stories. It'll be a limited run, about 500 copies, but I think it'll be a good book. Fifteen or sixteen of my best stories between '81 and '85 with one or two from this year thrown in.

As for short stories, there will be others, but not as frequently. I'm writing a different type of short story now than I used to—though I never really wrote any one type. But the stuff I've written in the last couple of years, with a few exceptions, has been darker and stranger. I think that will be my direction for a while. And longer stories.

But, as I said, fewer will appear, and even if I never wrote another, I have enough sold to appear in magazines for another year or so.

THS: Does the horror story have a solid future?

LANSDALE: As long as there are people and there are problems, there will be a love for terror. It's how we feed the alligators in the pit of our subconscious. If we don't feed the beasties, they just might crawl out. Some people, of course, can feed and feed, but their alligators are hungry rascals and crawl out anyway. But for the most part, I'm more frightened by the person who claims no need for that sort of stuff than one who does. One who doesn't feed the gators is breeding a big batch of ravenous critters, and someday, when he or she least expects it, they just might come crawling out.

I think horror is good for the soul and a catharsis to most of us.

THS: What are some things you believe might benefit the up-and-coming author?

LANSDALE: Advice is simple. No magic formula. Read. Put your ass in a chair in front of a typewriter and produce. The more you write, the better you get at it. If you find it's hard for you to sit there and write after a few months' practice, well, you just might be in the wrong business. Just having written is not enough for me; I also have to enjoy the process. And it seems to me the best and most successful writers feel that way. I'm not saying it isn't work and it isn't hard. But it's not work in the sense of having a part-time job at 7-Eleven.

It's a passionate hobby that pays.

Robert McCammon Interviews Joe R. Lansdale

Robert McCammon / 1989

Published in *Lights Out!*, October 1989. Reprinted by permission of the author.

If Texas writer Joe R. Lansdale had been born on a fantasy world, he might be a cross between a lion and a chameleon. His work is full of fierce nobility and resists being caged. His work changes colors and blends easily into a variety of backgrounds. Joe Lansdale has written horror, science fiction, fantasy, mystery, suspense, westerns, "men's adventure," and just about every other kind of writing you can think of. Joe has done it all, and he keeps on getting better. He won a Bram Stoker award for *The Night They Missed the Horror Show*, his novel *The Drive-In*—nominated for a World Fantasy Award—is like a ride on a runaway Tilt-a-Whirl, and his *Tight Little Stitches in a Dead Man's Back* is probably one of the finest pieces of writing I've ever had the pleasure to read. Just when you think you've got Joe pegged in a particular category, he goes chameleon again. His *The Magic Wagon* is a bona fide western, complete with a gunfighter and a wrestling monkey. Well, you can't say—you *dare* not say—Joe isn't an original talent. He knows one of those Oriental killing techniques that I can't pronounce, and he used to hire himself out as a personal bodyguard when he lived in San Francisco and had hair down to his butt.

I digress. Joe conducted one of the first interviews I ever did, for *Twilight Zone Magazine* back in 1986, and I'm glad to have the opportunity to turn the tables. Let's get one thing straight: I don't like everything Joe writes. I think he can be colder and crueller than Hell. He doesn't like everything I do, because he thinks I sentimentalize too much and that I overwrite. Joe is of the school of true grit and hard knocks, and he says what needs to be said and no more. One of his first jobs was picking roses. He says the smell made you sick after a while, and your hands got cut up by thorns. You need tough hands to pick roses, it seems to me. Joe's got 'em. And if his stories were roses, pulled from his imagination as if from a field under the hard, blue Texas sky, he leaves an occasional thorn on the stem so he can draw a drop of blood. That way, we can have a little pain with our pleasure. Which seems to me what writing might be all about.

Joe has a new collection of short stories out, called *By Bizarre Hands* and published by Mark V. Ziesing. It's a beautiful-looking book, and is a terrific scope of Joe's talent. Joe doesn't sit still very long, so it's time we got to the questions.

Robert McCammon: What's your favorite piece of your own work?

Joe R. Lansdale: *The Night They Missed the Horror Show.* That's my favorite. It's closer to me because it's been with me for a long time. It's based on real incidents. Things that happened to me, things that happened to friends of mine, stories that I heard that I knew were true. I wove all those things together, and I think I really captured a certain element there that I remember from growing up.

McCammon: Does that story particularly appeal to you because it mirrors something about you?

Lansdale: Yeah, I think so. It mirrors where I came from. That's not saying that everybody I grew up with dragged dogs behind cars or were racist. Racism is a thing that bothers me very, very deeply. My feeling about racism probably appears in my work more than any other thing. It's in almost every story. I know people who are otherwise really fine folks, except they've got this blind spot about racism.

McCammon: I do too, and that's probably because of growing up in the South. Racism used to be part of who you were, at least in an "Old South" sense. It's like the good old boys' mindset.

Lansdale: Right. And a lot of those people who might make racist remarks would never ever think of hurting anybody of another color. I left Texas for California partly to get away from that racist attitude, and I found out California wasn't a lot different, though people didn't make obviously racist remarks. But the South is an easy target. When you write about racism in the South, everybody figures that's the status quo. It's not, because racism is everywhere and certainly not just in the South.

McCammon: Is there a work you wish you hadn't done or wish you could change?

Lansdale: I could probably go back and rewrite a lot of things now, because I know more about writing now. But I don't regret anything I've written. I don't regret any of the viciousness . . . . you know, people may say this earlier book or short story I did was crude or too bloody or something like that, but I always knew what I was doing. I was always trying to push it as far as I could go. But I wish I could rewrite some of the prose, make it more clever or clear what I meant to say.

McCammon: You say you wanted to push things as far as you could go. Why was that?

Lansdale: Back when I did *Act of Love*, that was before Clive Barker or splatterpunk. I wanted to write something very powerful and visceral. This was before the movies were doing graphic horror, too. I guess this was late 1979 or 1980. The closest thing to what I wanted to do at that time was the work of Sam Peckinpah—which, if you look at it now, is pretty tame. I didn't want to make violence insignificant. I wanted to make violence nasty, I wanted to make it bother you, but I wanted to make the story compelling. The thing that made me write *Act of Love* was anger. I was angry that so much attention was directed to psychopaths and murderers and very little attention given to their victims. So when I wrote a scene of butchery, I wanted to build sympathy for the people the violence was done to.

McCammon: Your scenes of violence are intense, but they're usually short.

Lansdale: Yeah, they are. I try to tell it flat-out. It's funny, but most people usually think my violent scenes are longer than they are and bloodier than they are.

McCammon: Could you be happy if a publisher said, "Joe, we want you to write one thing: horror, mystery, westerns, or whatever. But just one"?

Lansdale: Uh-uh. No. It would break my heart. And it is said to me; it's said all the time. What I'm concentrating on right now are the novels and on suspense. I think suspense is a broad field, and that's what I need. I think I'll continue to write horror and science-fictional types of things in shorter pieces, but it looks like I'm moving away from doing those in novel length. I'm trying to do what I like to do without compromising my work, but also reaching a wider audience.

McCammon: I hate those labels publishers put on a writer's work, but that's how the business is.

Lansdale: I hate 'em, too. I've always known what I've wanted to do, but it's been hell on me. My friend Bill Nolan has been a major influence on me, and he advised me not to skip around from category to category. Bill has taught me to have a game plan, which is real important.

McCammon: But you basically write for yourself, don't you?

Lansdale: Yeah. I have a game plan in the sense that I think about my career and where it's going, but I write for myself. It's obvious. I've written Westerns, horror, mystery, science fiction, all kinds of things.

McCammon: And some things that defy a category, like *The Drive-In*. What is it? Fantasy? Horror? It's an excellent book, but I don't know how to define it, and defining it really isn't important.

Lansdale: I wish they'd just market my books as Lansdale books. I think I've proven myself. But *The Drive-In* is quirky as hell. It's kind of a cult book, and it's not for everybody.

McCammon: But it really has your voice.

Lansdale: Yeah, and I'm starting to think a voice is what makes a writer. I used to think it was plot. Then I thought it was character, and then I thought it was theme. I guess all those are important, but a writer's voice has to be there. Ultimately, a writer has to develop some sort of tone that keeps you turning the pages. I think Stephen King has a tremendous voice. That's been his biggest asset. His voice is easily recognizable, and that's pretty important too.

McCammon: Do you have a dream book you'd like to write?

Lansdale: Yeah, I do. A big, historical Western that would be realistic and funny at the same time. Sort of my *Little Big Man*, though the story isn't anything like that.

McCammon: You've been thinking about this for a while?

Lansdale: For years. But I feel like I could miss the time to do it. Even though I do write for myself, I believe that when you have any kind of commercial success, it affects how you think. When you reach a wide audience, you have a tendency to think, "God, what did I do right that time?" I don't know how many writers I've seen who write the same damn book over and over and over again. That's like me saying, "Well, I know what the public expects, so I've got to give it to them." I'm concerned with what *I* want to read. That doesn't mean I'm not going to screw up and make mistakes, but I want to do the best that I can do with every book and not think about having a public who expects a particular thing.

McCammon: I don't like to think about my books going out to thousands of people. That's nice and all, but it makes me nervous to think about. It's kind of unreal.

Lansdale: I'm flattered by the attention I'm getting, but it embarrasses me too. And there's a side of it that's seductive. I mean, you're going to get good and bad reviews, and just because you get good reviews doesn't mean somebody's not out there wondering what the hell you're trying to do. You can't be universally admired. It's seductive to believe you're doing everything right when you know you're not.

McCammon: Where would you like your career to be in five years?

Lansdale: I'd like to be doing suspense novels. I'd like to be out of what some people would call the labels ghetto and be marketing Lansdale books. I want to do suspense novels, but I'd like to continue to do what I'd call "off-beat" books for the smaller presses. Short story collections, too. Other than that, I want to keep on writing and not get bent into that seduction of success we were talking about. I want to keep on writing for myself, and if people like it, that's fine too.

Joe R. Lansdale at the World Fantasy Convention

The Scream Factory / 1989

Published in *The Scream Factory*, Fall 1989. Appears by permission of *The Scream Factory*.

THE SCREAM FACTORY: How long have you been writing?

JOE R. LANSDALE: Since I was nine.

TSF: What was your first published work?

JRL: When I was twenty-one, I wrote an article that was published in *Farm Journal*. I wrote it with my mother, as a matter of fact. It won a prize. I think we split $25. Then I wrote a number of articles for farm magazines. Then *Old West* and *True West*.

TSF: So you're heavily into Westerns?

JRL: Yeah, I always wanted to be a Western writer, but I was always interested in the other stuff. Now, I'm quite happy with what I'm doing. Actually, I started out wanting to be a science fiction writer, but I was more interested in the West. I became a horror writer sorta by accident.

TSF: The horror and Western genres blend naturally.

JRL: Yeah. Mysteries were actually the first things I sold as fiction, and the mysteries led to horror. I've been interested in it all my life. I read everything. I've written for literary magazines, mainstream publications too. So, I just write what interests me.

TSF: Which of your novels are you the proudest of?

JRL: *The Magic Wagon* did way more than I intended it to do. I felt more comfortable with it, I mean they all disappoint me, but that one probably pleased me the most. *Cold in July* is a close second.

TSF: Let's talk about *The Nightrunners*. You're obviously going to continue on with the God of the Razor character. Where is that leading to?

JRL: I haven't got a clue! The thing is, when I created The God of the Razor for *The Nightrunners*, I wrote him in such a way that you didn't know if he really existed or not. What happened is: I wrote *The Nightrunners* and *Act of Love* and nobody would buy it. Nobody would touch either one of them with a ten-foot pole. I sold *Act of Love* eventually after thirty-something rejections. People'd tell me I was sick, I was crazy, nobody'd ever print this kind of stuff! Then it sold (to Zebra) and I wrote *The Nightrunners* and *Dead in the West*, and *Nightrunners* sold six years after it was finished. By that time, Clive Barker was doing stuff and he sort of opened it up. Times have changed, [the public] was ready for that kind of thing. But I was doing it years before he was, which is no slight to him or credit to myself.

TSF: *Act of Love* was released in 1981.

JRL: Yeah. It was really radical then; now it just kinda falls in line. It got really good reviews and I did well with it. When I did *The Nightrunners*, I thought that the same company would pick it up. They wouldn't. They said it was like "*Clockwork Orange* from Hell" or something. They didn't know what to do with it. My agent didn't know what it was. He said it didn't fit in with horror or science fiction; it wasn't fantasy and he didn't want to try to market anything that didn't have a box to fit in. I said, "Well, I write what I write," and fired that agent! I lived off writing short stories for about three years and I ghosted some novels.

TSF: *The Nightrunners* was initially rejected because it was too radical?

JRL: Oh yeah, I got letters that stutter. I had people offended by it. Deeply offended.

TSF: The reader really wants Becky Jones (the heroine of *The Nightrunners*) to survive.

JRL: So did I, but things happen. Actually, I learned that technique from Stephen King. I was reading *'Salem's Lot*. There was a character named Susan, one of the main characters, love interest. All of a sudden, she's killed off, and you'd grown to like this person. I remember I read (the death scene) and just stood up, put the book down and said, "Goddamn him to do that." That was brilliant. That taught me that anyone can die at anytime, no matter how much you like him. Real life is like that. Real life doesn't care. But you can't just use it as a gimmick, killing the characters off, 'cuz then you'll have the opposite problem.

TSF: You said you wished that Becky had lived. Do your characters write themselves?

JRL: Yeah, it feels that way. I mean, obviously you're doing it. It's your subconscious that's working it out at some point. I feel like the characters take over. I never intended for (Becky) to die, I liked her too much. She'd been through so much, and I wanted to see her succeed. She'd started out as underprivileged, everything went wrong. She finally found someone she thought she could have some kind of life with, and then she got the chair kicked out from under her, so to speak.

TSF: *Dead in the West* has been optioned?

JRL: It's been in production a couple of years now.

TSF: Does that mean the book will see a mass release?

JRL: I don't know. I really hope so, but one of the problems is I haven't found anybody willing to do it, because it's so short. It may end up in a collection of novellas.

TSF: Like King's *Different Seasons*?

JRL: Yeah, probably. I've got a novella I think I'm going to do for Dark Harvest called *Captured by the Engines*.

TSF: Let's talk about your involvement in *The Further Adventures of Batman*. Your style of writing fits in perfectly with the Batman mythos.

JRL: I've always wanted to (write Batman). When I was growing up, I really enjoyed comics. Batman was my favorite character.

TSF: You were obviously given some kind of restrictions, since "Subway Jack" is not a typical Joe R. Lansdale story.

JRL: I felt it was a chance to write something I'd always wanted to write. Sort of a childhood thing. I didn't want to write something that was "Kiddie," but obviously I had some restrictions in the language. So I tried to write the best comic book I could.

TSF: You dedicated the story to your son, so you probably wanted to write a story he could read. It's a violent story, but violent in a tame sort of way. The violence happens off the page, if you will.

JRL: Yeah, that's exactly it. Another one I just did for my daughter, a Joker story called "Belly Laugh (or The Joker's Trick or Treat.)" That'll be in *The Further Adventures of The Joker*.

TSF: You've got three sets of characters. The cast of *The Drive-In*; The God of the Razor; and now The Pilots (from the short story of the same name found in Dark Harvest's *Stalkers*.) Are there more stories to come involving the Pilots?

JRL: I really have no intention of doing anything more [with the Pilots]. I wrote that nine years ago. I feel really uncomfortable with it; it looks old and creaky to me. I revised it for the paperback version. It's the same story. I just revised the prose. At one point, (co-author) Dan [Lowry] and I were going to do a screenplay of it. We figured it would make a hell of an action film. We still want to do it but . . . .

TSF: You set up the characters so well in *Pilots*, giving them origins. It almost begs to be a novel.

JRL: That story owes as much to Dan as to me. It's actually his idea.

TSF: Who is Dan Lowry?

JRL: I went to school with Dan; he's a couple years younger than me. He used to be one of my Karate students. He just had this idea he wanted to do. He writes, but it's just he's never written but three or four stories. He wanted to do the story, he just didn't have the skill at that time. I had written several stories. So I said, "That's a great story." He had the basic story, the plot, and I said, "Well, the characters can't just come out of nowhere. They've gotta have a past." So I created their past. I felt the story had to have the momentum of a truck going all the time, even when we fall back in the past, it should just move back and forth. We didn't succeed all the way through, but it was an interesting experiment. It was fun. But it laid in a drawer for eight or nine years, because nobody would buy it. It was rejected by all the good ones and all the bad ones.

TSF: You're getting to the point now though, where everyone wants a Joe Lansdale story.

JRL: Yeah, and I don't give people old stories unless I think they're good because you could fall into a trap there. People want something and you say, "Ah, I could get it published now!" But, I don't feel that way. One of my best stories, "By Bizarre Hands" appeared in a small press magazine. It was written back in 1983, and everybody passed on it. Anthologies, magazines, the whole works. But I think it's one of my better stories and when it was in *Hardboiled*, even in that little magazine, the response was terrific. Tom Monteleone just bought it for his anthology (*Borderlands*).

TSF: Some of your first appearances were in Bill Prozini's Chrestomathy series (*Werewolf! Voodoo! Creature! Mummy! Ghoul!*).

JRL: Bill Prozini had read a couple of my mysteries and we corresponded. He was doing these horror anthologies and he says, "Do you want to write a story for a mummy anthology?" So I wrote a story called "The Princess." That was my first published horror story. Then I wrote one for *Creature!* called "Waziah." For *Ghoul!*, I wrote "The White Rabbit," which I think is the first good short story I ever wrote. Then all of a sudden, I said, "Hey this is fun!"

TSF: You're a very down-to-earth guy. How do you handle being a celebrity?

JRL: I don't like being a celebrity. I like coming (to the World Fantasy Con) because I like talking about books. I like meeting people who are interested in books. But the celebrity part makes me a little uncomfortable, and that's not just me trying to be modest. I'm serious.

TSF: Meeting the people behind the books is an added plus.

JRL: Right! That's the way I see it too, because I used to come to meet the people behind the stories, and if you have any interest in writing stories yourself, it's encouraging to meet these people and find out that they're just regular folks. They can be just as normal, or just as much of an asshole as other people you meet! In fact, I found it enlightening, 'cuz when I was growing up in Texas, I figured every writer had to come from New York or California. At some point, I realized it's just people that write these stories. That's one of the things I try to make people realize, that my life is not all that different from other people's lives. Everybody has their own peculiar position in life. This is my job. It's more than a job, 'cuz it's not like something I gotta do. It's something I love to do. But I got a life outside of writing. I got a family, I got other concerns. So, for aspiring writers, it's good to see that it can be done. I mean, I worked two jobs while I was trying to get there. I was a janitor. I took only blue collar jobs because I didn't want anything to tempt me to relax, make money, and not write. I was a poor kid all my life, so it would have been easy to settle into something and say, "This is comfortable," and look up at my age right now. I'd be an unhappy man not having written the stories.

TSF: You're going to be working on a project at DC Comics.

JRL: DC is very interested in working with me and Mark Nelson (the artist of the Dark Horse Comics *Aliens* comic series), and they're interested in the idea we have. If we present our proposal and they don't like it, we won't be doing it, but it looks real good. It'll be horror and it will be in the prestige format.

TSF: What do you have coming out in the near future?

JRL: A new novel, *Icebirds*. [The publisher] doesn't like that title, so they've asked me to change it. It's gone through a couple of titles. They don't like any of my titles. Raymond Chandler used to say to his publisher, "I'm thinking up a little title for you to change right now!" It's a suspense novel somewhat in the vein of *Cold in July*. It'll be out in hardback next year. *Cold in July* will be out in hardback. Both *Drive-In*s will be done in hardback with a third *Drive-In* in one volume.

TSF: Will Joe Bob (a character from *Cold in July*) have another adventure?

JRL: You know, I've never written a book with any intention of using a character again. And it always amazes me when it does happen, like when The God of the Razor shows up, and the sequel to *The Drive-In*. Part of that was a commercial consideration, 'cuz I wanted the money, and part of it was because I thought I could do another book. Had it just been the money, I wouldn't have done it. Had it just been I thought I could do another good book . . . I might have done it! With The God of the Razor, I just find the idea intriguing, and he just keeps popping up.

TSF: You weren't too happy with the way Bantam/Spectra marketed *The Drive-In*.

JRL: I wasn't happy at all. [The sequel] was a lot better in the way it looked.

TSF: What about *The Drive-In 3*?

JRL: Yeah, I'm doing the first two together and then adding a third shorter book, a novella actually. It'll be one long novel. I'm making some changes in Part 2, the parts where I went back and filled in for people who might not have read Part 1. I'm gonna take that out, do some revisions, and write a real long introduction and that will be the end of the *Drive-In* books.

Joe R. Lansdale

Stanley Wiater / 1990

Appeared in Stanley Wiater, *Dark Dreamers: Conversations with Masters of Horror* (New York: Avon Books, 1990). Reprinted by permission of the author.

Like his friend and colleague Dean R. Koontz, native Texan Joe R. Lansdale is possessed of an enormous and varied talent which can't be locked into a single genre. With such controversial and violent novels as *Act of Love, The Nightrunners,* and *Cold in July,* it's obvious that Lansdale is on his way to becoming a master of psychological horror and suspense—even if he doesn't like to be labeled as favoring any genre. With such plain weird novels as *The Drive-In* and *The Drive-In 2 (Not Just One of Them Sequels),* Lansdale also shows a penchant for the utterly outrageous which is second to none. His Western-horror novel *Dead in the West* reads like Zane Grey's (and George A. Romero's) worst nightmare in its unflinching descriptions of mutilation and mayhem. Then again, a small gem like *The Magic Wagon* is poignant enough to bring tears to anyone who reads it and can still remember what it's like to be a child.

If his novels weren't enough to ensure his reputation, then the short stories (over one hundred to date) would certainly qualify this plain-talkin,' straight-shootin' Texan for at least cult status. Just three stories like "Tight Little Stitches in a Dead Man's Back" (*Year's Best Horror Stories XV*), the Stoker award-winning "Night They Missed the Horror Show" (*Silver Scream*), and "On the Far Side of the Cadillac Desert with Dead Folks" (*Book of the Dead*) were enough to declare to the critics that he had arrived. A collection, fitting entitled *By Bizarre Hands,* was published in 1989 by specialty publisher Mark Ziesing.

As a writer, Lansdale is possessed of the ability to make you laugh out loud and then retch in disgust—sometimes in the same sentence. His voice as a writer is unmistakably his own. In person, Lansdale is both funny and profane, and the last person in the world to think he deserves some special status on this earth just because he thinks and writes differently from just about anyone you'll encounter in the field.

STANLEY WIATER: There was a time when you were grouped in with the lads half-seriously referred to as the splatterpunks. It was a title that you didn't seem too pleased to carry.

JOE R. LANSDALE: I didn't like to be called a splatterpunk writer, *at all*. I was doing what I was doing long before anyone decided to call anything splatterpunk. I don't think it's a fair term anyway, in the sense that I do a wide variety of things. I don't mean to imply that I dislike splatterpunk or the people who write it; I don't like the title merely because I find it *limiting*. If people start thinking of you in that way, then they always expect you to write that sort of fiction. I don't like any kind of label at all—I don't even think of myself as a horror writer. And I don't mean that in the way those film directors say, "Oh my God, this isn't a horror film . . . !"

I, by God, *like* horror. And I write horror. But I write other things, too. It's no more fairer to call me a horror writer than a Western writer or a suspense writer, because I'm those, too. I'm a writer. So it doesn't bother me at all to be called a horror writer, but I don't want to mislead people into expecting that all the time. But it is the largest percentage of my work. And I think a lot of the novels and short stories I've written, which may not be thought of strictly as horror, always have *horrific* details. In my suspense work it's the same way.

WIATER: You may not like to use the term "horror," but there's a great deal of intense violence in your work, and for many critics, violence can often be equated with contemporary definitions of horror.

LANSDALE: That's true. A lot of stories I've written have no violence or your usual "action" in them, but I do lean in that direction. I'm fascinated by violence—I'll be the first one to say so. But my fascination with it doesn't necessarily mean I enjoy violence or that I'm a violent person any more than anyone else. But I suppose that all people who are involved with horror, action-adventure, suspense, or crime are in some way connected with that interest in violence. But then, that's what sells newspapers and television programs. So most of us—who are at least willing to admit it—are in some way or another interested in violence, even if our interest is to be incredibly repulsed by the whole idea of violence.

WIATER: But few writers seem to deal with violence so intensely; you almost gleefully rub the reader's nose in the sight and smell of it.

LANSDALE: There is a certain glee in my work, I'll admit. But for me, it heightens the horror. It's really a little trick learned from Robert Bloch. I think my approach and style is very different from Bloch's, but he is really the one who taught me—and so many others—that horror and humor are opposite sides of the sword. When I was growing up, Bloch was undoubtedly my favorite horror writer—and is still one of my favorite horror writers. Maybe the favorite horror writer of them all.

The hard-boiled mystery writers influenced me in terms of style and approach. In many ways, I consider Robert Bloch a hard-boiled writer, with *Psycho* and *The Scarf*. Those are masterpieces. I think the hard-boiled voice has influenced me a lot more than horror writers. In the same way, Flannery O'Connor has been an enormous influence. So I like that straightforward, here-it-is, "fuck you" attitude. Bloch gave me an attitude. He was an original I-don't-know-what-you-would-call-it, but he would always cackle on about the most unpleasant things in the world [*laughs*]! And I always liked that posture, because if I was going to read horror, I wanted it to be scary. For me, he *was* scarier that way. And when he wasn't scary, he was at least always interesting and entertaining.

I think there's nothing more frightening than to find horrible things somewhat amusing. Any horror movie or book—even a good one—if you stop and think about the majority of 'em, the idea's *stupid*. Unless you really believe in vampires and werewolves. Of course horror has moved in considerably different directions from that, which I believe it has to—we've outgrown it for the most part. Which is not to say people shouldn't write about these supernatural creatures—I'm not saying I wouldn't do it. But in modern times, they become more representative of modern themes rather than simply being vampires and witches and werewolves. They may have had some psychological representation in the past, but they must have even more now if they're to be used effectively. They represent today's society.

WIATER: That's why the traditional label of "Horror" doesn't quite fit you—your work is more concerned with the horror man has in fighting his inner demons rather than any supernatural forces from beyond.

LANSDALE: Yes, I really am. I find as time goes on I'm more and more bored with supernatural elements—a large percentage of my work doesn't contain them at all. I hadn't thought about it before, but it's almost Lovecraftian in that I often deal with the breakdown of what you think are the expected rules of existence. In a sense, I guess that's what H. P. Lovecraft was doing with his Cthulhu Mythos, expect he had them explained as aliens or entities.

WIATER: Where do you feel your strength lies as a writer—in a novel or short story form?

LANSDALE: I prefer the short story medium. I think if I could make a living as a short story writer, I would do that primarily. I do like to write novels, though, and I'm proud of all the novels with my name on 'em. But I feel better about the short stories in general, though I'm very proud of *The Magic Wagon* and *Cold in July*. They're my favorites of my novels, for whatever reason.

WIATER: *The Magic Wagon* is unique among your works to date; it's all but impossible to shoehorn into any one genre. What compelled you to write it?

LANSDALE: I feel a strong connection to that one because it's very much about East Texas, and it takes place the year my father was born. My father's "voice" is the voice I tried to capture, with my own voice mixed in. By that I mean it contains some of the stories and attitudes that he told me when I was growing up. And I added in my own tendencies toward fantasy and oddball elements. But I am also a great fan of Westerns. I wish I had written more Westerns, but fate just didn't work out that way. I have a great big Western novel that I would like to do at some point.

What I've begun to realize, and I could be wrong on this, is that one of the things that makes my horror work interesting is that I do come at it from the perspective of thinking of myself as a Western-of-suspense writer writing horror. So the blend comes out more interesting for me. If you analyze a lot of my stories, you'll see they are very Western oriented or have Western elements.

WIATER: *The Drive-In* and its sequel *The Drive-In 2* are again two novels which seem to fit into no set genre, but rather use elements of every fantasy-related genre one can imagine, plus some elements no sane person should be able to imagine.

LANSDALE: I usually enjoy every line when I'm writing. But I didn't enjoy writing either one of *The Drive-In* books. And they're the ones that seem the lightest and the "frothiest" in many ways. I had a very, very hard time writing them. I think the universe I set in them was confining. Also, I work better when I am dealing with normal situations that are screwed up, instead of abnormal situations that get screwed up even more! Because in a universe where anything can happen you have to rely very strongly on humor and on characters, and that just takes a lot out of you. Writing those two books was very much like being a stand-up comic. You're on stage, people paid their money, and by God you'd better be funny—'cause they got tomatoes . . . .

WIATER: Stephen King has often stated the theory of the three levels of horror, the third and most outrageous being "to go for the gross-out."

Some of your critics would state this is the level where Joe Lansdale typically begins.

LANSDALE: [*laughs*] I like to go for the gross-out if it has some irony. I'll probably put my foot in my mouth for saying so—and then they'll say, "That pretentious asshole!"—but I think of myself as a satirist a lot of times. Not every time out, but I often see what I do as being that way because some stuff is so over the top that it is humor. Like "Cadillac Desert . . . ." A number of people I'm told were deeply offended, which in one sense makes me feel real good. And in another sense, I'm not out to just write something that will offend. It's very easy to offend—but it's not that easy to offend deeply [*laughs*].

WIATER: Organized religion seems to be one of your favorite targets as a satirist, again most obviously in *The Drive-In* and its sequel.

LANSDALE: I seem to have this thing about religion. I step on it every chance I get. But it's not that I'm stepping people's beliefs in religion, I'm stepping on the *smugness* that people have about religion, about how everybody's got to believe in this to be a good person. I think that I'm a good person, and lead a good life, and don't have to go to church or necessarily believe in a Christian God—or any god—for that matter. I can believe that I live this life, I die, I go belly up, I'm meat for the worms. And if I can be a good person knowing that, that can be an accomplishment that may be greater than expecting some reward in the next life.

WIATER: Any boundaries you've set on yourself as a writer? You don't appear to be the sort who "precensors" his work to insure easy acceptance from an editor or publisher.

LANSDALE: No, I don't think so either. Much to the dissatisfaction of a lot of publishers, and to the audience, too, at some point. I'm sure I have some subconscious boundaries, like everybody else. Most of my boundaries would be that I would write about almost anything—except in the area where I feel it's already been overworked. Or this particular subject is something I can't give anything new to. My boundaries are: Try to avoid stupidity. Or trying to repeat what someone else has done because you like what they did. Those are the only real boundaries I have in mind.

WIATER: Do you ever use any of your personal fears or experiences in your stories?

LANSDALE: I use a *tremendous* amount of autobiographical material, and I use a lot of my own fears. I use a lot of the fears of other people, that they've told me. But usually if I can't put something of myself into the stories, I can't write them. Which is not the same thing as saying the stories represent all my beliefs, but they are boiled down from my subconscious. Mainly it's autobiographical elements from personal attitudes and beliefs or experiences. A lot comes from newspaper headlines.

WIATER: It's well known you had some trouble early in your career with publishers being afraid to deal with such violent and uncompromising novels as *Act of Love* and *The Nightrunners*. Is this still the case?

LANSDALE: You know, it's funny, but when I started out, I sure did have trouble. Now, publishers always expect for me to be over the top, and don't even think about it anymore. Maybe they should [*laughs*]. No, I hope it doesn't get to that again. I've had editors say, "I like the story, but I just can't ... because I'm afraid it will ruin my magazine." I had one story called "Boys Will Be Boys" that caused subscriptions to be canceled.

WIATER: Could you tell me what your typical workday is like?

LANSDALE: I usually get up with the wife and kids around seven-thirty and I try to get down to work within thirty minutes of when I get up and work till about noon. I take off an hour, hour and a half, for lunch, then go back to work till about three. And I do that seven days a week. Sometimes I'll pull a double-shift if I get a little behind. But mainly I'll do only that, because I have a family and I have interests other than writing. I don't live to put paper in the typewriter. I like to spend time with my wife and my kids. There's a lot of things I'm interested in that I try to devote time to because I think you can get very stale as a writer. Those people who just live to write eventually repeat themselves. Besides, what kind of life is that? Go out and get a life!

WIATER: I can see you now: practicing martial arts in your backyard, followed by a half-dozen Lone Star beers, right?

LANSDALE: I'm not much of a drinker, contrary to what people always assume—that I'm a big, two-fisted drinker. I very seldom ever do. There goes the image! I'm an iced tea and Diet Coke man.

WIATER: Speaking of image, what advice to you have for someone who imagines writing fiction to be an easy road to fame and fortune?

LANSDALE: Learn to be a plumber. I'm serious. You need to learn something where you can make money, set up your own hours, and then spend your spare time writing as you see fit. A plumber makes pretty good wages, doesn't have to work all the time, and doesn't have to take a specific job if he doesn't want to. I was a janitor and found that was good for me. The rest of the advice is put your ass in a chair, put some paper in a typewriter, and write.

WIATER: Early in your career you ghostwrote some novels and also did some pseudonymous work. For what reasons?

LANSDALE: First of all, there haven't been many ghostwritten or pseudonymous books. Oddly enough, there were a number of projects where I was hired to do writing on them, was paid, and then the projects were eventually canceled for a variety of reasons. I once wrote *one* chapter for an action-adventure novel. Don't ask me why [*laughs*]. One of the pseudonymous novels is fairly common knowledge, though I don't think it's much of a book. It's a Western by "Ray Slater." There's very few copies of it, so I don't worry about it, though I would never reprint it. But the reasons I did them was simply to put food on the table and also just practice.

WIATER: You've also edited a few very strange Western anthologies. Like your own work, they are a wild collage of Western elements, science fiction, horror, fantasy, mystery—you name it. What was the inspiration behind them?

LANSDALE: In many ways they were attempts to interest people in the cross-pollination of genres. *Best of the West* has perhaps more traditional Western material than the others. My love of Westerns is there, but I didn't hold anybody to any strict guidelines and clichés. Just take some idea of the Western in your mind and take it from there. It's the whole idea of blending genres and becoming a little less genre-conscious. Which is not a comment that I don't like horror or Westerns or science fiction—I like all of them— but I think one of the things that is wrong with all those fields is that they become *predictable*. They become what's *expected*. And that's the main reason I did the anthologies, and each one's a little bit different from the others. *The New Frontier* is the one I'm most proud of.

WIATER: I understand you're also anxious to become more involved with screenwriting or at least adapt your own work to the screen?

LANSDALE: *Dead in the West* has been optioned. The book itself was optioned—I've done a screenplay, and we'll see what happens to it. I've had a tremendous amount of film interest in all of my work. I haven't written a novel yet that there hasn't been film interest in. So we'll see what all pans out. But I like the idea of writing original screenplays and might even adapt a book someone else wrote. But I don't feel drive: "My God, I've got to work in the movies!" I want to do it, but I believe I can pick and choose the projects I want to work on. A few years ago, things might have been different; I might have needed the money and said, "Sure, I want to write the next sequel to *Piranha XII*."

WIATER: It was once said about Charles Beaumont that he was the sort of writer who wouldn't be remembered for the titles of his books, but for his name being *on* the books. Does this seem to hold as true as well for you?

LANSDALE: I generally just think, "This is the story I'm telling now. I will tell it to the best of my ability." I don't worry if I'm topping the last story or not. I don't worry if my audience is going to accept it or not. I don't think about my audience, and that's not an insult to the readers. I certainly care about the readers. But when I sit down behind the typewriter, *fuck the readers!* What I'm interested in then is *me* as a writer, or otherwise I cannot get this story down. And if I start worrying about my readership, then I'm going to repeat myself and burn out either me or my readers. Or I'm going to bore myself, which in that case, why not dig a ditch?

I'm just not going to open new gates if I say, "I've found what works!" I don't think I've ever found what works. There's a certain voice that comes through most of my stories, but I'm sort of like a weathervane—there's no telling where I'll point next time! I want to keep it that way, because I think in the long run I'll get more readers and the readers respect that more. I don't ever want to be a predictable commodity.

A Conversation with Joe R. Lansdale

Gary Raisor / 1991

Published in *Cemetery Dance*, Winter 1991. Reprinted by permission of the author.

GARY RAISOR: Would you introduce yourself, the vital stats, that sort of thing?

JOE R. LANSDALE: I'm thirty-nine years old. Born in Gladewater, Texas, 5′11″, 170 pounds. Married with two children. One boy, eight years old. One girl, four years old. I live in Nacogdoches, Texas. Have been a full-time writer since 1981.

GR: How did a poor boy and jack-of-all trades from East Texas ever get started writing in the first place?

JRL: I've always wanted to write; I can't remember not wanting to. It seemed to me to be the only profession I could do day in and day out and be happy with.

GR: You've written a lot of horror. Why?

JRL: First of all, one of the things that attracted me was I liked scary stories. I think we're all fascinated, to some degree, by violence and the unknown. Once we recognize the violent nature that we have in ourselves, we're more likely to do something about it. It's a way of giving ourselves short doses of the inevitable—death.

GR: You've said a time or two that you've said all you have to say in the horror field. Do you think you'll ever return to it?

JRL: Though I have said that, and sometimes feel that way, I never say never. I don't seem to have much to say in the traditional vein. A short story collection that I have forthcoming from Pulphouse Publishing called *Stories by Mama Lansdale's Youngest Boy* pretty well covers 50 percent of the stories that I wrote in the traditional horror vein, as least as traditional as I get. I think there will be more traditional stories, but I don't know that they'll be traditional horror stories.

GR: Why do you feel compelled to push what, many would say, are the bounds of good taste?

JRL: I don't consciously do that. I just write the stories that appeal to me. Stories that have some relationship to everyday life: things I see happening around me, hear from others, read in the newspaper. Sometimes I write stories purely as metaphors, things that surround me and scare me.

GR: Recently you've turned to writing crime and suspense. Why?

JRL: I really don't see a tremendous division between where my writing has been going over the past six or seven years, and the crime and suspense tales that I'm writing now. Remember that when I started writing, my first sales were in the mystery, crime, and suspense fields. And when you look at many of my horror tales, they often have a crime angle and many are not supernatural. I doubt that I can stay in any one field completely.

GR: You've said that your writing is going in a totally new direction. Can you tell us what to expect in the future?

JRL: I've shifted gears again, but I don't know how to describe it. In the next two years, around 1992, you're gonna start seeing totally different types of tales from me. That doesn't mean you won't recognize me, but I've never tried to keep up with my audience; they have to keep up with me, and if they can't or prefer not to, I'm sorry.

GR: How much of the real Joe Lansdale comes through in your writing? I.e., Are you really the sick puppy everyone thinks you are?

JRL: I don't know; I don't think I'm a sick puppy. I'm just fascinated by them. I'm very much a family man, and I hope at least a fairly good one. I'm a small-town kind of guy; reasonably conservative at heart. I'm more of a literary anarchist than a political anarchist. Politics, day-to-day life . . . I'm primarily a middle-of-the-road type person, but I think that's more of an advantage for a writer, because I'm less inclined to have a definite agenda. I fortunately, and unfortunately, can see a number of viewpoints and though I may not agree with all of them, I can get into their skins and write from different angles. The angles that fascinate me generally are those that are the farthest afield of my own views.

GR: What's the best thing about being a writer?

JRL: The writing.

GR: The worst?

JRL: The financial insecurity, and the fact that each time out you want to do a better job than before and that's not always possible.

GR: Have you ever written anything that made you stop and say: "Hey, maybe I went too far this time, maybe I should back off?"

JRL: I've written things that have disturbed me. "Drive-in Date" in *Night Visions 8* probably bothers me more than anything I've ever written. So I knew that little buddy had to be in print.

GR: Of your own writing, what's your favorite short story? Novel?

JRL: "Night They Missed the Horror Show." I think it did everything I wanted it to do within my human abilities. For novel, it varies between *The Magic Wagon*, *The Drive-In*, and *Cold in July*. Those three are very different from each other and yet each seems to be able to accomplish what I intended them to do as best as I've ever been able.

GR: A lot of your novels are very short, which goes against traditional wisdom in the publishing business. Why do you write short novels?

JRL: That's just how long the stories are. A novel that I'm planning to write next year probably will be long because that's how long the story is.

GR: A good part of your work concerns racism in our society. Why does this issue crop up again and again in your writing?

JRL: That's simple. It's one of the things that bothers me more than anything else. People worry about the atomic age and being blown off the planet, but I think it's much more likely that we'll self-destruct, and it's one of the things that frightens me and not just because I'm from the South. I see it everywhere. Personally, I don't see that the South is any more racist than anywhere else. I think it's funny when people in the North or West experience it they act surprised, but when it occurs in the South they act like it's status quo. I'm offended by that.

GR: These days, horror is hard pressed to keep pace with our violent reality, don't you think? What do you see in the future of horror? Can it keep pace?

JRL: I think that's one reason so many writers are turning to crime and suspense—to real horrors. I do think, however, that people will reach a barrier with that and that the trend will turn back to more supernatural traditional horrors, which will be used as a release, which is why many readers originally turned to horror, and which is why I feel that much of my work fails to satisfy readers' expectations. At least, in this point and time.

GR: Would you tell us a little about the Lansdale stories in this issue?

JRL: "Bestsellers Guaranteed" is one of the stories that I felt had not gotten enough play. I like the story and it is considerably different in voice and tone from my recent work. Strictly speaking, it's a more traditional tale, but it was written out of frustration because at the time, 1983, when I wrote "Bestsellers Guaranteed," I had already written a number of the stories that I'm now known for, but couldn't sell them anywhere. I was so frustrated that I decided to "mute" my voice and write a more traditional sort of story. But if you read between the lines you can certainly touch on the frustration that drives the story's engine.

"Drive-in Date"—the play version—is based on a short story in *Night Visions 8*. The story and the play are probably influenced by Henry Lee Lucas and his buddy Otis, or at least the stories they told about themselves. It makes no difference if those stories are false; the stories themselves disturbed me and frightened me enough that one night I woke up with this one in my head and had no choice—the same way that a constipated man has no choice but to shit—to take a laxative at the typewriter and get this nasty turd of a story out of my head.

GR: What upcoming projects can we look for?

JRL: I'm doing a Batman novel called *Captured by the Engines*, a Batman adventure in five gears. I'm hoping it will be fun and echo both Batman and Lansdale. There will be a comic book project with Mark Nelson for DC, prestige format, in four parts. Followed by a novel I've been nursing for two years, a novel that I think will be as fast-paced and exciting as *The Nightrunners*, but I hope will echo my more recent concerns as exemplified by *Cold in July* and *Savage Season*. To be perfectly honest, I'm avoiding talking about it directly. I don't normally feel that at least giving a general synopsis of a story will harm my ability to write it, but in this case I've developed a sort of superstition. Let's just say I have high hopes.

GR: What makes Joe Lansdale happy?

JRL: I'm happy right now. My family, my writing, reading good books and stories, good bowel movements, plenty of iced tea. I'm a pretty simple kind of guy, I guess.

GR: What keeps Joe Lansdale awake at night?

JRL: Mexican food, popcorn, and the kind of dreams they give me.

GR: When all is said and done, what would you like to be said about you, as a man, as a writer?

JRL: He was a good man and he did his best.

Chewin' the Fat with Mama Lansdale's Youngest Boy

Dwight Brown and Lawrence Person / 1992

Published in *Nova Express*, Summer 1992. Reprinted by permission of the authors.

Lawrence Person: To start off, I understand you're finishing up a Batman novel?

Joe R. Lansdale: Yeah. I've finished that, in fact. Called *Captured by the Engines*. A Batman novel with four gears and overdrive.

LP: How did you first get started with writing something like that?

JRL: Batman?

LP: Yeah.

JRL: The idea for the story had been with me a long time. I was called by DC when they were doing their *Further Adventures of Batman*; they asked me about a short story, a Batman short story. They had heard that I was a big Batman fan; I grew up on the comics and all that. It was one of those moments to kind of go back and be nostalgic and so I did. That led to *The Further Adventures of the Joker*. They read those stories, liked them so much they asked me to do a novel. I turned them down a couple of times, but the third time everything just hit me right, and I did it.

LP: Are you the only one who's doing a Batman besides . . . ?

JRL: There were two others. I think Craig Shaw Gardner did one, and Simon Hawke did one.

LP: Was that the first time you had done writing for any sort of comic medium?

JRL: It's not that kind of form, it's done like a regular novel. I'm now writing comic books for DC for Mark Nelson to illustrate. We're doing a four-volume Prestige format thing called *Blood and Shadows*. We have plans for other things we haven't officially submitted to DC, but we're hoping to pursue those.

LP: While we're talking about all this stuff you're doing outside the regular book channels, I understand there are several Joe Lansdale movies, either scripted by you or taken from your work, in the works.

JRL: Yeah. I wrote the screenplay for *Cold in July*, which was optioned by John Irving, who did *Dogs of War, Hamburger Hill, Turtle Diary, Tinker, Tailor, Soldier, Spy*, a couple of other things like that. He optioned *Cold in July* and asked me to write the screenplay. *The Drive-In*'s been optioned for a couple of years in a row using a screenplay written by somebody else, which I've seen. I think it's a pretty good screenplay. *Dead in the West* has been optioned five years in a row. "The Pit" has been optioned a couple of years in a row, and so has "On the Far Side of the Cadillac Desert with Dead Folks." Those screenplays will be written by other people.

LP: I can just imagine them trying to bring that one to the screen.

JRL: I don't expect that to happen. I'll be doing some more comic book work too. Probably over the next year or so. I'm sort of going through a period where I'm enjoying doing that. I've always wanted to do it, and I'm hoping that I'll get a little of that done before I start on my next novel. Which should be something to keep me occupied for a long time.

LP: Not to get too much into your finances, I'm given to understand that everything you've been talking about is generally pretty lucrative work.

JRL: Yeah, it is. It's kind of fun to do what you want to do and get paid for it. I seem to be going through a good period right now. Whether that will hold out, I don't know. I still seem to be surviving primarily off an extremely strong cult audience, and the peripheral fallout from that has made me comfortable.

LP: So you feel you've got an audience that will follow you just about anywhere you go?

JRL: I don't like to think of it like that, because that seems kind of pushy. I tend to think I'd better write what I want to and hope they follow me. That's better, because otherwise, if I start trying to identify who "they" are, then I may start trying to write for "them," and they may not exist. I like to think the reason people read my work is because I follow what interests me. That doesn't mean I think everything I do is brilliant, I'm just a guy doing the best I can. But I like to think that I have something interesting, something quirky, something original that people want to read. At least most of the time.

LP: There seem to be a lot of people in Texas that are doing something like that, Lew Shiner and Neal Barret Jr. . . .

JRL: Without a doubt. Neal is the best of us all.

LP: Is there anything . . . communicating with each other that helps you do this?

JRL: Well, it's funny. We all know each other, and we certainly talk to each other, but I don't know that we really discuss our work or think of ourselves as part of any movement or anything like that.

LP: A nonmovement.

JRL: Yeah, it's a nonmovement. I guess it's that we all tend to be extremely avid readers, and we don't just read in one field. We read a lot of different things, and we're looking for something different. I think that it must be in the air, but it seems to be in Texas air more than a lot of other places. Maybe that's just a Texas chauvinistic attitude, but it seems to me that Texas is producing some of the finest stuff coming out right now. Lew Shiner's *Deserted Cities of the Heart* and Neal's *The Hereafter Gang*, which is probably one of the most brilliant novels I've ever read.

LP: How did you first get started in writing at all?

JRL: I've always done it, since I was nine years old. I don't really know what the catalyst was. I was reading fairy tales and stuff like that—by the time I was eleven, the *Iliad* and the *Odyssey*. I was reading those things and mythology. I just loved it. When I read Edgar Rice Burroughs, it just kicked a gear in. I said, "Man, this is it," and I knew this was what I wanted. This assured me that I was making the right choice. Then I just never looked back. Strange that it's Edgar Rice Burroughs, my work's probably totally different from that kind of fiction. But if there was any single author that put the final excitement in me, it was him.

Dwight Brown: *Act of Love* was your first novel, right?

JRL: It was my first novel bearing my name, yeah. Probably the first novel of mine to appear.

DB: And it was one of the early serial killer novels. Don't remember off the top of my head when *Red Dragon* came out, but now, all of a sudden, it's like, "Hey! Everybody's into serial killers!" There's something like three serial killer books on the *Times* bestseller list. What do you think the reason is for this mass appeal of serial killers?

JRL: Well, first of all, I knew there were other serial killer books before mine. Dean Koontz had done some. I do think mine was different, in the fact that the intent was different. I had a standard police procedural with the serial killer element to it, and then cranked it *all the way up*. Now everybody's doing that, so it's not all that new, but back then, that novel was absolutely radical. It's hard to believe now, but it really was radical. I mean, some of the rejects I got off it, and *The Nightrunners* later, as I've said before, jokingly, "It's like the rejects stuttered." As to why, I think it's pretty obvious; for a while people thought those things were anomalies. Certainly I don't think everybody's a serial killer, but I'm sure a lot of unexplained murders in the past, we're beginning to realize now, were probably serial killers. I think it's more an awareness than anything else. People are less and less willing to believe in the supernatural right now. They'll swing back, it always does. They're looking for a realistic horror, but at some point it'll get beyond the thrill. I think it already has for some. I mean, even for me—and I've written the stuff—it wasn't just the thrill. There's always that element in anything scary, no matter how horrible it is, there's a certain thrill to it. But it was an attempt to explore something that you are concerned about and worried about and terrified about. I think it's just an outgrowth of where society is right now. It has a lot to do with the fact that, used to be when people got put in prison, they stayed there. They don't now. Used to be that people had to be responsible for their actions. Now it's something else causing it. I'm not saying which is right or wrong, but I think it's a totally different mind-set and awareness that makes us think about these things more. Makes us frightened.

LP: We mentioned *Red Dragon* briefly. Obviously when *Red Dragon* came out, it was a phenomenal hit, and deservedly so. But, did you feel a little bit of jealousy over that?

JRL: I felt a twang, . . . I don't know, of jealousy. I thought the book was too damned good to be jealous of; it was much better than mine. But I felt a twinge of regret because I was there first. For its time, mine was an extremely good and radical book. I think it deserved more serious publication. I think I can write a lot better now. But it has its power. I think to this day it's got power. Not as much as before because it's been done so much, but yeah, I felt a twang of disappointment that mine had not been noticed. But I certainly couldn't fault *Red Dragon* any. It's a far superior novel to mine, and it deserves it.

LP: We've touched on this a little before, but you write in a lot of different genres, horror and mystery and Western. Is there any you feel particularly comfortable in? Or that you're finding now that you've written all of them, you like this one a little better?

JRL: I don't think I could ever say, "This is what I'm gonna do." I feel real comfortable with crime and suspense and Westerns. I think crime/suspense more than anything else. I like Westerns tremendously, but I couldn't write Western after Western, because I don't like standard traditional Westerns, and those don't come to me often. But the crime field, I find I do that more naturally than anything else. I can take what is normally a standard plot, start writing it, and something quirky will come out without me trying. It seems to be my stuff, and yet it's more. I think it's more accessible to readers. Which is not necessarily why I do it, but because I'm so comfortable doing it. I'm glad that if that's an offshoot of it, that it is accessible to readers and that they enjoy it, because that seems to be the thing I enjoy the best. At least right at this moment. Who knows later?

LP: You've done one excellent straight Western, or "straight Western," *The Magic Wagon* and also *Dead in the West*, which is a Western/horror hybrid. Are you thinking of doing any more in the future?

JRL: I wouldn't be surprised. It seems like what's happening is that in the novels I tend to be moving more and more toward crime and suspense, and the short stories tend to be moving towards more quirky and . . . maintaining that sort of thing that I've been doing. I don't think you're going to continue to see the same kind of stories from me, because I think that's a dead end. I don't want to start repeating myself, and everybody looks to me to do the same thing. I've got some real different and unusual things in mind. But I do think that, novel-wise, I tend to be moving more towards crime and suspense.

DB: Just as a casual observer, it seems to me like you're one of the leaders of a movement that's trying to change the direction of the Western away from what it's been for the past thousand years. Have you encountered a lot of resistance from the traditional Western [reader]?

JRL: Not in a real direct way, but in subtle ways. Most of them I get along with pretty good, and I think they respect my writing. But I think the traditionalists are really upset by it. I think they think I'm antitraditional. Some of my favorite books are very traditional, but what I'm saying is that most of the traditional stuff that goes under the label of traditional is just the same old shit. Traditional is a type of novel which can be done brilliantly. *True Grit* is a traditional novel, but hell, it isn't like anything else either. All I'm trying to do is say that, if a Western's going to survive, people have to realize that those elements of the West can be moved into other areas. I think that I'm sort of a Western kind of guy myself. But I live in a modern time, and I think you have to look at it from all angles.

LP: I want to expand a little on that. Back when I was doing my splatterpunk article, you wrote me back . . . .

JRL: Yeah. Yeah, excellent article. I think it was the definitive article on splatterpunk. I think it's the best that's been done.

LP: Oh. Thank you. The Mutual Appreciation Society's in full swing here . . . .

JRL: The only one that comes close would be Paul Sammon, when he did his piece on the splatterpunks.

LP: The big one? Yeah. I personally had a lot of respect for R. S. Hadji's article. He got some things that I missed.

JRL: Well, you always do.

LP: But back when I was writing that, you wrote me, and at the bottom you just signed "Joe Lansdale, The Cowpunk." And then you said: "Just joking."

JRL: Yeah. "Just joking," really.

LP: But since then, that term has bubbled up in recent months related to your work, and some of Neal's work, and etc., to the point where you labeled *Razored Saddles* "the cowpunk anthology" . . .

JRL: *They* labeled it that.

LP: Oh, they labeled it that.

JRL: I don't know it was on there until I saw it.

LP: Do you feel that's perhaps not an accurate tag?

JRL: I'm more comfortable with that than I am "splatterpunk." On the other hand, I wouldn't want to have that one label. I said it as a joke, but it's the same thing, you've got to watch your mouth. Schow said the "splatterpunk" thing as a joke, and it was picked up. Then they really got into defending it. I think it's an unfortunate term. It's very, very threatening. If they had called it "outlaw fiction" or something like that, it would have been more acceptable, because it has such a broader range. It means "not the same old stuff." "Splatterpunk" seems to imply a very, very narrow vision. "Here's splatter." Then all this stuff has to be bloody. And that really isn't true of the stuff that's going on.

LP: Since you're really very different people, I'd like to know how you got to know Lew Shiner.

JRL: Lew and I have known each other for a long time. I met him in the late seventies at a World Fantasy Convention in Fort Worth. We were the only ones there that were reading detective fiction and talked about it. We wanted to talk about mainstream literary fiction we were reading and nobody else did. George Procter introduced me to Lew, and boy, we've just been bosom buddies ever since. We don't see eye-to-eye on a lot of stuff, but we're very close friends. I think we care about a lot of the same things in our lives.

LP: I heard this story secondhand, but I'm given to understand that at one point the editor of a mystery magazine said you and Lew were the future of P.I. fiction, and the next issue he was gone.

JRL: Yeah, that's right. That's true. That was *Mike Shayne*. Larry Shaw, I think, was the editor. He was the editor for about one month. We wrote a story called "Black as the Night," that he bought and published—I think it may have even been bought by the editor previous to him. But he says, "Man, this is what I want. Y'all are the models for what we're gonna do with this magazine." Well, we threw our chest out. We were happy sumbitches, and we wrote that next one and sent it in. The time it got there, Chuck Fritch says, "You know, I don't understand this kind of stuff at all." Because Larry Shaw was *gone*. He was there about a month and he was *gone*. So there went our careers. Looking back on it, we weren't all that radical, but for *Mike Shayne*, it was different. It was more of a sensibility to the story that made the difference, I think.

LP: One more thing on Lew Shiner. What's the story behind "Western Action-Adventure: As You Like It!"?

JRL: Well, Lew once came to the house, and we once wrote a novel in four days under a pen name. We wrote it in four days, so to keep it going, we would do the old Marvel thing, "Western Action—As You Like It!" I'd go in and write for twenty or thirty pages, and come out, and he'd go "Western Action—As You Like It!" Every time we'd start to fade down, we'd go "Western Action—As You Like It!" to get ourselves geared up. About the time we got ready to leave, my wife was ready to kill us both. She says, "I hear that one more time, you're both gonna die." We named characters after people we knew. What Chad Oliver always says is, "Now, when you write a Western, shoot the sheriff on the first page," so we did. There were people riding off into the sunset and stuff. It was a parody, but it was lovingly done and fun. It's probably a little bit of a hoot, but I'm glad it didn't get published.

LP: So, pretty much irrecoverable, you think?

JRL: I've not looked at it in years. Just a few years ago, somebody wanted to buy it, and I went "Aaaaaah!" I was *real* enthused, yeah. It was under a pen name—I don't remember what name we came up with.

DB: Canonical Nova Express question number one: But there's a different spin on this. You strike me as possibly having the most curious set of literary influences of anybody we've ever met, and I'd like to know what some of them are. I have some speculations of people that seem to have influenced your work, but I'm curious what you have to say.

JRL: Like a lot of writers, I seem to be influenced by a tremendous number of people. My father couldn't read or write, and my mother had about an eleventh-grade education, so nobody could say, "This isn't good" or "This isn't bad." They just encouraged me to read, so I read everybody. I think the hard-boiled writers of the Gold Medal school certainly had a lot to do with influencing me. Flannery O'Connor is a tremendous influence. I would say that Hemingway and James Cain are strong influences. Henry Kuttner, Ray Bradbury, Richard Matheson, this is kind of a mixed bag. Western writers like Glendon Swarthout, I'm trying to think who else . . .

LP: Harper Lee?

JRL: Harper Lee without a doubt. My favorite novel's *To Kill a Mockingbird*. I love that novel above all novels. I've read that thing, I don't know, three or four times, and every time I read it, I like it better. I guess Flannery O'Conner is probably my single favorite writer. There are a lot of people that for some reason I can't even think of right now. They're mostly people not in the field. The people in the field I named are very prominent. Bradbury, Charles Beaumont, I like him a lot, Gerald Kersh. That's all I can think of off the top of my head.

DB: I've always thought there was strong Cornell Woolrich influence in your work.

JRL: You know, that's funny, because I don't like Cornell Woolrich's work, and I've been compared to him a couple of times. I think we're alike in that we have a nightmare sort of vision. There was one story by him, "The Number's Up," that was an influence for "Night They Missed the Horror Show." I think that's the best Cornell Woolrich story I read. What I like by Woolrich, I like a lot. So I may be more influenced by him than I realized. But certainly those type of writers that wrote those dark—David Goodis . . .

DB: Chester Himes?

JRL: Chester Himes, without a doubt, is a major, major . . . . I love Chester Himes. That guy was a genius. He had that dark humor angle I so admire.

DB: Jim Thompson?

JRL: Jim Thompson I didn't know about until recently, but a lot of people thought I had read him, that's one reason I did. People kept saying, "I think this guy writes like Jim." "Who's that?" I thought I was pretty well-read. I missed him till five years ago.

DB: Till the revival started?

JRL: Yeah. With the Black Lizards.

DB: What did you think of the *The Killer inside Me*?

JRL: I liked the book. I liked it quite a bit. I'm not as fond of some of the others, but I really liked it. Thought they made a pretty good film out of it, with Stacy Keach.

DB: Which of the others have you read? *Pop. 1280*?

JRL: Yeah, I've read that one. I've read one he did about oil field days, it's kind of autobiographical.

DB: *Roughneck*?

JRL: That's it. And I read one, *After Dark, My Sweet*. There's another or two I've read, and I can't remember . . . *The Grifters*. And then there was one other that I can't think of right off.

DB: Did you read Hammett or Chandler when you were younger?

JRL: You bet. Chandler's one of my favorites. I like Hammett, too. James Cain. I like all that stuff. A lot of writers that people don't know about, like Robert Kyle, all the Gold Medal people . . .

DB: Yeah, people who are coming back out from Black Lizard. Charles Willeford?

JRL: Charles Willeford. Oh, my God, I love Charles Willeford. Charles Williams is good. I like all those people. Stylistically, you look at my work, you see more of the hard-boiled writers than you see horror or science fiction. John D. MacDonald's another one.

DB: Of course John D. MacDonald. I was thinking about that. Travis McGee in specific, or . . .

JRL: The early stuff, before Travis McGee, really is what I always liked. *Soft Touch* is a big influence on me. Ed Gorman's a good writer, too, off the subject.

DB: Well, I figured that. I've been reading the Black Lizard stuff. Getting away from literary influences and into something else, who are you reading for pleasure now?

JRL: A lot of the people we've named. I tend to reread things. I like Robert F. Jones a lot right now. He's only done four books.

DB: I've never heard of him.

JRL: Yeah, afraid too many people haven't. They're awful titles, usually, one title, *Bloodsport*, is really, really neat. There are some novels named *Bloodsport*, but this is Robert F. Jones. Then there's *The Diamond Bogo*, which I like a lot, and one called *Bloodtide*, which is recent. In spite of those horrible titles, they're brilliant books. *Bloodtide*, they tried to market with "If you like Clive Cussler, you'll like this." I see Clive Cussler people picking this up and going, "Let me have it, yep," and then reading it and being disappointed. And I can also see people that would have really liked this novel not picking it up because they don't want to read Clive Cussler clones. It's nothing like that. Robert F. Jones is really unusual. *Bloodtide* is probably his most conventional novel in some ways.

DB: Have you ever read any Andrew Vachss?

JRL: Yeah, as a matter of fact, I like his stuff. I bought a story from him recently for an anthology Karen and I are editing.

DB: What's the anthology?

JRL: It's called *Dark at Heart*. It's crime, dark crime, it's suspense. This is for Dark Harvest.

LP: We've touched on this before, but I know about your pseudonyms. It's pretty much open knowledge that you wrote *Texas Nightriders* . . .

JRL: Yeah. That's open knowledge.

LP: . . . as Jack Slater.

JRL: Ray Slater.

LP: Ray Slater. And also, the infamous *Molly's Sexual Follies* with Brad Foster, which was a Ballantine book. What was the name that one came under?

JRL: You know, I don't remember. You'd have to ask Brad. It was a pseudonym he had used before on several, and we just took the pseudonym that he'd been using. But I don't remember what the pseudonym was.

LP: It would be easier if we found the number, I think. What are some other ones that you're willing to admit to?

JRL: Those are them. I wasn't willing to admit to those. I had a guy come up at a World Fantasy Convention and bring two of the three books I wrote in a series and says, "sign these." And I looked at him and I say, "What makes you think I wrote those?" And he says, "I can tell by the writing style, and you mentioned Nacogdoches, and . . ." So I signed them, as the pseudonym.

LP: Was there a particular reason you did them as a pseudonym?

JRL: Money. I had to have money . . . to pay my bills, to write the books I wanted, to afford *The Nightrunners*, you know. They were three books, and they were *The MIA Hunter*. I'll go ahead and tell you, it was Jack Buchanan. You can mention that, but I won't say which ones I wrote. It's getting to be common knowledge, it can't hurt the guy I did them for, because he has reached that point where the series is about gone. The main reason I didn't tell was . . . you've got to keep in mind that these were all tampered with. There were things like "he grunted" and "he growled" added that I would never, in a hundred years, have said. I guess that's an exclusive, I don't think I've ever told anybody that. I mean, who gives a shit, right?

LP: I assume you've read Dave Schow's *The Pulpmeister*?

JRL: Yes. And . . . .

LP: And it's that sort of thing.

JRL: Well, I guess so. Yeah, pretty much.

LP: "The rain fell down wetly" is my favorite line.

JRL: Yeah, and it's very much that. I think that's on the money.

LP: Almost every one of your novels or short stories has dealt with racism, in one form or another.

JRL: Happens a lot, yeah.

LP: Is there a particular reason this particular subject is so strong with you? Is it from being brought up in the South?

JRL: I guess that's part of it. When I got older and got into other places, I saw it everywhere. When I was in the North, it was more open. Growing up and seeing Black people go into the back of a building to get their food turned my stomach. It always did. My mother just hated it. My father was very racist in his rhetoric, but he was never racist in the way he treated people. He could say some awful things about other people—but he was a John Wayne type character, in the best sense. I mean, he lived by his word and all that stuff. I know that when Black kids were hungry and they'd come around, he'd give them money, five dollars a hit. So, I think rhetoricwise, he had been raised that way, but in his heart, he just wasn't. He couldn't mistreat somebody. So, though I grew up understanding racism, from the standpoint of my father's talk, it bothered me so much because it seemed such a flaw in such an honorable man. That and the fact of seeing water fountains that said "Colored" and seeing washeterias that said "N----r" on them. I saw that, and I just can't reconcile that somehow. It never occurred to me that these people should not be treated as people. It hurts me deeply. It still does. You see, I'm not scared of atomic wars or such, I'm scared of racism. I'm scared of things of that nature more than anything else.

LP: Do you think it's gotten better?

JRL: Yeah. People say, "It's not better." Well, hell it ain't better, it's a *lot* better. I remember when you'd walk down the sidewalk and a Black man'd step off the sidewalk if he was coming the other way to let you pass. When I was a child, and I'm forty-one this year, that was in the mid-sixties when these things began to change, and I think really noticeable where I lived in the late sixties. There was so much turmoil at that time. The Vietnam War was probably a big influence on how I think. That whole period, the sixties, I think that had a lot to do with it. I'm coming from a different perspective than a lot of other people of the sixties. But I think that era affected all of us who lived through it. It's a very interesting time, a very strange time. Positive and negative.

LP: You put a lot, both positive and negative, into *Savage Season*. Was there anyone you particularly had in mind, or rather I should say, did you have any particular person whom you knew, that had—obviously, not that had found $100,000 or whatever, but had something like what happened to Hap happen to them?

JRL: You're talking about the Vietnam experience? That happened to me. Except I was drafted, I dropped out of school to be drafted, and I was. I went and refused to accept induction. They didn't know what exactly to do with me. They told me I was going to prison, and I said, "I understand. I'll get my stuff in order." I went home, and they wanted me to come back. They sent me to a psychiatrist, and the psychiatrist said, "You know, you're not fit for military service. I think you're dangerous. I think that if somebody told you to do something that you thought was wrong, you'd shoot 'em, so go home." They gave me a 1-Y or something like that. Not long after that, draft cards were abolished, so I would have gone to prison. I mean, I was prepared to. Which is strange, because I'm not a conscientious objector. I wouldn't sign papers. I believe there's some wars that should be fought. In fact, I believe the war we just fought [the Gulf War] should have been fought, although I don't think it's all clear cut. Also, I felt there were questions like this, "If someone attacks you in your house at night, would you defend yourself?" Right, you know, yeah. And, "Would you have fought in World War I and World War II," and I said, "From what I know historically, probably." See, I couldn't in all conscience say I was a conscientious objector. So *Savage Season* is based on me, for better or worse.

LP: Based in a very, very personal way, obviously.

JRL: Yeah. Leonard's based on a couple of people I know. *Cold In July* has a lot of personal things in it, too. A lot of my fiction is very, very personal. I was busy when I was young.

LP: Touching again on when you were young, I remember from a workshop with you that you had, what you consider at least, a pretty normal, happy childhood.

JRL: Yeah, I had a very happy childhood. We were poor by standards—I got older, I realized it. But I don't think it was any detriment to me because nobody had money, we were all poor. Occasionally somebody we knew had money, but everybody was just about the same. We always thought of ourselves as broke, not poor. There is a difference, a psychological difference. My mother encouraged me to read. I had a father that was almost bigger than life in many, many ways. He had a big bark, but his bite wasn't that bad. He was an intelligent man, not an educated man, but yeah, I had a good home life.

LP: What did you father do for a living?

JRL: Worked with engines. He was a mechanic. Self-taught. My mother bought him a Model T or a Model A, I get them mixed up, and he just took it apart and took it apart and took it apart. This was before I was born. He just took it apart so he could do it, and he just kept doing it till he became a mechanic. So yeah, I had a real happy childhood. I had friends, I wasn't unpopular. I wasn't the class geek, and yet I wasn't the class bigwig, you know—I was very popular in school. I had no troubles.

LP: You failed Karen Fowler's "prominetics" test.

JRL: What's that? I don't know.

LP: Well, Lew mentioned it at the workshop, it's basically, if you didn't go to your senior prom, you're more likely to end up a writer.

JRL: I went to both of them, junior and senior. I married, first time, when I was eighteen. When I went to Tyler Junior College, I had hair that was probably about as long as Dwight's here. And they said, "You're not going in this, you're not going to this school." You've got to remember this was 1970.

LP: We'd like to note that Dwight's hair, although a little longer than average, is not below his collar.

JRL: Yeah. "You're not going to this school." And I said, "Well, we'll see." And so we took it to court, and we won an injunction. It's in the law books, it's *Lansdale et al., vs. TJC*, and retroactive in East Texas, everybody could wear their hair the way they wanted to, dress the way they wanted to. There were a lot of things going on then, and those were just ways of saying, "We're not gonna do these stupid games. We're not gonna be bossed around." It was very important then to be individual, and I miss those times. I think that a lot of things, probably negative, came out of that too. But, it seemed like a more exciting and interesting group of folks.

LP: So you were pretty darn radical for someone of your background.

JRL: Yeah, I was pretty darn radical. I sort of pride myself on being middle of the road, but at that time, what would be middle of the road now was radical. I was for women's rights, and I was for civil rights and all this stuff. I was anti-Vietnam. I had hair down to my waist nearly, and people used to say, "Hey, honey, you give head?" And I had to fight everybody, you know? I was a tough kid, too, martial arts and all that stuff. So I don't seem to fit a lot of what would be the classic profiles for that. But I didn't become a writer because I grew up with science fiction fandom. I never knew it existed until I was in my midtwenties. I just wrote what interested me.

DB: Sketching in background, how much education did you get? Did you go to college and get a degree, or . . . ?

JRL: No. I got a high school education, then I went to college, I rode out a four-year period to get about two years' worth of work. I was just taking a couple of courses. I was in anthropology and archaeology. I think I changed to humanities for a while, and I just said, "You know, I want to write. I don't want anything to get in my way of being a writer."

DB: You don't want to put pots together.

JRL: Yeah. I love anthropology and archaeology, but not as a career. I still read the stuff and am interested in it. I think anthropology had a lot to do with the way I think as a writer, I think that affected me too. My father was a storyteller, too. He could tell stories, he was a very oral tradition. I think my work shows an oral tradition, and I think that comes from my father.

DB: What did you do to support yourself before you could make a living full-time writing?

JRL: I literally dug ditches. I farmed with a mule. Karen and I had a mule and I had truck crops . . . .

LP: Did you have forty acres?

JRL: No, we didn't have forty acres. I had more like four acres and a mule, and some of that I rented. But we did that. I worked in an aluminum chair factory—I'm not doing these in order, but I'm trying to get to all the things I've done. I was a janitor for several years, that was the last job I had before I began to crack into writing.

LP: Another thing up there on the Joe Lansdale list of things to hate is snuff films. I wonder if there's a particular incident or particular reason that also turns up in your work now and then.

JRL: I think it's that when I'm trying to think of something that really upsets me it's just the vilest thing to think that people's death is entertainment. In a sense it sounds hypocritical because I'm writing about it, but I think there's a difference in writing about the horror of it. We're all attracted to horrors, whether we admit it or not. But I think I'm condemning it, that's obvious. It's one of those things that scares me. I think it's the inhumanity in man, the fact that I don't think there's that much difference in you and I and some of those horrible, horrible people, in the sense that we all have the potential for tremendous evil, and we all have this potential for tremendous good. We hope that our balances are there. You just keep wondering, "What happened to this guy?"

DB: I ran across a comment somewhere fairly recently—I think it was Howard Waldrop, writing in the *Austin Chronicle*—talking about *Henry: Portrait of a Serial Killer*. He made a passing reference to how you wouldn't watch that movie again.

JRL: No.

DB: Were you disturbed by it because you felt it was a snuff film, or were there other reasons?

JRL: I think that scene where they're filming this family being slaughtered . . . you get this feel of this happy family, and then there's somebody that comes and destroys it. I have a very happy family, we're crazy as hell, but we're happy. I have kids. I'm not saying there's anything wrong with him making that movie or doing it that way. I think it's a brilliant piece of work. I just can't watch it again. But, as a writer, I will write about those things. I feel that it's one way of dealing with it and one way of trying to get rid of some of that booger-bear. You don't necessarily get rid of all of it, but it helps you deal with it.

LP: Along those lines, have you ever written anything that, later on, you were sorry you'd written because it deeply disturbed you?

JRL: No, I've never written anything I was sorry I'd written. I've written things that deeply disturbed me, but I felt that was their point. "Drive-In Date" bothers me a lot. I have another story that's unwritten, that will probably get written, that bothers me tremendously.

LP: Ed Bryant said of "Drive-In Date," "It's like 'Night They Missed the Horror Show,' but not as warm and funny."

JRL: Well, I'd have to say that's pretty correct.

DB: What was the deal with the play *Horrorshow*? Did that ever open?

JRL: *Screamplay*, they called it. What happened is they asked several of us to write one-acts. Out of that, they bought two from me. I know Neal Barrett did one, and several other people did one. I think Nancy Collins did one. They were going to do it in October. They had the Astor Place booked, and then one of their financiers pulled out. They just never got it going again. They're still trying, but I don't look for it to happen. The plays have been reprinted.

DB: I know that "By Bizarre Hands" is in *Cold Blood* . . .

JRL: The other one was in *Cemetery Dance*, the "Drive-In Date" play.

LP: Just the sort of thing that Broadway's gonna *love*.

JRL: Yeah.

DB: "The Feel-Good Play of the Year!"

[general laughter]

JRL: The two of them are probably going to go together, probably Roadkill Press is going to do that. They're going to be printing three or four of my stories. I was asked to do a Broadway play too, but I had to turn it down, because I'd already decided to do this one. I don't know if that's even gotten off the ground.

LP: You mentioned Roadkill Press, and *By Bizarre Hands* came out from Ziesing, and you've done lots with Dark Harvest. What's the difference in working with a small press than with a big press?

JRL: Well, some small presses can be just awful. But people like Ziesing and Dark Harvest, I've found that they're pleasures to work with for the most part, because you get to have more say in the way you want the book to look and the way you want the book to turn out. I think some of the more peculiar things I've done I probably couldn't have gotten into regular presses up front. But if the books go out there and get good reviews, then they'll buy them anyway, like *By Bizarre Hands* coming out from Avon. I seem to be at the point where I don't need the small press to do that for me, but I certainly appreciate it. Also, I like the way they do books, and I don't want to forget where I got a lot of support.

LP: Do you find them easier to work with than the mainstream press?

JRL: In some ways. There's less money, usually. The mainstream presses pay me more. But they do very attractive books. I get a lot of personal care. Ziesing sent me on a signing tour, a *very* successful tour. Bantam didn't send me on any. I've found that my book publisher has handled my books very, very poorly, in spite of the fact that I have a good cult audience and good reviews. I seemed to be poised on the edge of something of a breakthrough. I feel the reason I haven't done that is my publisher. I'm not going to be the next bestseller, but I think I can reach a much larger audience than I'm reaching.

DB: What anthologies have you done? You did *Razored Saddles*, you did the upcoming one . . .

JRL: I did *Best of the West, New Frontiers*, and *Razored Saddles*. I'm doing *Dark at Heart*, and I'm doing one originally called *The Second Coming*, but we broadened the grounds for it. Right now it's called *It May Be Weird* [since changed to *Good Stories Don't Sell*], with Pat LoBrutto. That's all.

DB: I think I saw a reference to another anthology you had done. With somebody else, Bill somebody . . .

JRL: I know what you're talking about. A few years ago, Bill Prozini and I had a contract to write a novel for Walker called *The Gallows Land*. It was based on an idea of his. I knew Bill had time, and I think he just wanted to collaborate with it. I wrote a first draft, he didn't like it, so I ended up pulling myself out of the deal.

LP: Did you have any intent when you did *The Drive-In* to do *The Drive-In 2*?

JRL: It was sort of a mixed thing. When I wrote the proposal it mentioned a second book. Then what came along was a happy medium of financial need and the fact that I had some ideas left over that I wanted to do. I think the same thing has happened to a lot of other writers, but I didn't want to do the same book over. Some people were disappointed in the sequel because they wanted the same book. They wanted the exact same experience. I knew that would be there before I started writing, so I just said, "Well, I can't worry about that." The third one will basically be different from the other two, and that will be the end.

LP: So, there is a third one coming out.

JRL: There will be. From Joe Stefko, from Charnel House. All three of them are going to be bound together with an introduction and some recollection about the *Drive-In* novels. The third one may, in fact, be printed separately. I don't have any deal as to how long it has to be, so if it's a novella or a short story or whatever, fine. I just have some things I would like to do that are left over from *The Drive-In 2* that I think are very interesting. If it comes out book-length, it'll probably be a book somewhere. If not, then I'll make sure it appears later, where people can see it and read it, in a short story collection or something, because that Stefko stuff is expensive. But they're good books, they're beautiful books.

DB: I don't think that our readers will let us get away with not asking the man who wrote *The Drive-In* what his favorite movies are.

JRL: Well, let's see. I like a real mixed bag. Of the low budget stuff, I like *Basket Case*, I like *The Beast Within*. I like *Night of the Living Dead*, of course, *Chainsaw Massacre*, of course. I like *Eaten Alive*, it's also called *Legend of the Bayou*. That is the *trashiest* piece of shit I ever saw. One of the things there is almost like an East Texas joke. This guy gets wounded very, very awful, and he sits down, opens this powder and starts snuffing it up his nose, like cocaine. So he says, "Boy, that B.C. powder made me feel better already." All those people in East Texas, that grew up with Faren Young saying, "You take a B.C. powder and you come back strong," that's very humorous. You can always tell if a person's from East Texas when they watch the movie, because they let out a scream, you know? Anybody from New York, they say, "What? I don't get it." My favorite person to watch low budget movies with is David Webb. He and I are writing a low-budget movie column for *Cemetery Dance*. It's been delayed because of different things, but those are among my favorites. I really like those movies a lot, but I also like a lot of other movies—Westerns, film noir, you know. I like *She Wore a Yellow Ribbon* and *The Searchers* and *The Shootist* and—I love the novel, *The Shootist*, a lot. It's written by Glendon Swarthout.

DB: I haven't read the novel, but I love the movie.

JRL: Oh, the book's even better. Man, the book is good. Little bitty book, you can read it in no time, it just knocks you flat. Beautiful writer, beautiful characterization, provocative voice, and the times come alive.

LP: There are some other movies, as long as we're on the topic. *Brazil*?

JRL: I saw that, and I thought it was curious. I can't say that I really loved that.

LP: Any foreign films, like Kurosawa, or . . .

JRL: I like all that stuff, yeah. *The Seven Samurai*, especially. I'm not much of foreign films in general, but Japanese stuff is what I like the most. French stuff doesn't do much for me. I like some of it, but I don't lean in that direction. I like the Japanese stuff, I don't mean Godzilla movies, but *The Seven Samurai*, things like that, I really like those a lot.

LP: Back to low budget horror movies, how about things like *Evil Dead* and *Evil Dead* 2?

JRL: Yeah, I love those.

LP: And *Reanimator*?

JRL: Oh, I love *Reanimator*. Yeah, yeah. I think *Reanimator*'s great.

LP: We touched on *Henry: Portrait of a Serial Killer*. Are there other films that you would not want to watch again?

JRL: I think that's about it. I find *In Cold Blood* a little hard to watch. I like it, it's an extremely good, excellent movie, but I find it almost too depressing to watch. A marvelous book, too. Truman Capote was a wonderful writer. The last years of his life his stuff was just shiny and bright and nothing to it. But, man, when he was on. With *Tree of Night*, that collection . . .

DB: I read *In Cold Blood*, and I understand why he got the reputation he did.

JRL: It's an astounding book. *In Cold Blood* was his peak. He reached it right there. Harper Lee, by the way, was his research assistant. One of those connections you never hear about. People wouldn't talk to him, but she was a country person. She could go in and talk to them, and they liked her. They would get very close to her, very friendly. And she was very much the research assistant. I think a lot of it sounds like her. I'm not saying she wrote any of it, but I'm thinking her influence was there.

DB: Have you seen Demme's adaptation of *Silence of the Lambs*?

JRL: Yes.

DB: What did you think of it?

JRL: I liked it. I like the book, and I like the movie. I think the movie did one thing better than the book and that was that the character of Starling was better. In the book, I felt it could have been a man, woman, or a talking dog.

LP: "Agent Starling, fetch."

JRL: Yeah.

LP: Who among the people that are contemporaneous with you, in the various genres you write in do you think is doing really good, important work?

JRL: Ed Gorman is doing very important work. I think he is so clean and has such simple storylines a lot of people really just don't know how good he is. I think he fools them, he's so smooth. Neal Barrett, obviously, in whatever the hell he's doing, is doing great work. It's hard to figure that out. Lew Shiner . . . I don't mean it to sound like old home week or something, but those guys, they impress me, and I read them for fun. I don't read them because they're my friends; I read them because I *enjoy* them. A guy that's coming up in the horror field who's kind of fun is Gary Raisor. I think people have seen enough of his stuff to know it. I kind of know Gary, so I know more about what he's doing, but I think he's going to be interesting. Let's see, I like Jeter, K. W. Jeter. Andrew Vachss is great.

LP: More Jeter's horror, or . . .?

JRL: Yeah, I like the horror best. All of his stuff is interesting, though, but I like the horror best. I think his *In the Land of the Dead*'s great.

LP: As long as we're on horror, we mentioned the Splatterpunk article, and the Splatterpunk tag, earlier. How do you feel about the "movement" in general, and also, as applied to, if not all of your work, to specific stories?

JRL: I don't really care if somebody says it. I would prefer them not do that. But if they want to say specific stories are splatterpunk stories, that doesn't really bother me much. I mean, I agreed to be in a book called *Splatterpunks*. I'm not fanatic about it. I don't want to get fanatic about anything, because then you start going to the other extreme. I think it was an important period for the horror field, I really do. It was like the New Wave in science fiction, just unfortunately titled, because it narrowed its focus and didn't have the impact it would have had had it been called something else. I really believe horror is going down the tubes as a genre. I think it'd be more prominent right now, had that label not been applied to it. I do believe innovative work was being done by a lot of people tagged that way. I also think a lot of people tagged that way were doing godawful work. A lot of it is transient, and it's gone. You know, it's not going to be interesting the next year. I do think there is a group of people right now, not just in horror, coming out of the genres. People that grew up and loved it like so many of us, that have been influenced by mainstream writers, literary writers, nonfiction, films, and things of that nature. You're getting a new group of people that are trying to weld all this stuff together. Trying to make a more interesting stew. We're not just trying to do Campbell's soup. At least, I hope. I think that in the next five years you're going to see some real interesting stuff. I think the horror field is going to really bite the moose for a while, tell you the truth.

LP: What do you think is the reason behind that?

JRL: I think it's a variety of reasons. I think the horror field became a marketing tool. Then the publishers started producing a lot of it and glutted the market. You couldn't tell the good from the bad the way it was marketed. A very few writers were pushed beyond that; even those writers that had a lot of promise within the field never got the chance to go out there and be pushed into a wider audience or have something done with them beyond being packaged with the usual "Book of the Month Club" look. I think that's a lot of it. I also think that it became popular because of the films. You ended up with a lot of people that could not write at all. Their whole sensibility was watching *Friday the 13th*. A lot of the people who read that sort of thing built the field up, read it for a little while, got bored with it and moved on to something else, like Twinkie gorging or something.

DB: One of the things that I've noticed people talking a lot about recently—at least in the places I hang out—is the Dave Schow/Ed Bryant/Somtow Surcharitkul ongoing debate/orgy/thing in *Pulphouse*. Do you have an opinion on this?

JRL: I pretty well agree with Somtow. I think his was the one that kind of capped it. It's like David had been bitten by a rabid dog or something. I read Ed's article, and I thought it was interesting, but I didn't see anything in there that was offensive. The things Schow started talking about, "I didn't do that! I didn't do that!" Nobody would ever have thought he had. I think he way over-reacted to a more or less general statement. Somtow's article was probably the most balanced, and I don't agree with everything Somtow said. I agree with him more than everybody else. I think David takes the whole splatter-punk thing a little too personal. It's probably because he came up with the name, and I think he probably feels some ownership, without meaning to.

LP: Getting back to the small press. We know you've been generous with us with your stories, and they've also appeared in places like *Cemetery Dance*, *Grue*, and *The Horror Show*, when it was alive. Do you think the horror small press is going to survive?

JRL: Yeah, I do. I think that you're going to see people like Dark Harvest moving more towards dark suspense. But I think they're still going to be able to sell horror, if they do one thing. They're going to have to develop new writers that people are interested in reading, because they're not going to keep getting Robert McCammon, F. Paul Wilson, or me. We're going to have to move on; we have no choice. We've done that gig, and we've got to move on. It's harder and harder for me to take time to do a story for little or nothing, when I can do the exact same story and sell it for ten to twenty times what would be offered. That's what you're up against. If Dark Harvest develops more horror writers, slants towards crime and dark suspense for a little while, they will survive and do quite well. Ziesing has the potential to do tremendous things, but I think his marketing skills need work. He is more versatile than Dark Harvest, but I think they're both excellent presses. Borderlands Press is going to try some interesting experiments, it's too early to see. I think they may be all right, I don't know. They're too new to really know yet. Of the magazines, *Cemetery Dance* seems real interesting, like they're really trying. He started out pretty rough, but advanced very quickly. *Grue* is hanging in there. I think those things will survive, because when the field started out that was what *Whispers* and *Weirdbook* were really about. They didn't pay but maybe half-a-cent a word or something, but they had Fritz Leiber. People that like the stuff will continue to write it. I think that most of us that have liked it are probably a little burned out on it. I know I am. I've done what I wanted to do there, for now . . .

DB: Do you think it also has something to do with small press being less conservative and more willing to take risks, in this environment.

JRL: Oh, without a doubt. But I think a lot of the small press prides itself on not being conservative, being wild to read, but it's the same old crap, because they haven't read anything. They don't know. I'm sorry, *Weird Tales* did this twenty years ago. I find a lot of the stuff the small press loves is obviously old and worn out. But the best of the small press will continue, and they will produce good work.

DB: Do you think violence against women has been done to death? I seem to notice a trend away from that.

JRL: I think it's moving away from that. I think a lot of it was not so much thinking, "I'm gonna be mean against women," it was just ignorance. When you write about serial killers and that sort of thing, that is your realistic victim. That doesn't mean they don't kill men and women, but when you look at crimes of that nature, they're usually men against women. So it's unrealistic for that not to be there. I've done it from both angles. I've never tried to write it where my message was how joyful this is.

LP: There's not a lot of joy in "Drive-In Date."

JRL: There's none.

LP: Speaking of plotting elements, I've noticed that a lot of your novels end with a climactic fight or gun battle. Is this conscious structure in your mind, or is it just a . . .?

JRL: In *The Drive-In 2* I was experimenting, it led up to one and it didn't happen. I did this because that was pointed out to me. I realized then that, in many ways, I'm very much a traditionalist. My stories have that build, that idea of storytelling as building to a point, and it reaches this point, goes down a little bit, and then BAM! But I think that's the influence of pulp fiction. I haven't lost that, and it's not necessarily a bad thing. It's learning how to use it so you can grab the reader that normally wouldn't do anything but see a movie or read pulp fiction. They get those elements they're looking for, but I'm able to do all these other things with it. So I've come to peace with that. That doesn't mean every one of them will reach that climax, but I tend to think that way. I just build and build, like a truck going downhill.

LP: Now, of all the books that have been published under your own name . . . when, for example, was *The Nightrunners* written, as opposed to published?

JRL: 1980 was when a large portion of it was written, and '82 it was finished. It was published in '87. Then I borrowed from it, and revamped, and— I never thought it was going to be published.

LP: Was it written before or concurrently with *Act of Love*?

JRL: It was written the same year. I finished *Act of Love*, took fifteen days off and wrote *Dead in the West* in fifteen days. Then I went and spent the rest of the year writing *The Nightrunners*. Of course, I stopped for a lot of other things too, I don't know how I wrote all that much.

LP: You mentioned the Batman novel. What is the novel you're going to be working on after that?

JRL: I'm being real quiet about it. It's one of the few that I've come up with that I don't want to talk about too much. All I want to say is, it's suspenseful.

LP: What sort of music do you listen to? And what sort of work environment do you like to work in?

JRL: I like quiet when I work. I don't listen to music much. I find it distracting to me. The Batman novel's the only one I listened to music while I was writing, and I mention that in the foreword, and that was Roy Orbison and Sam Cooke. What I listen to mostly is country and Western. I like Dwight Yoakam and Garth Brooks and things like that. I listen to old rock 'n' roll. And rockabilly, and stuff like that. Soul music, I like. And blues.

LP: What do you think of the "new country"?

JRL: I like a lot of the new country. It's like anything else: I think a lot of country just sounds awful. But I think that of rock 'n' roll, too. It's just what I like. The new country stuff is interesting to me. I really find it interesting. I probably listen to country music more than anything else now.

LP: How long, on average, does it take you to finish a novel? From when you actually sit down and start writing.

JRL: It varies. I'd say four months is pretty good, because my novels are short. This other one'll be longer than four months, because it's not short, at least comparatively.

LP: Have you received any flack from your publishers about working in so many genres? Have they ever told you, you shouldn't do this?

JRL: Yeah. It's come up.

DB: What did you tell them?

JRL: Told them I'd do my work. And whatever that is, that's what it is. I understand their marketing considerations, but I don't see that they make great careers for a lot of people they design careers for. I got where I got because I did my work, and I still believe there's an audience out there willing to move around a little bit. I think the voice of the writing carries some of the readers.

LP: What sort of writer does your publisher want you to be? Do they want you to be just a horror writer, or just a mystery writer?

JRL: I think they want me to be a suspense writer. Right now that doesn't hurt me too bad, because I seem to be moving in that direction anyway. But I'm also going to do a book for Mark Ziesing that takes place in the 1930s, kind of an East Texas novel. And I'm going to go back and do *The Drive-In 3*, and another collection of short stories, *Writer of the Purple Rage*, from *Cemetery Dance*.

DB: I wanted to ask about "dark suspense" in general. That seems to be the new genre, the successor to splatterpunk, which was the successor to cyberpunk, which was the successor to . . ?

JRL: New Wave.

DB: Yeah. Do you think there really is something new going on here?

JRL: In the "dark suspense" field?

DB: Yeah.

JRL: I don't know if there really is. I think it's interesting right now. In many ways a lot of people are writing the same stories that they were writing in horror, and they're calling it "dark suspense." It's a marketing angle. Some of my stuff was always crime and suspense oriented. "Night They Missed the Horror Show" doesn't have a supernatural element in it. So no,

I think a lot of it is more traditional crime stories, with maybe a darker element, like Vachss. David Morell did a novella for us that's very, very grim. Good novella, real good. Dark suspense is going to give people a chance to air out a lot of things, and I think it's going to give people a chance to get away from a currently more destructive label, which is horror.

LP: Do you think "horror" is going to disappear, or bifurcate, or just eventually, after all of the crap falls out of the market, come back in vogue as its own market category?

JRL: I think it'll come back. I don't think it's going to do what the gothics did, but I think it's going to mutate some. There are a lot of things that could have been called horror two years ago that are being called "suspense" or "crime" or "dark suspense," or they'll be labeled just as mainstream, or whatever. As far as the fiction itself, it's not going to die. The label will be less used over the next few years, but it'll come back.

LP: As long as we're talking about the word "horror," you and your wife, Karen, were very involved in creating the Horror Writers of America. How did that come about?

JRL: It was Robert McCammon's idea, but he didn't want to do it, so my wife decided to. She actually did it. Then Dean Koontz made it professional. I served in the background, doing odds and ends, making contracts and stuff like that. If any one person deserves credit for the Horror Writes of America existing, it is Karen. Not because she's my wife—she never gets that credit. It always angers me, because I see things that are always saying, "Well, Robert McCammon and Dean Koontz and Joe Lansdale . . ." Well yeah, we were there. But Karen did it. She's the one that took those names. It was just a Xerox thing because there was no money, and she did the best she could with what there was, built that thing up to the point where Dean could take over.

LP: Do you think the Horror Writers of America has had any effect out in the real world?

JRL: Yeah, I think it has. I don't think it's been a tremendous impact, but it really pulled together a group of respected professionals, and I think their award, the Bram Stoker, means as much as any of them does. Personally, I don't think any of them mean all that much.

LP: Although you've won a fair number of the small number of Stokers that have been given out.

JRL: I've won two Stokers. One for a short story, one for a novella. A British Fantasy Award, and an American Horror Award.

LP: That's the one where the World Horror Convention or whatever . . .?

JRL: No, this is one that the *Mystery Scene* crowd does.

LP: Given your caveat about awards, do they still sort of give you a nice ego boost?

JRL: Oh, sure. I'm not one of those people, "Aaaaah, awards." I'm very sincere when I say, "Well, that's nice. That really is." But I see so many people manipulating people, trying to get people to vote for them, and I know at least I didn't do that. So I can feel good. The biggest award is that I can see how readers are responding, and I think that's good. I like the awards, they're good for your ego, but you set them on the shelf, and they don't do a thing. I don't think that's helped my career any is what I'm saying.

LP: Do you think they help careers who haven't had the sort of exposure you have?

JRL: I think they can. If you're on a roll already, and you got them, then they help. And if you're not, I don't think they necessarily do.

LP: Just one final question about HWA, do you think now that it does exist, that the publishers take notice of it? That's had any sort of effect on things like contracts?

JRL: I think it has. I don't think it's been a tremendous effect, nowhere near what I think it should have been. What happened is, I had invested so much time in it, by the time it got to the point where it could do stuff, I couldn't do any more. I was worn out. We ought to have more in the way of funds for writers that are ill, for writers that are aged, sort of insurance background, like the science fiction writers are trying to do. I really think that's what it's about. One of the funniest things I keep hearing, "Oh, that it always squabbles," but I don't see a squabble. I look in the newsletter, and I don't see any. Four people got in a fight, about four years ago, and those guys were just upset because they weren't published, most of them. So I don't really see that. I don't see that at all. I know what a lot of people don't know—behind the scenes—because I used to be the Vice President. I was also on the Grievance Committee and, I think Chet Williamson can tell you this too, numerous times I have helped people straighten out their contracts. I managed to get people better deals. But you don't hear about it, because you can't go and say, "Well, you know, old Joe Blow, they only gave him $4,000." People don't want that mentioned. So all the good work, all of the fires you put out, and all of the stuff you deal with never gets reported. All that does get reported is a few squabbles. If nothing else, it gives everybody a community, and a chance to talk to people that are of a like mind.

DB: Stephen King has written some about this, do you get a lot of real weird fan mail?

JRL: I've been a little lucky in that I do get a ton of fan mail, and I've really appreciated that. I used to answer all of it, but I'm getting to where I can't keep up with it anymore. That's certainly pleasant, to be able to get it, but I'm disappointed that I can't keep up with it as well. I also get a lot of phone calls. I've gotten a few strange ones, but I've never gotten anything as weird as King has gotten. Most of mine are pretty intelligent. Once in a while I'll get a real strange one, but I've never gotten anything that I thought was scary, or deadly, or anything like that. I'm beginning to get phone calls a lot, and I've considered getting a private line and a new address and all that. But I really hate that, because I like being myself, just a regular guy. I think you start believing your own bullshit, and I hate that. I'm just a guy, doing what I do.

DB: Sounds a lot like something Shelby Foote said, about how, all he ever wanted was to have his name in the phone book and be able for people to be able to reach him.

JRL: That's me, too. That's exactly the way I feel. I like to know that I can be called up.

LP: Along those lines, is it ever at the back of your mind, a fear that some-day some wacko's going to read what you wrote in *Act of Love* or *The Night-runners*, and go out and do it?

JRL: It certainly crossed my mind. I honestly believe—if I didn't believe this, I wouldn't write this stuff—*no one* reads stuff like this and is influenced to kill. I think people may look for a method of operation and they may find it from one of your books, and . . . who's to say if maybe that did set them off, that final moment? But, saying that is foolish in the sense that the people that read this, and see films that are related, are us. I don't think that if you look through well-known horror writers, or whatever, that we've ever had anybody that's committed a murder. I'm not saying it can't happen or won't happen, but I'm saying, on the whole, we seem reasonably sane in that area. It's like saying people who read romance novels are romantic. I'm sorry, I don't buy it. I read this stuff and I think I'm a normal human being. Maybe more normal than a lot of people who don't read it. Certainly I would feel bad, if someone were to use some method from a book, but I don't think I would carry the responsibility.

DB: I was going to ask you specifically about some of the characters in *Cold in July* because at least one of them is almost too good not to be real, the private detective.

JRL: He was kind of based on an over-the-top good ol' boy; he's almost a caricature at times. But that's his front, because as it progresses, you see there's more to him than that. But that's the way he comes off; he sets people off guard. People think he's dumb as a post. I think people that don't know me have perceived me that way, sometimes. So there's a little bit of me in that character. If you talk a certain way, or you have an accent, people sometimes immediately say, "Aw, he's dumb," and that's what I was playing with. He's based on several people I've known, but there's no one person that's like that. Over the years, there's been people I've found that talked that way, that used those terms, that, on the surface, didn't seem particularly bright, and were really sharp cookies. The more you knew them, the more clever you realized they were.

LP: You've written a lot of both novels and short stories. Do you feel comfortable working in both forms?

JRL: Yeah, I do. I like short stories best, but I'm becoming more and more comfortable with novels. Short stories, I don't know what it is about them, they just have a real impact for me. One thing I will say about *Savage Season*, I think there is another Hap and Leonard adventure. In fact, Jim Bob shows up in that one too. And I say "think," because it isn't finished. It's going to be a short novel, and I've written a quarter of it already. I think it's better than *Savage Season*. I really like it, and right now, Jim Bob looks like he's going to show up. So we get Jim Bob meeting Leonard, that ought to be a treat.

LP: That ought to be good indeed. What's your personal favorite of your own works published so far?

JRL: If I had to pick one, it'd be *By Bizarre Hands*. I like it because it's a collection of short stories, which I like very much. I think it shows a wide variety of things that I can do. It even gives you some idea of some of the novels, because there's pieces of novels in there, and the influence for *The Drive-In*. So I guess that's my favorite book. But of the novels, it's kind of a three-way tie between *The Magic Wagon*, *The Drive-In*, and *Cold in July*. Those three are my favorite books. Just depends on which day you ask me.

DB: Are there any of them that you're particularly unhappy with?

JRL: There's always things I'm disappointed in. I've never written a book yet that I was happy with, really. Those are the ones that I'm most content with. And I've never written a story that I was totally happy with. I can look at them all and see flaws. But I know they were the best I could do at the time, and I still think—or I would not have let them be published—that they're good stories. *The Drive-In 2* disappointed me some, because it didn't do all I wanted it to do.

DB: I've become specifically curious about *Cold in July*. Did you write that all in one draft? Or was it extensively edited and reworked? Because that is one *hell* of a tight book.

JRL: It was pretty much written in one draft. Neal Barrett and I write alike in that way, we both average three to five pages a day and it's finished. When we get through with it, we go in and touch up little things, obviously. Once in a while, I'll see an entire chapter or page I want to rewrite. No telling how many drafts a day, but we keep throwing pages out until they're right. He does it longhand, and, then has it transcribed. I tend to do it on the word processor. I was on the typewriter. I didn't start using a word processor until *Captured by the Engines*. Back then I would lay it beside the typewriter, and just retype the whole thing. Usually, it was just like it was, except neater. I would occasionally change words and stuff like that. When I write crime, I find that I immediately edit myself better. I don't know why that is, I really haven't got a clue.

LP: We've touched on some of the things you're doing in the immediate future, the Batman novel, the one beyond that, and some of the other works you've got in progress. Where do you see yourself, say, ten or twenty years from now? Do you see yourself moving away from the dark suspense genre into something new, or just . . .?

JRL: I really don't know what to tell you on that. I just always hope that I'm changing, and that my work is interesting. That I don't feel like I've found something that works. That's all.

Author Spotlight: Joe R. Lansdale

Lisa Morton / 2013

Published in *Nightmare Magazine*, June 2013. Appears by permission of the author.

Few writers can authentically claim to be their own distinct genre, but there's no question that Joe R. Lansdale is a category unto himself. He's written award-winning horror, mystery, suspense, Westerns, graphic novels and comics, media tie-ins, screenplays, and mainstream literature, yet each new work fits recognizably into the East Texas-slang-filled, fast-paced, fluid storytelling style that defines the Joe R. Lansdale genre. His most recent works include the novel *The Thicket* (which critics have compared to some of Mark Twain's books), and the feature film *Christmas with the Dead*, which Lansdale's son Keith adapted from Joe's short story of the same name (Lansdale also served as producer on the film). Lansdale's novel *Cold in July* has also recently been adapted into a movie starring Michael C. Hall, Don Johnson, and Sam Shepard.

Lisa Morton: You were a full-time writer by 1981, and about 1989 was when your work suddenly seemed to be *everywhere*.

Joe R. Lansdale: I feel like 1986 was a big turning point for me, because *The Magic Wagon* came out that year from Doubleday and got reviewed in the *New York Times*, so it kind of got that train going. At the same time, *Dead in the West* came out, so I also had the small press thing going on. And then "Tight Little Stitches" came out and was nominated for a World Fantasy Award, so that was a big year. It sort of built momentum toward 1989, which is when *Cold in July* came out.

LM: For many of us, our introduction to your work probably came via the story "On the Far Side of the Cadillac Desert with Dead Folks" from the seminal anthology *The Book of the Dead*.

JRL: Right. I'd been selling short fiction in the seventies and eighties, and probably by about 1983 I'd started writing my stuff, in the sense that I'd sort of gotten out of the vein of the apprenticeship of writing like other people. I mean, you're always influenced by other people, but from that point on my momentum was growing, and I think by 1986 somebody had started to take notice and the novels helped give that notice. By 1989 I was starting to get film options, and *Cold in July* came out, and that book was my second film option—I'd gotten *Dead in the West* before that.

LM: So your career was kind of like a series of little plateaus.

JRL: Yeah, it's funny, when you look back on it. Nineteen seventy-three is when I started, and I was selling nonfiction exclusively—in fact, I wrote nothing but nonfiction.

LM: It was farm reports, wasn't it?

JRL: Farm articles. I wrote an article with my mom, under her name, and sold it first crack out of the box, and then I sold every nonfiction article that I wrote, and I thought, "Well, this is easy." But I wanted to write fiction—that was what I'd always wanted to do—and that took me a couple of years. I was working in the rose fields, and my wife was working in a meat-packing plant, and she told me to take three months off and just write. So I wrote a story a day, because I didn't know you couldn't do that. I wrote roughly ninety stories in ninety days. And over the next three years I got about a thousand rejections, because there used to be ten or twenty markets you could submit every story to.

LM: And all this was on the old typewriter, not even using a word processor!

JRL: That's right! It was a manual, too. I'd had those big old Underwoods, which were terrible. My wife had this little Montgomery Ward's typewriter, and it was easy to use. I used that until I could afford an electric typewriter.

But anyway, that was a big turning point for me. Then in 1981, I started selling. Then came 1983, when I realized that I didn't really want to write the stuff I'd been doing—I was doing ghostwriting work, and suddenly I realized I didn't want to do that. By 1986 I was doing my stuff, and it just kept rolling.

The real turning point for me was probably "Tight Little Stitches in a Dead Man's Back," which I wrote in 1986 and was followed by "The Night They Missed the Horror Show," which David Schow bought for the movie-themed anthology *Silver Scream*, and then after that was "On the Far Side of the Cadillac Desert with Dead Folks." I had a bunch of stories I'd written that I couldn't sell because everyone thought they were too odd, and then all of a sudden "The Pit" sold, and that had been rejected by everybody! Now it's been reprinted and it's being reprinted again next year. My wife always said that Kasey was born in 1986, and we knew it was going to cost money!

LM: You were (and still are) frequently grouped with the 1980s "splatter-punk" trend. Were you comfortable with that label?

JRL: I hated it. I'm gonna kill David Schow for it! I think a lot of people were just trying to look for a humorous way to identify what they were doing, but as soon as they did that, I said, "Man, you're gonna rue the day you did this, because it's gonna box you in." And I was afraid it would box me in, because they would keep sayin' it—it still pops up now and again. But I just refused to accept it. There were two or three stories of mine that fit very well there and that's fine, but I always thought the attitude was different. So when I started writing other stuff, for ninety percent of the readers I didn't stick in that box. Of course, there's that ten percent of the readers who, any time you change and move on they say, "What happened to that one?" and you say, "Well, I wrote that one already!" Been there, done that.

LM: Horror was booming in the 1980s, but that boom turned into an explosion that decimated much of the market. In one interview, you said, "Horror failed to mutate when it was most necessary. There was just too much of it. It's kind of like if you saw a ghost every day—after a while, who gives a shit?" Did you make a conscious decision then to move away from the genre more into mystery?

JRL: Well, you know, the truth of the matter is that by 1981 I'd sold a crime novel already called *Act of Love*, so my first novel was a crime novel, and my first short story sales were all crime stories, mainly to *Mike Shayne Mystery Magazine*. But I was also writing for *Twilight Zone Magazine*, so my interests were always broad. I think I started out to be a science fiction writer, but I wasn't having any luck with it. So I all of a sudden discovered crime and mystery—I'd grown up with it, but I'd never thought about writing it, and when I did I just became a nut for it. Then that kind of segued into one of my other childhood interests, which was horror.

Some of it was planned, but I don't want to make myself sound smarter than I really am. I did a lot of stuff just because I wanted to do it! But I did think horror was filled to the brim, and I was tired of it. I feel like if I sit down to write something that's mechanical, I don't want to do it. And if I feel like everybody's expecting the "boo," I don't want to do it. I came back to it later, of course.

LM: Well, you never really left. Even the first Hap and Leonard novel was nominated for the Bram Stoker Award.

JRL: *Savage Season* was a nomination that I almost asked them to remove because I couldn't understand why it was there. It's a crime novel, very clearly.

LM: In a 1997 interview, you said, "You're starting to see more horror films again as well, and I think that you're starting to see a trend back to that sort of thing. It's almost a fifties, B-movie sensibility. It's really coming back, though. Not that it ever really left." Did horror come back to stay then? Or has it mutated since?

JRL: I don't think anything ever really disappears. It has different levels and different degrees. Horror is still here, but it's not like it was in the eighties. I think what happened in the eighties was you had an insane moment when you had . . . well, I think a lot of people forget this: They forget that people like me and David Schow and a lot of others came along and we hit horror at a time when it was changing, and we were changing it. For better or worse, we were the vehicles of that change. It cycles in and cycles out. I think it's now cycled back to more traditional things. Like in the films, there are a lot of ghost stories and monsters. It goes through cycles until it gets tiring. I borrowed the tools and furniture from it for other things.

LM: I agree 100 percent with the idea that Joe R. Lansdale stories are their own genre, because they are so recognizably your work, regardless of whether they're horror, mystery, graphic novels, whatever. Are you ever conscious of genre when you sit down to write?

JRL: Well, I'm conscious of it when somebody says, "I've got an anthology and I'm doing stories about Jack the Ripper." Even then I can go mystery or I can go horror. Internally, I don't worry too much about it. I know I've got a basic idea, and I might think, "Okay, it's going to be horrific . . . but to what level, what angle, what degree, what method of attack . . ." And then some of the stories I'll write for anthologies like that will later get reprinted in crime or mystery anthologies or different things.

LM: You've mentioned before that you have a particular fondness for novellas.

JRL: It's my favorite form.

LM: Is it the best form for horror?

JRL: I think novellas and short stories are the best form for horror. There are some really good horror novels, but for me horror novels usually play out at about forty or fifty pages. There are exceptions, of course.

LM: When you wrote *Savage Season* in 1990, did you expect to carry on the saga of Hap and Leonard for so long?

JRL: No! I wrote *Savage Season* because I was very much a big fan of the Gold Medal novels. So *Cold in July* and *Savage Season* are in many respects my Gold Medal novels. Aspects of that continued throughout the series, along with the noir. But I really think that *Savage Season* is the most Gold

Medal novel. And *Cold in July* is the most Gold Medal of the non-Hap and Leonard novels. Or maybe *Waltz in Shadows*.

LM: For some reason, I'm always surprised when I see the word "quirky" applied to your work, as it often is with the Hap and Leonard books in particular; I think "quirky" implies "arch" to me, whereas your style seems to honestly reflect a particular place.

JRL: I don't like that label; I don't think they're "quirky." I think they're different in some ways, but I also think they're some of the most traditional stuff I do. I guess it's because of what I do they apply that word quirky; it's like they apply that word "cult." But I'm a pretty big cult now!

LM: Did you hear a lot of that East Texas patois growing up?

JRL: Oh, absolutely. People give me a lot of credit that I don't deserve because a lot of that's just . . . y'know, ignorance has been a great boon for me. I'm not terribly educated—I've got a high school education and a couple of years of college, but I don't have degrees and stuff like that. Most of my stuff I learned from doing. I never took a writing class or anything like that; I just wrote. Some of the benefits for me have been not knowing the proper way to do certain things.

LM: Your latest novel, *The Thicket*, is not obviously a horror novel, but it does open with gruesome disease deaths, a violent murder, and an act-of-God storm, and leaves the reader with that sense of unease that great horror should provoke.

JRL: Yes. I think that goes back to that constant blending of genres. I grew up on all those things, a mish-mash. I grew up on comics, which mish-mashed everything anyway. I used to watch, in the 1950s and 1960s, a lot of old movies and serials they brought to TV. I used to watch all the Flash Gordon serials and the old Tarzan films, and all that stuff just sort of ran together. And then I was reading, too. My parents never said, "This is bad for you," so I was reading everything from Burroughs to Hemingway (Edgar Rice Burroughs, not William S.—that was later!). So you read all these things, you don't think, "Oh this one's good for me and this one isn't." I just *read*.

LM: Is the definition of horror sometimes narrower than it should be?

JRL: It depends on the definition. For some people if you expand it, it's no longer horror. But for me, horror aspects are in a large percentage of what I write; horror is certainly an engine behind a lot of my stuff. Horror and mystery. I have one unpublished novel (that will be published) called *Fender Lizards*. It has no horror, no mystery, no science fiction whatsoever, but there's something about the way it's written . . . it almost feels like a mystery without the mystery. The tone and the attitude and the feeling come across in the prose.

LM: You've written a lot of work in other writers' universes—Jonas Hex graphic novels, Batman animated series scripts, and Tarzan novels. Is it ever difficult to slip into someone else's world?

JRL: Sometimes it is. It used to not be as much; I did some of those things just because I loved them and I wanted to do them. But I've been turning down things like that because as time's gone on I've thought, I don't really want to leave some things behind that are somebody else's. Especially since I don't get any more money out of it, so my family's not going to get any more money out of it, either. So my take on it is that if something comes along that I just really have to do or want to do, or I'm just really driven to touch some childhood dream like Batman or Tarzan, then I'm going to do it. But those are becoming smaller and smaller; I've done most of them.

LM: I really enjoy your Facebook and Twitter posts, and you've obviously embraced these new forms of social media. How important is that direct connection to your readers?

JRL: I like to stay connected with things like that. I don't really enjoy doing it all that much because I'd rather write, but I know it's a part of the business now. I also have a lot of people wanting to know things, and I can cover a lot of ground that way instead of writing fifty letters or a thousand emails. I do that and I'm done. And I can promote my books. Publishing has changed so much that it's harder and harder for even publishers to promote books, or at least to promote them well. The competition has changed, it's very different, so I feel like that's my way of doing it. And I always remember all these things that people will teach you about writing, that work for some people, but they don't work for everybody. A lot of it's just like cliché—you know, "this is this, and that is that"—and I probably do that, too. I'm just saying my way is one way, I'm not saying it's *the* way.

LM: You recently talked on Facebook about writers who complain about loneliness and other aspects of the craft, and you noted, "If you want to be miserable writing, that's your choice." Why do you think some writers describe it as some painful, soul-sapping drudge?

JRL: I'm sure there are some people out there who are just miserable . . .

LM: They'd be miserable if they were plumbers.

JRL: Right. But I think also it's a pose for a lot of people, because they think they're doing something that doesn't require that they dig a ditch or fix a car. I think because it's intangible. When you take a job, you get paid when you first start out whether you know what you're doing or not, but in writing you're not necessarily getting paid when you're starting out, so are you a writer or are you not a writer? So I think a lot of it too is insecurity, that feeling that it's like, "Look, I'm really working, this really is important and it's really hard." And it's not that it isn't hard sometimes—it is. I'm not saying it isn't hard work; I beat my head against the wall sometimes thinking, I just can't get that right. But that's not the same thing as saying I'm miserable doing it. It may be a hard thing to do, but I enjoy doing it. And I feel lucky, because I've never wanted to do anything else. It's not the same for everybody, but I feel like I just got the best break in the world.

LM: One recent tip you offered was, "Actually start out with 'Once upon a time' and continue." Have you done that?

JRL: Yeah, I've done it. I even have one story that begins, "Once upon a time." I've done it several times. I just type "Once upon a time," and then I'm into it.

LM: You've probably written more screenplays than most of your readers realize, and you've even taught screenwriting. Is that a form that you enjoy?

JRL: Yeah . . . when I'm in the mood for it. It's a nice break. I find it easier than novels and short stories, but not as satisfying. My son and I are working on one together right now that I hope to direct, if we can raise the money.

LM: I was wondering if you'd ever thought about directing . . .

JRL: I never really wanted to direct. I just want more control. I'm sort of producing some of the films that are coming out. It's sort of a title that comes with a check, but that's about it.

LM: David Lynch was attached to a film adaptation of *The Two-Bear Mambo* at one point, wasn't he?

JRL: Yeah, he was. It was always a vague thing, and I don't remember much about it. He also had *The Big Blow* for two or three years. Then Ridley Scott picked it up, and I did the screenplay, but they never made it. They had it optioned for several years, and then they finally bought the film rights outright.

[Joe's son, Keith Lansdale, joins us.]

LM: *Christmas with the Dead* started as one of your dad's short stories, then you adapted it into a screenplay. That must have been an interesting experience.

Keith Lansdale: Yeah, it was a lot of fun, actually! He was trying to find somebody to write it, and I was like, "Well, I could give it a go." I had no experience whatsoever doing screenplays, but I figured if I had any questions I had somebody I could go to. I was willing to take that leap. And I thought that the original story was a fun idea, anyway—a guy who's just tired of the apocalypse.

He gave me advice. "There is no dog," he said. "And your sister's going to play a part, and we have a guy who's going to be the co-star . . .," so it was like being given a bunch of puzzle pieces and you're not quite sure how they fit together. I still had a lot of room to do something with the original idea.

JRL: I told him he had to take the dog out, because we couldn't afford it. And it had to have more scenes so it could be longer—otherwise it would have been a twenty-minute film. That's about it; then I just turned him loose on it.

LM: Keith, was it ever intimidating?

KL: Well, yeah, of course. I don't know if I was "intimidated," though. I know I was getting into something I'd never done before, but I wasn't nervous about it. I felt pretty okay with it, actually.

LM: So you had your very first screenplay produced! That doesn't happen for a lot of writers.

Keith: That's true. It was kind of handy to have him as the producer because I knew that meant it would get made somehow.

JRL: When he complained, Lee (the director) and I would tell him, "You're getting treated nicer than anyone in Hollywood, because they don't even let the writer on the set a lot of the time!" I did get to go on the set of other things, but usually they don't.

LM: Were you on the set for this, Keith?

KL: A little bit here and there. It was unfortunate that it was in the hottest part of the summer, and of course you can't run the air conditioner when they're shooting. I'd stay as long as I could stand it, then I'd say, "I've gotta go home."

JRL: It was so hot we just left Lee and them there and we went to Italy. It was so hot the makeup would melt as fast as they'd put it on. It was one of the hottest summers on record. In Texas, you know you're going to have hot summers, but this one was just unrelenting. They were filming at three in the morning, and it was still eighty-five.

LM: So it was all shot on location?

KL: It was all shot right there in Nacogdoches, except for one scene that was shot in Lufkin, which is right down the road from Nacogdoches.

LM: Joe, as producer, were you ever conscious of reining in Keith as the screenwriter?

JRL: Not really. It's like he and I have the same brain, it's actually pretty amazing. What I did was just help him with the format. But he was fine with the storyline. I'd have an idea, but he was already doing it, so that was funny.

LM: Keith, do you plan to continue screenwriting?

KL: Yeah. Sure thing. He mentioned the one we're doing together—that's been a lot of fun. There's a lot of kind of going back and forth. Sometimes I find myself arguing about little minute details that I know are not going to matter, but it's just when you're in the minute and you're thinking, "It's got to be exactly this way!" If something really comes up, I can say, "You're probably right because you've been doing this a long time," but I'm definitely getting my words in there. No question.

JRL: And I encourage that, too. He's written comic books—he wrote for Antarctic Press—and I think that helps. The framing of comics owes something to film and vice versa.

KL: And it's more visual than just a regular novel.

LM: So, Joe, can you tell us anything about this project?

JRL: "Fried-pie noir" is what I call it. It's about a guy who's a fried-pie king. Or just a pie king. We haven't decided if it's fried pies or just pies. But the problem lies with the pies, or the ownership of the pie recipe, and that's about all we can say. It's kind of noir, it's kind of funny, it's kind of Western. It's got characters with names like Birdhouse Willie.

LM: You don't often collaborate . . .

JRL: No. I actually collaborate with my children best. Kasey and I did a story together that's coming out in *Dark Duets*, edited by Christopher Golden. She and I are doing another story together. The kids wrote stories together back when they were eight and twelve—one was published by Random House. The kids have been around it all the time—people who are writers or directors used to come to the house, people were always there.

LM: What else is coming up for you?

JRL: Well, besides this screenplay Keith and I are working on, I'm working on a new novel. And *Cold in July* has been filmed and is coming out next year. They're editing it now, and what I've seen of it looks great. It's got Michael C. Hall and Don Johnson and Sam Shepard and Vinessa Shaw . . . it's going to be really, really good. What I saw just impressed the hell out of me.

Darkness on the Edge of Town

Eric Benson / 2016

Published in *Texas Monthly*, February 2016. Appears by permission of the author and *Texas Monthly*.

Let's clear up one thing before we begin: Joe R. Lansdale—author of more than forty-five novels and 400 short stories, essays, comic books, and screenplays, ranging in genre from historical fiction to grind-house pulp—is a hell of a nice guy, maybe the nicest in East Texas. An avuncular fixty-four-year-old with piercing blue eyes, a Matterhorn nose, and a slightly crooked grin, Lansdale is a big-hearted pillar of the Nacogdoches community, a still-smitten husband to his wife of four decades, and a proud-as-pie dad of two children. Lansdale rescues stray dogs. He has been known to house kids in need. He runs a local martial arts school at a loss. He offers advice to aspiring writers—on his Facebook page, in emails, in person. When he walks into any of his familiar haunts—the Starbucks on North Street, the Japanese restaurant Nijiya, the General Mercantile and Oldtime String Shop—he addresses employees by name, inquires about their lives, and leaves pretty much everyone smiling.

Tim Bryant, a Nacogdoches crime writer who studied screenwriting under Lansdale, swears that his former professor is the "friendliest, most down-to-earth" man that he's ever known. This comes as a surprise to some, Bryant attests. "A lot of people think he must be the craziest, darkest, most twisted person."

That's because Lansdale is not only the nicest guy in East Texas, he's also the man who wrote this: "Ellen stooped and grabbed the dead child by the ankle and struck Moon Face with it as if it were a club. Once in the face, once in the midsection. The rotting child burst into a spray of desiccated flesh and innards." And this: "As they roared along, parts of the dog, like crumbs from a flaky loaf of bread, came off. A tooth here. Some hair there. A string of guts. A dew claw. And some unidentifiable pink stuff. The metal-studded collar and chain threw up sparks now and then like fiery crickets. Finally they hit seventy-five and the dog was swinging wider and wider on the chain." And, just last year, this: "In the next instant Uncle Bob was dangling by a rope from a tree and had been set on fire by lighting his pants leg with a kitchen match. That was done after a nice churchgoing lady had opened his fly, sawed off his manhood with a pocketknife, and tossed it to a dog."

When I first met Lansdale, I had a hard time fathoming where he found such darkness. It was a mid-November afternoon, and Lansdale was sitting with his family at their favorite Starbucks. They were a picture of suburban bliss: sipping lattes, making plans for dinner, and reminding one another not to forget the "puppaccino" for Lansdale's one-year-old pit bull, Nicholas. ("He knows when we've been to Starbucks and expects it!" Lansdale laughed.) His daughter, Kasey, a twenty-nine-year-old country singer, was on her way to teach a yoga class, but she would soon be moving to Los Angeles. You could tell. She was wearing full makeup, movie-star shades, platform heels, and a pink T-shirt emblazoned with the words "La Di Da." (A bracelet with tiny skulls on it was the only accessory that betrayed the macabre sensibility she had inherited from her dad.) Her brother, Keith, a thirty-three-year-old 911 dispatcher and screenwriter with a laid-back surfer vibe, simply looked exhausted. He'd woken up from a nap after his graveyard shift and had stumbled into Starbucks to power up before another night fielding emergency calls. Their mother, Karen—the poised, flaxen-haired matriarch, who manages the business end of Lansdale's creative pursuits—sat smiling at her husband and children. She injected the occasional quip as they bantered back and forth about film festivals in Italy, blues festivals in Norway, Kasey's impending move, and the family's decades-long collaborations.

"We did our first story together when they were kids," Lansdale said happily. "Keith was twelve and Kasey was eight. It was for Random House, *Great Writers & Kids Write Spooky Stories.* Kasey wrote this hanging scene and it was really good, but they said we had to take it out. It was too intense for other eight-year-olds."

I'd come to Nacogdoches to spend a few days with Lansdale, because after decades as an object of fan-boy adulation, he looked to be on the brink of the kind of above-the-title celebrity that rarely accrues to a writer, much less one who has spent his life behind the Pine Curtain. Starting in the late eighties, Lansdale made his reputation by leaping across genres (Western, horror, crime, sci-fi), bounding through tones (from campy to bleak to tender and back again), and skewering bigots, Bible-thumpers, and plain old hypocrites along the way. That fearlessness had done more than earn Lansdale fans; as Steven L. Davis, the curator of the Southwestern Writers Collection at Texas State University, once wrote, it had established him as "the unabashed conscience of East Texas." But even as he's won an ardent following with works like *Bubba Ho-Tep* (in which JFK and Elvis, both still very much alive, battle a reanimated mummy in their nursing home), the Southern-fried noir *Cold in July*, and, especially, his sublime Hap and Leonard series, Lansdale's stories and novels have remained niche products, his readers members of a devoted and select cadre.

Lately, though, Lansdale's writing has attracted a broader audience. His recent novels *Edge of Dark Water*, *The Thicket*, and *Paradise Sky*—all published by Little, Brown's Mulholland Books imprint—have balanced his penchant for absurdity and visceral horror with a style that's a little more accessible, albeit still happily in-your-face. After decades of false starts, *Cold in July* was finally made into a movie, and Hollywood is pursuing other adaptations, with Bill Paxton planning to direct a screen version of Lansdale's coming-of-age fable *The Bottoms* and Peter Dinklage's production company developing a project based on *The Thicket*. And Hap and Leonard, Lansdale's crime-fighting odd couple (Hap: white, liberal, straight; Leonard: Black, Republican, gay), will soon swagger into the big time. Over the next two months, Lansdale will release a complete collection of Hap and Leonard short stories as well as the ninth Hap and Leonard novel, *Honky Tonk Samurai*. But the really big occasion arrives on March 2, when Sundance TV will air the first episode of its *Hap and Leonard* series, starring the classically trained English actor James Purefoy as Hap and Michael Kenneth Williams, best known for his work as Omar Little on HBO's *The Wire*, as Leonard. (Christina Hendricks of *Mad Men* plays Hap's bad-news ex-wife.)

So life should have been grand at the moment when I met Lansdale. But no matter how joyful things look, he never loses sight of the ghoulish lingering nearby. One afternoon, he decided to take me on a tour of Nacogdoches in his Prius (Lansdale has written enough dystopian stories to be a committed environmentalist). The weather was mild and sunny. His two favorite women, Karen and Kasey, were riding with us.

Cruising down North Street, we passed by Stephen F. Austin State University, the site of Lansdale's own American dream story. In the seventies, he worked there as a janitor. In the aughts, he became the English department's writer-in-residence. "And you still don't have a degree!" Karen said.

"But I got 'sperience," Lansdale drawled.

Then, a few blocks south, we drove by a seemingly nondescript corner. "Hey, is that where the two sisters burned to death because they were wearing their nightclothes?" Lansdale asked his wife and daughter. They nodded. "You ever hear about that?" he said, glancing at me, before recounting the shocking and perhaps apocryphal tale of two women who refused to leave their fire-engulfed house because the clothes they had on were immodest.

When we got to Main Street, we parked and strolled over to Lansdale's brick on Nacogdoches's unofficial Texas walk of fame, where he shares real estate with Buddy Holly, Tommy Lee Jones, and Molly Ivins. Lansdale was proud to point this out, but he was far more eager to take me inside the city's visitors center to show me a grainy black and white photo memorializing the site's past.

"They had the last public hanging in East Texas right here," Lansdale yelped, pointing to the image of a Black man named James Buchanan ascending to the gallows in 1902. "They said, 'We can give you a trial and then we'll hang you, or we can hang you now.' And he said, 'Just hang me.' He probably hadn't done the murder, but he was Black."

Later, as Lansdale and I were driving back to his house on the outskirts of town, another "puppacino" in tow, I told him that I was beginning to understand where he gets his stories. "You can go through my books and pick out things that happened here or they happened in Gladewater or they happened in Tyler or they happened in Starrville," Lansdale said. "A lot of friends I went to school with were criminals. Like, one of my best friends growing up, he went to prison for locking his wife in a closet or something, and he died in prison. I have so many friends who died in prison, were killed, committed suicide. It's a big list."

Back at the house, Lansdale was greeted by a barking Nicholas. Hundred-foot-tall pines, oaks, and maples swayed in a soft breeze, and soon we were tramping down to his pond, the trunks of bone-white trees sticking up from the water like the ruins of a postdiluvian city. It was the kind of marshy landscape that appears often in Lansdale's work, a place where Hap and Leonard might discover a sunken van with a corpse inside, or where young Harry Collins and his sister, Thomasina, would go searching for the Goat Man in *The Bottoms*.

"This is where you watch for snakes," Lansdale said as we climbed over some logs. "Right here it's mostly copperheads, and around the water you tend to get water moccasins. But in East Texas, there's every kind of poisonous snake there is."

Lansdale has been scampering around creeks and woods like this since he was boy growing up in the towns of Mount Enterprise and Gladewater. His father, Alceebe (he went by Bud), was a shade-tree mechanic—a wrench man who couldn't afford his own garage so he literally worked under a tree—and his mother, O'Reta, held a string of sales jobs, peddling World Book Encyclopedias and flower arrangements. Lansdale's only sibling, John, is seventeen years his senior, so the younger Lansdale grew up more or less an only child. For entertainment, he had the swampy river bottoms, a place where a boy, his dog, and his imagination could run wild. Early on, his family couldn't afford a television set, so when Lansdale was at home, he would stare through a window at a neighboring drive-in theater, watching the images of Warner Bros. cartoons while his mother improvised her own version of the dialogue. "We were poor, but we never thought of ourselves that way," Lansdale says. "We thought of ourselves as broke, and that's a different psychology."

What the family did have were stories. Lansdale's father had never learned to read or write, but as a young man he had lived an outsized, itinerant lifestyle, and with his baritone voice he would unspool absorbing yarns about his days as a boxer and a wrestler during the Great Depression, when he'd hop freight trains to fight at fairs across the country. Lansdale's mother didn't have such outlandish tales, but she was in possession of something even more valuable: books. "She loved writers and she loved reading, and she instilled that in me very early," Lansdale says. "More like instilled it in me."

From the moment he could read, Lansdale was devouring any text on which he could train his eyes: comic books and Hardy Boys mysteries as well as the works of Shakespeare, Twain, Kipling, and Tarzan creator Edgar Rice Burroughs. He kept a copy of the *Iliad* under his pillow at night because he had read that Alexander the Great had done so. He imagined a life beyond the Piney Woods, inspired by the exploits of Batman, although he conceived of a more literary variety of heroism.

"I think there are some people for whom words are like food," Lansdale says. "I tried to draw and write comics when I was four. By the time I was nine, I had written my first story—about my dog, of course."

Lansdale figured out early on that he wanted to be a writer, but he didn't know anyone who held such a profession and didn't have a clue how to become one. He was a blue-collar kid from hard-luck towns, and he partially fit that profile. At sixteen he went to work part-time for the "street department," cutting grass and putting in shifts on a garbage truck. At seventeen, now living in Starrville, he got an after-school job on the assembly line at an aluminum chair factory, and after graduating from high school, he went to work building mobile homes.

College was an intermittent pursuit. Lansdale spent a year at Tyler Junior College, then went to the University of Texas at Austin before dropping out in the middle of his second semester. After leaving UT, he joined a friend in Berkeley, California, where he found employment as a bodyguard for a used-clothing salesman. "He kept having these unsavory people come by, and I thought, 'Man, are used clothes that popular?'" Lansdale remembers. "It turned out he was selling drugs on the side. I quit when I found out."

Lansdale returned to East Texas after a few months ("Berkeley wasn't for me," he says), enrolled at Stephen F. Austin, and not long after met Karen in an anthropology class. In 1973, just after their wedding, the couple moved from Nacogdoches to join his parents in Starrville. They had dreams of living off the land, and they raised goats, hogs, and chickens while laboring in the Tyler rose fields. Lansdale liked the work—he rubbed shoulders with people of every race, and he got to be outdoors—but he had other ambitions. He sold some nonfiction pieces to *Countryside Magazine*, and he kept a journal about his and Karen's farming experience, imagining that they might one day turn his notes into their own version of the back-to-nature classic *Living the Good Life*. But it wasn't enough. "All this time I'm thinking, 'I gotta write, I'm about to explode,'" Lansdale says.

The problem was that Lansdale, by his own estimation, wasn't a very good writer, and he didn't really have the time to improve. But he was determined to succeed, and Karen supported her husband's dream. In the fall of 1974 Lansdale was working in the rose fields, but the weather was icy and cold and the work schedule erratic. "My wife said, 'Just take three months off and write—it's what you want to do, just do it,'" Lansdale says. For the next ninety days, he wrote from morning until night, producing a story a day. Many were short: three to four pages. Others were shockingly long for a day's work: twenty-five pages or more. At the end of the three months, Lansdale had nearly 1,000 pages of text. "They were some of the worst stories ever written; I was just flushing out all the crap," he says. "But I learned to type real good."

The dream at that point was to get published—anywhere. Lansdale couldn't spell, he didn't know grammar, and editors rejected his stories by the bundle. In 1975, the couple moved back to Nacogdoches, and he went to work as a janitor at Stephen F. Austin. In 1976, he finally made his fiction debut, landing a detective story, "The Full Count," in a pulp outlet called *Mike Shayne Mystery Magazine*. More followed, mostly in *Mike Shayne*, although it was hardly a living and it wasn't his endgame.

"We were both really eager to get published any way we could—horror, sci-fi, detective, Western, you name it," Lansdale's longtime friend, the novelist Lewis Shiner, told me. "But we always saw markets like *Mike Shayne* as milestones to get past. The short-term goal was to be making a full-time living at writing, but the longer-term goal for both of us was to make a real impact."

In 1980, Lansdale took a big step toward that first goal, selling his first two novels: *Texas Night Riders*, a Western that he wrote in eleven days under the pen name Ray Slater, and *Act of Love*, the tale of a Houston serial killer. Soon after, he quit his janitorial job to write full-time.

The publishing world did not, at first, reward his audacity. For the next several years, as his writerly voice grew darker, more personal, and more satirical, he sold only a few short stories and couldn't get another book deal. It took until 1986 for Lansdale to have his first real breakthrough, with the publication of his horror serial *Dead in the West*, his postapocalyptic short story "Tight Little Stitches in a Dead Man's Back," and his Western *The Magic Wagon*, which got a hardback release from Doubleday and Lansdale's first notice in the *New York Times*. (The reviewer praised Lansdale's "subtle discussion of racism and the myths people create for themselves," while also noting the "expected emphasis on nose picking and wind breaking and cow piles.")

Over the next three years, Lansdale followed up on his nascent success with a prolific run that won him a substantial cult audience. The short story "Night They Missed the Horror Show," a pitch-black comedy of entrenched racism and good-ol'-boy goobers, won Lansdale his first Bram Stoker Award. *The Drive-In*, a novella about a horror-movie screening that descends into a cannibalistic melee, established Lansdale as a figurehead—somewhat unwillingly—of what critics dubbed the "splatterpunk" genre. *Cold in July*—a twisty noir that begins with the shooting of a home intruder and ends with FBI informants, the Dixie Mafia, and snuff films—marked a new level of plot and character sophistication and was quickly optioned by Hollywood.

Still, Lansdale was always one step short of crossover success, a little too vulgar, a little too bleak, his humor a little too politically incorrect—or maybe he was just always a little bit unlucky. "The only thing more certain than Lansdale's eventual fame is tomorrow's sunrise," the best-selling horror writer Dean Koontz wrote in 1989. "I suspect, however, that he is going to be one of those writers who takes a long time to build, who has to find his own readership with little assistance from his publishers."

Koontz's words proved prophetic. Over the past three decades, Lansdale has battled his way through the book industry. He has run through a string of genre publishers—lowbrow outlets like Zebra and Leisure Books—many of which, in his opinion, didn't do nearly enough to promote his work. ("They had their eye on some other people, or they didn't care, or they just wanted me to be a mass producer.") He has fired more agents than he can count—some sleazy, some lazy, some who just didn't believe in him. ("I had one who said, 'Ahh, you're all over with.' The only thing he wanted me to do was ghostwriting.") He has chased down money from deadbeats. (He once pretended to be Norman Mailer to get the top editor of an unscrupulous publishing house to take his phone call.) Despite all of that, he was always on the verge of becoming the Next Big Thing.

In 1994, the *Dallas Morning News* celebrated the publication of *Mucho Mojo,* the second and best-loved of Lansdale's Hap and Leonard novels, by writing, "If you haven't heard of him, chances are getting better that you will. . . . [*Mucho Mojo*] may be his 'breakthrough' book." In 1997, soon after he had resurrected the Jonah Hex franchise for DC Comics, written episodes for *Batman: The Animated Series,* and published the *Mucho Mojo* follow-ups *The Two Bear Mambo* and *Bad Chili,* the *Austin Chronicle* wondered if Lansdale wasn't the "most famous unknown writer working today." Seven years later, on the eve of Lansdale's debut for "Tiffany publisher" Knopf—his first major-league book contract—the *Houston Chronicle* judged that Lansdale "stands poised for a big breakout." Eight years after that, in 2012, with rumors of movie adaptations of Lansdale's work swirling around, this magazine wondered, "Why is Lansdale finally having a moment, after three-plus decades toiling in semi-obscurity?"

It's 2016. Here we are again. Lansdale is still most revered by the kinds of passionate genre fans who read websites like *Macabre Republic* and *Apex Magazine.* He is still influential to younger genre writers like Tim Bryant, Stephen Graham Jones, and Joe Hill. (Hill, whose father is Stephen King, got hooked on Lansdale as a teenager after reading *The Drive-In.* "My own story ideas were goofy and gory and silly and it would've been natural to keep them to myself," Hill wrote to me in an email. "Lansdale suggested another possibility: he seemed to be saying you could stick your crazy right in people's faces.") Lansdale is still significantly less well-known than contemporaries like Koontz and his old friend George R. R. Martin, the author of the Game of Thrones series. And his most intense fan base can be found in Italy, which he visits often. ("I think the humor translates well," Lansdale's sometime interpreter Seba Pezzani told me. "We get the Southern humor and his larger-than-life view on life itself.") But the vast cultural reach of a television series, the possibility of more screen adaptations, and the strong reception for his latest major novel, *Paradise Sky*—an exuberant imagining of the life of the African American cowboy Nat Love, which Lansdale believes is the best thing he's ever written—makes this "breakout moment" feel a little different.

Lansdale, though, remains unapologetically eclectic, happy to mix prestige with pulp. The epic *Paradise Sky* wasn't his only work published last year. He also wrote the young-adult novel *Fender Lizards*, co-created the comic book series *The Steam Man*, and, with Keith, dashed off a story about the cartoon heroine Vampirella. (What you'd expect: big boobs, blood lust, bad attitude.)

"I always felt that Ray Bradbury was kind of a role model for me, because he said, 'Leap off the cliff and build your wings on the way down,'" Lansdale says. "That's kind of what I've done my entire career. I've been told time after time, by editors and other writers, 'Don't do that, it'll ruin your career,' or 'What are you doing? Stop writing that Batman novel. You're getting recognition, this is the dumbest thing.' But I like Batman. Sometimes I want to write the Batman novel."

On my first night in Nacogdoches, Lansdale and I drove to the south side and pulled off Stallings Drive at the sight of an illuminated sign that read "Lansdale Self-defense Systems." Next to it stood a one-story metal-framed building, little more than a garage with Sheetrock walls. We parked and stepped through a side door to the sound of thwacking flesh and foam.

Two men circled each other covered in sweat. They traded strikes, grappled for position, then one would toss the other to the floor. Behind them, a painting of a cobra stared down from the wall, the emblem for Lansdale's own form of martial arts, which he calls Shen Chuan, Chinese for "Spirit Fist." The master stood watching. "Not bad, not bad," Lansdale said. "But we're working on perfection here!"

The men, thirty-five-year-old Terry Lee and twenty-three-year-old Daniel Sherrer, continued to rehearse their moves. Sherrer, the less experienced of the two, was struggling to get the hang of a combination that would immobilize his opponent. His face scrunched up in frustration. "You're too hard on yourself, kid," Lansdale said, a verbal backslap. "Learn to mess up happily!"

Lansdale has practiced martial arts since he was a boy, and for the past three decades he has been teaching Shen Chuan, first as an unofficial melding of arts like hapkido, kenpo, and jujitsu and since 1996 as an established school unto itself. For much of his adulthood, Lansdale fought in sanctioned matches (he is an inductee in both the U.S. and International Martial Arts halls of fame), but he has gone into semiretirement, no longer competing and relinquishing most of his teaching duties to longtime students.

At first glance, Lansdale doesn't look like a guy who could beat you up. He's got a pot belly. His shoulders are slightly hunched. And with his Batman watch and black-and-pink "Nacogdilla!!!" T-shirt, he seems more like a comic-book guy than like the kind of crime-fighting ninja that comic-book guys dream about being. But when Lansdale stepped onto the mat, he transformed as surely as Bruce Wayne.

As Sherrer watched, Lansdale demonstrated a series of moves on Lee. First, Lansdale backed Lee across the mat, his hands moving in a blur of strikes. Having gained an opening, he grabbed Lee's left wrist and twisted it to the inside. The joint seemed just a few millimeters away from snapping. Lansdale paused and looked toward Sherrer.

"This bone on top of the wrist presses against an artery," Lansdale said. Then he took a deep breath, deploying a technique he calls "ghost hands." He didn't appear to move at all, but as Lansdale sucked in air, the younger man dropped to the floor and tapped his hands in submission. It's all about subtle shifts in weight, Lansdale explained. "I've been doing this for fifty-three years and I still go, 'That's weird.'"

A few minutes later, Lansdale was palming Lee's face, demonstrating another technique for bringing an opponent tumbling to the ground. Lansdale moved his hand from over Lee's mouth to his forehead. "You don't want to put your hand there or he'll bite the hell out of it," Lansdale said, addressing Sherrer. "And they will bite you. I would."

Under the tutelage of his father, Lansdale first learned the rudiments of martial arts when he was eleven, and he's been fighting ever since. Originally, he learned because he wanted to defend himself against bullies. He was a bookish kid who questioned authority, which wasn't always easy in the East Texas of the fifties and sixties. There were plenty of people who wanted to know what the hell his problem was, and sometimes they tried to get him to conform to their own ideas, school-yard-style.

But Lansdale wasn't simply looking to defend himself; he wanted to learn to fight for the same reason his hero Batman did: he saw injustice everywhere he looked, and he wanted to play a part in making it right. He saw the sting and violence of racism. He saw the oppression of poverty. He saw the difficult lives of anyone who was a little different.

"I would just see all kinds of cruelty and stupidity," Lansdale says. "If I could take you back in time to the fifties and walk you around to some of the places where I grew up, you'd be trying to get back in your time machine. It wasn't all sock hops—matter of fact, I never saw a sock hop. When I was growing up, it was a lot of thuggish bullshit."

By the early seventies, Lansdale was an avowed atheist and a liberal with long, shaggy hair. When he'd walk down the street, he'd be greeted with taunts of "Hey, baby, you give head?" One afternoon while he was working on a construction site, Lansdale finally struck back. The foreman had been "jacking me for weeks," Lansdale remembers. "And one day he grabbed me, and then he pulled his other hand back." Lansdale realized that he was about to get his lights punched out. He delivered the first blow instead. "I put him in the hospital. I felt bad about it, but he was going to hit me."

Lansdale kept fighting back. At Tyler Junior College, administrators told him he had to cut his hair. He not only refused but, with two other students, brought a federal lawsuit against the school. They won. When he was drafted by the Army, in 1971, he sought to take a stand. He wouldn't go, he said, but he would also refuse to register as a conscientious objector, because, he said, he would have fought in a just war. He also refused to flee. "When I was at the draft board, one of the Marines told me, 'This thing is terrible. Go to Canada.' I said, 'I'm not running. Because once I run, I'm going to keep running.'" Lansdale says he was ready to go to federal prison, but a psychiatrist gave him a 1-Y, a general deferment. "I think they threw me a bone," he says. "The war was winding down, and they knew I was sincere."

Not running became the defining feature of Lansdale's life. In East Texas he is very much a native son, but he's also deeply skeptical of religion, loathes gun culture, and is a social progressive. Jim Mickle, who directed the film adaptation of *Cold in July* and co-created the *Hap and Leonard* television series, told me that when he visited Lansdale in Nacogdoches he felt that "the whole family seemed like they were from another planet." There are lots of people who grow up in places that don't match their personalities, ambitions, and views. If they can, most of them leave.

But Lansdale never did. "I know Joe's not entirely happy with the culture here, but I think it's been really great that he's stayed," John McDermott, a colleague of Lansdale's in the Stephen F. Austin English department, told me. "He's sort of the opposite of Willa Cather. Willa Cather moved to New York so she could write about Nebraska. Joe stayed here so he could write about here."

When Lansdale was starting his career as a writer, his work lacked a distinctive regional style; he might as well have been from New York or Nebraska.

"I was trying to write to market," he says. "And what I found is, that's exactly what doesn't work for me. Then I started thinking about the way my dad talked, and I said, 'You know, the people that I know don't talk like the way I'm writing.'"

Lansdale began to experiment with a more vernacular voice, and he embraced the contradictions and humor of his native soil. His stories—once set in largely anonymous locations—began to take place in fictionalized East Texas towns like LaBorde and Mud Creek, and landmarks like the Sabine, the bottoms, and the area's drive-in theaters almost became characters themselves. His language, once timid, got caked in dirt and ash and attitude, sounding like the last gasps of an oral tradition. Elaborate and bizarre metaphors and similes started cropping up all over his prose. "The sound of the wind in the bottle tree came to me, like the faraway hooting of ghostly owls," he writes in *Mucho Mojo*. "Evil waddled about like a duck looking for a spot to squat," he writes in *Bubba Ho-Tep*.

Once Lansdale found his voice, his work became awfully strong stuff. His personal motto is "Write like everyone you know is dead." In other words, don't worry about what anyone else thinks, don't hold back, write the truth. For Lansdale, that meant confronting East Texas's real-life horrors in impolite ways, particularly when it came to its grim racial history, a history that, as the 1998 execution-by-dragging of James Byrd Jr. made clear, has a disturbing tendency to come hurtling back into the present.

Lansdale's favorite weapons for skewering racism are satire and explicit violence, and deploying them can be a risky gambit, an easy way to get denounced and misinterpreted. Lansdale has faced his share of both. He has received letters from racists that read, "I hate them too." Editors, especially early on, recoiled at work that was so raw, failing to appreciate his social aims. "They'd say, 'If you drop a happy ending on it, we'll take it,'" he remembers. "I said, 'Nah.' So it was a battle."

One group that hasn't been sure of what to make of Lansdale is Hollywood. Since the late eighties, his novels, stories, and screenplays have been frequently optioned, and directors like Ridley Scott and David Lynch have been attached to his projects. But it wasn't until the horror filmmaker Don Coscarelli adapted *Bubba Ho-Tep* into a delightfully campy B movie in 2003 that one of Lansdale's stories actually made it to the screen, and since then, adaptations have been few and far between. Mickle and the screenwriter Nick Damici secured the rights to *Cold in July* in 2006, but it took them seven years to get it made. "A lot of people were a little afraid of the tone," Mickle says. "It was a little darker than felt safe."

Cold in July—which stars Michael C. Hall, Sam Shepherd, and Don Johnson—debuted at the 2014 Sundance Film Festival, earned generally good reviews in limited release, and paved the way for Mickle and Damici to take on *Hap and Leonard*. If *Cold in July* seemed tonally difficult—with its stark violence and heavy Oedipal themes comingling with the likes of a preening, red Cadillac–driving bounty hunter named Jim Bob Luke—then the Hap and Leonard books present an even more challenging mash-up.

The first Hap and Leonard novel, 1990's *Savage Season*, which serves as the basis for most of the TV show's first six episodes, begins with a classic noir setup: a femme fatale from Hap's past turns up at his house and offers him a job that's too good to be true. But before long, Lansdale has taken us far from Sam Spade territory and into the hideout of a hippie goon squad that speaks primarily in peace-and-love platitudes. Then Lansdale throws in some guns, and a story that has been cruising along as an adult Hardy Boys mystery (they're after sunken treasure) darkens into a blood-soaked face-off that's as violent as anything envisioned by Sam Peckinpah or Quentin Tarantino.

The action is secondary, though. In both the books and the TV series, the heart of Hap and Leonard is their banter. The boys bond over seventies-era tough-guy cinema and Hank Williams records. They counsel each other on relationship troubles. And they spar verbally over more-weighty matters: the welfare state, the myth of the self-made man, and the nature of morality. (Hap: "I guess there's part of me thinks somewhere along the line everyone could have been saved." Leonard: "Evil's real, man. Same as good.") The conversations are Lansdale at his most naked. You can hear him arguing both sides, trying to tease out the secret order of the world around him.

"East Texas is an odd, complex thing," Lansdale says. "I love it, but I'm not blind to the things that I see here as warped. My dad was the biggest racist ever, yet I saw him do the kindest things for people, both Black and white. He's my hero in spite of his faults. In East Texas there's a kindness and a violence that's like a two-edged sword. You can find the kindest, most hospitable people here—and they'll shoot you over what I might think of as a mere slight."

The last afternoon that I was in Nacogdoches, I went back to see Lansdale at his house. The sun, as he writes in *Honky Tonk Samurai*, "was beginning its slide to the west, like a fried egg on a tilted Teflon skillet," and Lansdale stood over his stove, reading glasses perched on top of his head, cooking chicken biryani in a wok. "It's an East Texas variation," Lansdale said. "We make it with squirrel. You ever eaten squirrel?"

I told him I had not.

"People say it tastes like chicken. It does not taste like chicken. It tastes a whole lot like squirrel." Lansdale laughed. "Used to eat a lot of it when I was a kid. I don't know if I would have the taste for wild meat now."

Lansdale was joking about the squirrel. The biryani was made with pre-cut chicken slices that he'd purchased at Walmart. But he rarely misses a chance to play up his roots as an "ignorant country boy," especially when he's talking about how he's simultaneously traveled very far from them and remained very close to them.

As Lansdale finished cooking the biryani, Kasey arrived at the house with her friend Adam Lamar, an extravagantly bearded guitarist and illustrator with whom she has toured. Lansdale doesn't play music, but he's a lifelong fan of country and the blues, and he's an enthusiastic booster of Kasey's career. (In *Honky Tonk Samurai*, Hap and Leonard become Kasey Lansdale fans.) After dinner, Kasey sat cross-legged in the living room, Lamar perched in front of the fireplace beside her.

"Fame and fortune is a funny thing. It can take you down, make you lose your way," Kasey belted. They were lyrics of a song she had written based on her father's 2012 novel *Edge of Dark Water*, about a small-town girl who dreamed of Hollywood stardom only to end up as a corpse floating in the Sabine. Lansdale watched transfixed while his daughter's eyes rolled back as if channeling a spirit.

"It can lift you up higher than the moon," Kasey continued. "If you sell your soul, all your dreams will come true."

It was both a creepy and an ironic song to sing at such a moment. In January, Kasey would make her own jump at stardom with her move to Los Angeles, and in less than two weeks Lansdale would be traveling to the resort town of Courmayeur, in the Italian Alps, to accept the Raymond Chandler Award for lifetime achievement in crime writing. But he wouldn't be away from Nacogdoches for long, which seems to suit him just fine.

A few hours earlier Lansdale and I had been sitting in his kitchen, and I'd asked him if he'd ever considered moving. He has lots of buddies in the movie and book-publishing worlds, and no doubt he'd find plenty of kindred spirits in Venice Beach or Park Slope. I figured it was a question he got a lot. But Lansdale looked genuinely perplexed, as if the idea had never crossed his mind.

"When I went to Berkeley, I might as well have been on the moon. They had the same kind of racists, but they were more disguised—I couldn't see them coming," Lansdale said. "Here, I can see those sumbitches coming."

Onscreen Mojo: An Interview with Joe R. Lansdale

Chris Hallock / 2017

Published in *Cemetery Dance*, March 15, 2017. Reprinted by permission of the author.

Many colorful descriptors have been affixed to describe the work of ten-time Bram Stoker award-winning author Joe R. Lansdale, but reigning *champion of mojo storytelling* (coined by Lansdale's friend and webmaster Lou Bark) is the most fitting way to express his dynamic style. Throughout a prolific career, Lansdale has produced an astounding assortment of unique tales gracefully two-stepping between the pulp and the profound. His work is gritty, funny, and violent, characterized by biting dialogue and Lansdale's ability to seamlessly cross genres while remaining conscious of history and storytelling tradition. Lansdale's distinct literary voice regals his readers with tales of rough-and-tumble antiheroes ready to throw down against dangerous criminals, serial killers, and occasional otherworldly monsters running amok in East Texas.

Producer interest in his work began in the 1980s, but nothing manifested onscreen until Lansdale contributed teleplays to Warner Bros.' *Batman: The Animated Series* (1992–1996) for the episodes "Perchance to Dream" (1992), "Read My Lips" (1993); and "Showdown" (1995). Translations of Lansdale's original work began in earnest with Don Coscarelli's vision for the novella *Bubba Ho-Tep* (2002), a critical and cult hit. Coscarelli (*Phantasm* series) followed up with *Incident On and Off a Mountain Road* (2005) for the short-live Masters of Horror anthology series (2005–2007). Terrell Lee Lankford dove headfirst into *Christmas with the Dead* (2012) shooting the postapocalyptic zombie film in sweltering conditions. Indie stalwart Jim Mickle (*Stake Land, We Are What We Are*) helmed *Cold in July* (2014) from Lansdale's revered crime thriller, and recently tackled the eponymous Hap and Leonard for Sundance TV, featuring James Purefoy and Michael K. Williams as the East Texan firebrand private investigators and best friends.

Mr. Lansdale spoke with *Cemetery Dance* about the experience witnessing his literary work translated to screen, crafting relatable stories with thematic heft, and hints at the possibility of sitting in the director's chair himself.

Cemetery Dance: You've had opportunities to work with producers on projects that didn't necessarily pan out, and *Cold in July* bounced around for a while before Jim Mickle and Nick Damici tackled it in 2014.

Joe R. Lansdale: I'd worked with some directors and we just didn't get it made. Sometimes I've worked with them peripherally, and sometimes more directly. *Cold in July* was optioned by John Irving who did *Dogs of War* and *Ghost Story*. John Irving was a great director, I really liked John, but we could just never get it off the ground. They just kept wanting to change it to something we never meant for it to be—*Cold in July* was always difficult to film. Jim and Nick had a terrible time getting it set up, too, because people didn't know what it was. That's a problem with a lot of my work, producers always liked the cinematic aspects, but they feel driven at some point to define it—to put it in a box. They just kept on until it finally got made. I also dealt with other directors—I sold a screenplay to Ridley Scott's company and his son Jake was going to do it for a while, then it never happened. David Lynch was attached to *The Big Blow* for a while. The interest has always been there, it's just been slow in happening.

CD: How are you emotionally when negotiating with producers: do you get your hopes up, or do you get nervous about your work being misrepresented?

JRL: No, I don't. I mean, you have to have your hopes up enough to even go into it, but it doesn't shatter me. I mean, I'm disappointed, but it doesn't have any weight on my life, on my continuing projects, because I never put all my eggs in one basket. I just don't work that way. I always think of that Twain quote, "if you put all your eggs in one basket, watch that basket."

CD: It helps to have creators like Mickle and Coscarelli who get you, right?

JRL: Yeah, well they get it. Some of the others don't really get it, or they get pieces of it. The thing about people in film—and this is understandable—what they're doing is a job where they're already worried about their next job as soon as they start. So they live in constant fear of messing something up or not being able to put their imprint on it so that they can get another job. The best adaptation—if you think of works of good art—the best adaptation is one that comes as close as possible. You don't always get that. Occasionally you'll get something that varies, that's even better than the original, but it doesn't happen very often.

CD: Does it bother you when producers make significant changes to the story and characters to accommodate time or budgetary restrictions? In *Cold in July*, there's a change that doesn't necessarily account for those limits—in the book, the intruder shoots at Dane first, but not in the film. Is it difficult to reconcile such a fundamental difference?

JRL: I actually thought that was a very good change (in *Cold in July*), especially cinematically. When he shoots the guy and it turns out he doesn't have a gun, it makes the guilt even heavier. In the book it works either way because you have plenty of time to explore the inner feelings of the character. In the film, that's a way of establishing a lot instantly. That was one change I really liked. *Bubba Ho-Tep* didn't require much changing because it was a long story. It was almost—and I wouldn't have thought it at the time—but once Don adapted it, it's almost verbatim, the story. There are a few additions, little character parts at the first, but most of the dialogue, most of the scenes, most everything is right out of the story. In fact, when I reread it some years ago, I was shocked at how similar it was. Same way with *Incident On and Off a Mountain Road*, although it was a little short and they did have to add some things, it was so close to the story it was amazing. With *Christmas with the Dead*, my son wrote that script, he actually did change it up quite a bit. That's because it was a such a short story you'd have had about a twenty-minute film.

CD: Writing is such a solitary thing, did you appreciate being able to experience that with an audience around you?

JRL: It's fun, but you know, nothing takes the place of writing. People say it's a lonely thing, but I never feel alone at all. I mean, I feel alone, but not lonely. So to me, I enjoy writing a lot. I've worked on screenplays, too, but I think on some level that it's not an art—it's a craft. You're writing something, and immediately as soon as you write it, even if you're artistic in your moment, as soon as you finish and hand it to somebody—for other people to interpret—as soon as that happens, it's already got other eyes, other ideas and visions involved. Once the actors come into it, they all have their own take on the material—they have their own sound and their own look, their own body movements which change it to some degree. The director has their own ideas about it, even the stage direction, the cinematography, all that combination of things. I don't believe in the auteur theory at all. I believe the director's the general and I believe the writer's the engine. Everything after that is just different philosophies and interpretations.

CD: It looks like *Hap and Leonard* is a big hit for Sundance.

JRL: It was their number one show.

CD: Do they shoot that in Louisiana?

JRL: They did the first season in Baton Rouge, but I think some of the tax credits changed. They ended up shooting the second season in Atlanta, Georgia.

CD: Do you think the environment they created is suited to the atmosphere of the stories?

JRL: I really do. I haven't seen the second season; I wasn't on the set for it. My daughter was in it; she's in the fifth episode. She's playing a singer. She does a couple of songs, an old Carter Family song and one of hers, a song she wrote when she was seventeen or eighteen.

CD: I was hoping you and your family would make an appearance in there in some way.

JRL: Well, Kasey and I both were in the first season, but we're in the background in the café. Unless you're looking, you won't see it. But, she's in it this season. They gave her a Dolly Parton look, it's really kind of clever. Watch for her in the fifth episode in the carnival.

CD: I'm curious who's going to play Jim Bob Luke, who was portrayed by Don Johnson in *Cold in July*.

JRL: Well, right now there are some contractual problems about that because he was in *Cold in July*, but that doesn't mean they can't be solved. I think they can, in fact. I think Don would be very interested in playing that character again, but I don't know how that's going to play out.

CD: Fantasy fiction is typically looked at as a means of escapism, but you don't let your readers off the hook so easily. How important is it to you to confront them with relatable challenges like aging, racism, marital strife, financial struggle as found in both print and filmed versions of *Bubba Ho-Tep*, *Cold in July*, and *Hap and Leonard*?

JRL: It's very important to me. I've written some things that I think are just fun and they're nothing more than that, but I think that things that are difficult are fun, too, in a different way. I don't think my stuff is difficult to read, but I mean it's difficult subject matter for some people. For me, I think probably growing up in the sixties and early seventies—I reached my early manhood in the seventies, I was eighteen when I graduated in 1970. All through that era, that was a time of change. It was a time of civil rights, the Vietnam War—people for it, people who ditched it, antisexism and women's liberation, gay rights were beginning to have a stronger formation then. A lot of those different things, they were so much a part of the fabric of who I was that I always wanted to write about them.

CD: You accomplish that without anything feeling heavy-handed. If you take a look at *Bubba Ho-Tep*, one might look at it as being one of your lighter stories, but it's really not; it's one of the most devastating.

JRL: I don't consider it light at all; it's funny, but it's not light. It's sort of like *The Drive-In*. *The Drive-In* has got a lot of humor to it, but it's not light at all. It's about something totally different. It's about trying to find purpose in life and about meaning and the best laid plans of mice and men. There's a lot of stuff in there that I felt I was trying to say, and I was trying to use drive-in characters that were more caricatures than they were common characters. I have this belief that there are some books and stories where the main character is the book itself. Examples of that I were some of Ray Bradbury's stories—which I don't think the characters are particularly real, but the overall flow and the dynamics and the political aspects when all put together—the story itself becomes the character. Or like some of Vonnegut's work which he very seldom deals in real characters or feelings of bright characterization, especially his later works. The overall book itself, the tonality of it, becomes a character. The themes and the elements and the little things he brings into it as he writes are all part of that fabric. I tried to do that with *The Drive-In*. Most of the time I prefer a more realistic approach to character, but in that I was trying to make this broader statement to pull the reader in before they knew they were there.

CD: How do you balance the realistic consequences versus an over-the-top character like Jim Bob Luke or Bruce Campbell as Elvis, these tell-tale type characters. How do you keep these exaggerated characters from outgrowing the gravity of the stories?

JRL: The influences for those kinds of characters go way back to Walt Disney's *Davy Crockett* where they had Fess Parker play Davy Crockett. Davy Crockett was a real guy, but he was also bigger than life. Like Daniel Boone, "Wild" Bill Hickok, Buffalo Bill, they're all real people. Even my dad in some ways was bigger than life. What I always try to do to make sure it doesn't go too far is never forget the humanity of that person, the strengths and weaknesses that they have, their common strengths and weaknesses as human beings. As long as you keep that core, you can run out there pretty far before pulling it back in.

CD: Had you been writing comics for DC at the time you were approached to write for *Batman: The Animated Series*? How did you get involved in the beginning?

JRL: What got me onto it was not writing comics, but I was writing some short stories that were based on Batman. So they asked me to do a short story for a thing called *The Further Adventures of Batman* and I wrote a thing called "Subway Jack." Then I was supposed to do another one, I think it was called *The Adventures of the Joker*; it was a book where the Joker was the main character, and of course Batman was in it as well. I did those two and I think somewhere along there I might have done the Batman novel I did *Captured by the Indians*. I believe that's what got the interest. A friend of mine, Bob Wayne whom I'd known in Dallas went to work up there, he just retired there recently, and I think he threw my name in the pot along with the fact that I'd actually done some Batman stuff so they could look at it and see I knew the character. That changed everything, and I think it was Michael Reeves who called me and said, "Are you interested in doing this," and I said, "Yeah." They had ideas and storylines that they put together and they would pick a writer they thought might fit. They sent me one of them and allowed me to do dialogue and trail off where I wanted to go. It was one of the better experiences in my career dealing with cinema.

CD: How much experience have you gathered behind the camera being on set for these projects?

JRL: Quite a bit, actually. Not as much as the people assigned those jobs, but a lot of osmosis, as I like to joke. You absorb a lot of it just from observation and from being around it. I helped produce *Christmas with the Dead*, and Karen and I could afford to do a large part of that. We didn't do it all, but we did over half of it. Now we're talking about bigger money, so I have to go out and do what everybody else does. When you're working, you have to dedicate yourself to what you're doing so you don't do it halfway. You also have to have a way of compartmentalizing to go over and work on something else.

CD: So that only galvanized your interest and didn't scare you away?

JRL: No, I loved being on those sets. I enjoyed it. Some are more pleasant than others, some are more interesting than others, but it didn't scare me at all. I've been around a lot of directors in my lifetime, over thirty years being around directors. I've certainly been involved in it peripherally. I've read a lot of different things about it. So I'm not scared of it at all.

CD: You mentioned you're considering directing something yourself.

JRL: If things go well, I'll be directing my first one next year; it's called *The Projectionist* and it's based on a short story of mine in the new anthology by Lawrence Block called *In Sunlight or in Shadow*. It was never my driving force in life to be a director and it still isn't; I want to be a writer. Sometimes you look at it and think, "This is a way to project your work to people who might not ever see it." Writers like to think that everybody's reading their work, but I don't feel that way because I know they're not—you're not universally admired. What happens though is the more darts you have heading in different directions, the more possibility of hitting targets. If you did something based on one of your books or a TV series based on a series of books, that draws attention to them and gets readers you might not have otherwise. That's part of why I'm doing it, along with the love I have for film. It's fun to work with my son, and my daughter and I are working on some stories, so it's a way of continuing to work with my family.

CD: What are some other projects on the horizon?

JRL: Not counting the TV series, there's Hap and Leonard *Rusty Puppy* that comes out in February I think. *Blood and Lemonade*, which is a collection of early stories about Hap and Leonard when they were teenagers, mostly Hap but some with Leonard, is coming out at that same time. I've also got a collection coming out any day now *Dead on the Bones*, which is a tribute to the old pulps and those kind of TV shows I was mentioning. There's *Coco Butternut*, which is a Hap and Leonard novella coming out from Subterranean. There's another Hap and Leonard short story, "Hoodoo Harry," coming out from Otto Penzler, in a little chapbook that they do and also a hardback version of it. I'm writing another Hap and Leonard novel right now *Jackrabbit Smile*, and I'm writing an e-book that I promised. After that, I'll probably put Hap and Leonard on the shelf while I do other things.

Soundscapes: Joe R. Lansdale

Mark Slade / 2018

Transcribed from *Soundscapes Podcast*. This episode premiered in March 2018.

Years ago, as a teenager, I stumbled across Joe Lansdale by reading an anthology of horror stories. Which one, I'm no longer remember. I do remember the story, though. "Dog, Cat, and Baby." After I read it, I realized this is a different kind of writer than the ones I'd read before. His style was not only different, but his stories resembled no one else's. They were far out, strange, and engaging. Mostly, you could tell he put his heart and soul in them.

Flash forward several years later. I started a podcast of audio stories called *Dark Dreams*. I found quite a few of the writers I admired were on Facebook. So I messaged them about having their work read on the show. Some were receptive, some were hostile. Joe? Well, Joe went beyond kind. He said yes. He never criticized. He never threatened me to remove his stories. He always answered my questions and even offered advice on a few things. He granted me several interviews over the past eight or nine years. He was always warm and friendly.

This particular interview stands out to me because it was a cold and snowy January day in 2018. I live in Virginia, and Joe lives in Texas, but we were both snowed in that day. Joe gave me his phone number, and I assured him I would promptly lose it afterward. He said I didn't have to. I felt I did out of respect for his privacy, but the fanboy inside me was squealing. Thankfully, the realistic me had a better grip on things. Mostly. I didn't have a smartphone back then and used my daughter's phone to record the interview. Joe talked about his life and his journey as a writer, and I didn't intrude. I asked very few questions as this interview was for a failed podcast I was planning. I just let Joe tell his story, and I think it worked best that way.

A few months later, the worst thing in the world happened to me. My wife, Tracey, had a stroke. As young as she was, none of us expected it. The signs were there, and me being me, I ignored them. I feel that guilt every day. After she was admitted to the hospital and fighting for better health, I returned home. I didn't know what to do. I was bored and surfing Facebook. It was late at night, so all my family and friends were in bed. I came across a post by Joe about one of his books coming out. Now, out of respect, I don't bother Joe. I messaged him to ask how he was. He responded right away, and we started chatting. I told him about Tracey, and he said he was sorry and hoped she got better soon. I hit him up with a special request although I didn't think he would do it. I asked Joe if he would call my wife and leave her a message. He responded immediately, saying, "Of course. What's her number?" I gave it to him, and, to my astonishment, Joe called her. When I got to the hospital the next day, I told her about it. She wasn't sure who Joe was. She was still recovering. She handed me her phone, and we listened together. That meant a lot to both of us.

Recently we talked about Joe and this forthcoming book, and I reminded her that he left a message on her phone. She told me she still has it. Both of us will forever be grateful to Joe for the kindness he showed.

Mark Slade: Let's start out with your early life, where you were born and what the town where you grew up was like.

Joe R. Lansdale: Okay, I'll try to nutshell it as much as possible. I was born in a place called Gladewater, Texas, and it's in East Texas. From the first grade to about the fifth I lived in a town of around 150 called Mount Enterprise, and then we moved back to Gladewater at that point. That's where I graduated high school, and then I left there and did some college in Tyler, Texas, and some at the University of Texas. Eventually I got married early and I got a divorce not long after. I dropped out of college and went out to California for a while, came back and went back to the University a little bit. But I dropped out of college to be drafted, because I wanted to protest war by being drafted and refusing to go is such youthful idealism. I didn't want to go to Canada to avoid the draft, and I didn't want to be a conscientious objector because that was a whole different belief system, at least as defined by the military. They asked me things like, "Would you have fought in WWII?" And I said, "Yeah." They asked, how do I feel about the Vietnam War, and I said that I felt it's a mistake (and I still do), and I think time has proved that. We gave it up and we lost fifty-four thousand soldiers. I think the Viet Cong lost about nine-hundred thousand, and then three or four hundred thousand or so South Vietnamese, which accomplished noth-ing. Now they're one of our biggest trade partners, and our people go there for vacation, so it makes you feel like, yeah, that war probably wasn't the right thing. Anyway. I think they threw me a bone because I was straightforward about it. I don't know, but they gave me a 1-Y, which is kind of unfit for military service, and sent me home.

Shortly after, I met my wife and we've been together for forty-seven years. We now live in Nacogdoches, Texas.

My father was a mechanic. My mother was primarily in sales, but she was also artistic; she painted and she sold paintings. There's only one of those [paintings] in existence that I know of. My brother has it, and it's somewhat water damaged and time damaged. But she was a great inspiration for me. My father couldn't read or write. He was forty-something when I was born. My brother and I have about seventeen years between us. Now and again, my father rode the rails during the thirties, and he occasionally fought in fairs as a wrestler and/or boxer. He also worked in a cannery, odd jobs, lots of stuff. My mother bought him a car because he said he wanted to be a mechanic. She bought him an old car and told him to take it apart, until he could do it blindfolded, and he did.

He never truly learned to read or write. Towards the end of his life, he could write his name, poorly, you know, and he learned to make out the newspaper a little bit. My mom helped him learn, and I helped him a little bit, but you could never have called him a functionally-literate person.

So I guess that's kind of my story in a nutshell. My brother, on the other hand . . . we did a book together, and a screenplay, and some comics. He went to Vietnam. He wanted to be a soldier, and he had a different viewpoint than I did. He was there for a while. He was in Thailand. I think he was in army intelligence at that time. We had different views, but we accepted that. You know, I was the long-haired rebellious kid, and he was the guy that was following the norm. I'm not saying that was necessarily bad, but we were different. He has four kids and about twenty-four grandchildren and great-grandchildren.

I have a beautiful, talented daughter, and a handsome, smart son, both of whom decided to go into business on their own, like their dad. My daughter is a singer and a songwriter. She also works in film a little bit. She does some model work, some commercials, and she writes. My son sells comic scripts, and he's starting to sell screenplays, and he works as a dispatcher here in Nacogdoches, Texas. That is a job my wife had until shortly after I went full-time in 1981 as a writer, leaving my job as a janitor. Then, in about 1988, she dropped working where and went to work for me full-time, and that's how it's been ever since.

So, that's my nutshell.

Slade: I kept silent, but I wanted to say, "Oh, man, that's awesome," you know, because there are a lot of really good ideas for stories in the things you just said.

Lansdale: A lot of stories come from my real life, real events. It gives me a base from which to work with. When I was growing up in Gladewater, Texas, in the 1960s, it was a different world then. There were different worldviews and there were different experiences that people had or had to have. People, when they were seventeen, eighteen years old, were often leaving home and nobody said, "Oh my God, what are they doing?" That was expected. Now you have people who live with their parents who are over thirty. And I'm not making a judgment call. It was a different world. You were expected at that time . . . you know, you're raised, you've had what education you're gonna get, high school, whatever . . . . Maybe your parents are helping you pay for college. My parents helped me, I think, for the first semester, but after that I had to get loans and I kind of went on my own. It's one reason I never finished. But the other reason was I wanted to write. I knew I always wanted to write.

I thought I would have to do other things before I wrote, and I did. I thought that I would probably get a career out of the university, although I always went to the university not for a career but because I really thought learning gave you a better view of your own life and of the world. And then you get a job out of it, too, if you're lucky. Ultimately what I wanted to do was be an anthropologist and archaeologist and then write fiction. I also thought I might get a degree teaching fiction. But I couldn't afford to keep going, and then, at some point I realized there was no reason to wait to write. I started selling when I was twenty-one. My first piece was sold when I was twenty-one, and by the time I was about twenty-five or twenty-six, I began to realize I had to sort of invest myself in fiction if I was going to do it. By 1981, I was full time.

Slade: Who were your influences as a writer?

Lansdale: Oh, my God. There are a phenomenal number of influences. It's a very loaded question, because there are certain things and certain writers that influence you at certain times in your life, and then there are some writers who stay with you your entire life, and then there are a few that sort of sneak up on you and you don't even realize how much they've affected you until maybe one day, you know, you stop and analyze it, and you go, "Holy cow!" But I would say that the first great influences on me were comic books because they mix genres. And that's something that's stayed with me from the time I was four years old. As I got a little older, comics got a little more advanced and went from funny animals to superhero comics. There was a thing called Classics Illustrated back then. They've tried to revive it a couple times, but they always screw it up by trying to write their own stories instead of the ones they're based on. The original Classics Illustrated sometimes cut certain secondary plot lines, but they stayed pretty close, and through those I read everybody. I mean, there was Dickens, there was Poe, H. G. Wells, you name it. *Classics Illustrated* had beautiful art and really great adaptations. So those led me to read a lot of the original books and stories. Those things were big influences on me, and they led me to fiction.

Another important thing for me was television. I was born in 1951, so by the time I'm really aware of television, I'm probably four years old. That's the first time we actually owned a television, because I still remember radio, and I faintly remember some of the radio shows. *The Shadow* was still on. I think I remember hearing that. I think a lot of that stuff sunk in. My mother used to listen to soap operas on the radio. What happened is that, as TV developed into the late fifties, they began reprogramming. So they took a lot of the radio shows and turned them into television shows. *Gunsmoke* would be an example. One of the longest-running shows period, if you consider from radio and television both. A lot of soap operas and adventure things like *Superman*, started as radio shows and then became TV shows. When I was a kid, I was reading comics, watching TV shows, and watching movies. Things like the Tarzan movies. They started coming to television. The (Johnny) Weissmuller ones were the most famous. There was Gordon Scott, Lex Barker, and others that played Tarzan. Buster Crabbe played Tarzan as well as a lot of other characters like Flash Gordon and Buck Rogers. I watched all of those Flash Gordon and Buck Rogers serials . . . . I watched all of that stuff and it led me to want to read science fiction.

That wasn't really available to me, especially when I lived in Mount Enterprise. I would have to wait until I went to Gladewater where I had a library card, and somewhere there I discovered Edgar Rice Burroughs and I just went nuts. I mean I was reading (Jack) London and all of these people, Twain, Kipling, and so on, but at that time in my life Burroughs was the most influential writer. I think from eleven to fourteen, I just lived in Burroughs's worlds, as Tarzan, as John Carter of Mars, Pellucidar, *The Land That Time Forgot* . . . . All of it was tremendously imaginative, colorful, and inspiring. And that led to other things. When I got older, I discovered writers like Phillip Jose Farmer. If you were to break down my favorite science fiction writer, it would be him. I certainly read some Phillip K. Dick. I read a lot of it. I read probably all of Farmer, and I would find old paperbacks and I would read people like Henry Kuttner and Cyril Kornbluth. Some of it was in magazines. There weren't many science fiction magazines in the town where I lived, and I couldn't always afford them, but I bought them when they popped up. They were really erratic on the newsstand, but at least the magazines existed, and a lot of different ones, even if where I lived they were hard to find. There were comics and there were paperbacks in the spinner rack, so good grief, I read all kinds of things. Whatever fell into my hands.

Then when I was in Gladewater I used to go to the library on Saturday. We would sometimes go over to visit relatives when we got the chance, and I would go in there. They had a room that was for young adults. I quickly went through that and found a lot of it, like Tom Swift Jr., just boring. I read some Heinlein and some Asimov. I read some Bradbury, but Bradbury didn't really interest me until I was a little older. I didn't understand the metaphorical aspects of it. A few years later, I went nuts for it. But I'd just go to this library and start reading books. I remember reading Hitler's *Mein Kampf* 'cause it was just there in the library. Nobody was censoring anything. I read Mark Twain's *Huckleberry Finn*, which really gave me an understanding about what I was seeing in race as a kid in the South. People don't understand how graphic and wonderful that novel really is. How satirical and amazing it is. Then of course I read *To Kill a Mockingbird* after I saw the movie on television. A lot of the movies I saw then on TV were science fiction movies. Later on they started adding shows late at night, and I would stay up and watch them. There was no recording them, and they didn't always play at the theater, so you tried to grab them when you could.

When I was younger, they didn't have television late at night. It didn't exist. The television went off, I think in the afternoon. Then they started going, "You know what? I think we could get more programming." That's when they started adding programs. You would have the news at night at about 10:00, and at 10:30 the TV went off. It just had a test pattern. Ours had an Indian head, as they called it. It had a picture of a Native American with a feather in his hair, and that would just be it. You'd hear the national anthem and then it would run that thing all night. And then they thought, why not add something? So Steve Allen came up with this thing called *The Tonight Show*, and then it went to Jack Paar. Then it went to Johnny Carson, and so on. But during that time it was a revolutionary idea, and I think it was ninety minutes. Then, why not after this add the late show? Then why don't we add the late, late show? And morning programs like the *Today Show*.

This was before twenty-four-hour news, and the news was meant to be news then, and not there for profit or talking heads discussing what it means, what it might mean, and what it meant. So all of those things were fascinating to me and it's because they were, relatively speaking, new. So I would stay up and watch those late, late shows when *Forbidden Planet* was on or *This Island Earth* or maybe *The Day the Earth Stood Still*. All of the old films, some of which stand up to me today and some which don't. I watched the Roger Corman films. Many of those, by the standards of today, were just awful, like *The Attack of the Giant Leeches*.

All of this stuff sort of went into a mental reservoir, and I'd be wandering around that library picking up adventure books by Richard Halliburton, picking up Burroughs, even *Mein Kampf*, which completely convinced me that, "Oh my God, this motherfucker was terrible!" *Huckleberry Finn*, which made me think, "You know what? Black people aren't getting a fair shake here," and so on and so on. All of that stuff just sort of ran through my head.

Later, I was introduced to other writers because of the *Twilight Zone* and *Alfred Hitchcock Presents*. I read the credits and saw they were written by writers and were often based on stories by writers. Sometimes the same writer did the screenplay, so I'm: "Who's Richard Matheson?" I started looking that stuff up in the 60s. "Who's Charles Beaumont? Who is this writer Robert Bloch on *Alfred Hitchcock Presents*?" All of those writers really heavily influenced me and there began to be a shift away from the child's view of Burroughs, which I'm not knocking in any way. They're sexist, they're racist, all that and even more, but you can still read them for the adventure and for the imagination. If you're smart enough to divide that out, they're still somewhat fascinating but probably faded to the point that they will never have the kind of impact they once had on imagination. Without Burroughs there wouldn't be a lot of scientists. There wouldn't be a Ray Bradbury. There wouldn't be a ton of people, myself included, writing and trying to find our own adventures, trying to sculpt this stuff in our heads and put it out there for people to see.

When I went to college I began to read in an unassuming way. I had actually read *The Old Man and the Sea*. I think it was in *Life* magazine and my mother had all these old magazines she kept in stacks, so I would go through those and find stories. The *Saturday Evening Post* would have these stories about a character named Alexander Botts, who was the world's greatest tractor salesman, and those were really funny. I also read the Tugboat Annie stories, and some of them were made into movies and TV shows, so for me it was just like this big soup of all these things I loved. Then I got interested in martial arts and had that stuff seeping in too, and all of that affected the way I wrote. And growing up with people who were poor, blue collar, I had different experiences than maybe some people, and those went into the soup, too. As time went on, all of those things that I studied and learned (and still love and study) played a role.

So this is a long way of trying to explain some of the writers, because that list could go on. Flannery O'Connor was a tremendous influence by the time I was in my late twenties. Then I discovered Keith Laumer. I loved his first-person style even when the stories might disappoint me, but man, *Plague of Demons*, *A Trace of Memory*, *Dinosaur Beach*, were great. But he did a crime novel as well, a private-eye book, called *Fat Chance* in paperback. I read that and it hit me hard. The style, the attitude, the whole private-eye thing. The dedication was to Chandler and Philip Marlowe, his detective, and then I discovered the real thing. I began to read Raymond Chandler, James Cain, and Dashiell Hamett. I had seen movies made from their work, but finally I was reading the source.

Slade: I was going to ask you about the martial arts. Why did you get into martial arts and what have you learned from it?

Lansdale: I've been in it about fifty-seven years. My father, like I said, fought in fairs and stuff in the thirties, and he was my first instructor. He taught me boxing and wrestling techniques and things that would probably be for self-defense at a time when I didn't totally understand what I was learning. I was eleven when I started, nearly twelve. But that got me interested in self-defense. Also a parallel thing that really had me interested was Batman, who would mention boxing and judo and wrestling in some of the stories I was reading. I wanted to be like that. I thought, I can't be Superman; I can't be The Flash; I can't be Green Lantern. But I can possibly take the idea of Batman and try to become as good at martial arts as I could.

Pretty soon I started Judo classes and Hapkido classes, which was new to the US. I was probably one of the first people to study Hapkido in Texas. Then there's Kenpo and Thai boxing and, of course, Tae Kwan Do was being developed. It was very different than it is now. Self-defense. It wasn't sport in the way we think of it now, so I started studying all that stuff. Somewhere along the line, many years later, I realized I was doing something a little different, and I trained with some grandmasters in other arts to learn different things. At some point somebody said, "You know whatever you're doing is really good and it's not exactly this or exactly that," so over time I became recognized for my own system called Shen Chuan.

For what it's worth, I'm in the International Martial Arts Hall of Fame and the United States Martial Arts Hall of fame. I've been doing it a long time. I'm still learning. I'm sixty-eight and I'm still teaching, and except for a few injuries, I still do it, and I'm going to do it as long as I feel capable and I'm not missing a step.

I am a different martial artist then that I am now. I have a different approach, but it's working for me and, even if you get past what you can see—the physical—it's the mental and emotional exercises that help you have confidence in life, at least if you study it correctly. I don't mean if you go to a makeshift dojo and just do this as exercise. I'm talking about if it becomes a part of your lifestyle, because it gave me the confidence to write. It gave me the confidence to go out and take chances as a writer. It gave me the discipline to do it, and it taught me economy of motion and all sorts of things you can apply to the work.

Slade: I also wanted to ask you about the humor in your stories. I always believed it was intentional, but it's so subdued sometimes. But then sometimes it's way out there . . . . I also wanted to ask you about where the idea for "Tight Little Stitches on a Dead Man's Back" came from?

Lansdale: I'll talk about the humor first. When I was growing up, the way a lot of people handled things, especially when your life is a little rougher, maybe blue collar, was with humor, you know? My dad was not a big talker, but when he talked, he was interesting and he was a good storyteller when he decided to tell stories. He also had a lot of wisecracks and one-liners. They weren't all made up by him but were things that were part of the culture. I remember him saying about some man that he was the kind of guy who would rather climb a tree and lie than stand on the ground and tell the truth. A lot of the people around me had all these similes and metaphors. I think a lot of it may have grown out of the fact that some of these people were not particularly educated, so instead of trying to use big words they didn't know, they tried to use comparisons or they tried to use examples. I was also told all these stories, some of which I think were true and some of which were folklore. So I was heavily influenced by folklore, and folklore is frequently funny and it's frequently broad. It goes way out on a limb and then saws it off with you sitting on the other end.

And I think that kind of background and atmosphere influence humor. Some of the writers I read, like Robert Bloch, used humor in their work. Bloch's horror and humor were opposite sides of a coin. You know, he could flip it either way, so I think I learned from writers and I learned from people around me.

As for the second part of your question, the part about "Tight Little Stitches," I was asked to write that one. John McClay had a little publishing company at the time. There was a writer named J. N. Williamson, who was the editor of this particular house. At the time, I was starting to develop as a writer. I had written what I thought were some pretty good stories, and I had some that I had written that I couldn't sell at that time, like "By Bizarre Hands" and "On the Far Side of the Cadillac Desert with Dead Folks," and I had written the opening of "Night They Missed the Horror Show" and stopped because there was no market for it. Nobody knew what they hell they were and they didn't know what to do with them.

On "Stitches" I thought, "Man, this isn't going well. This is a loser." I worked and I worked and I worked, really hard, and I wrote it, and when I got through I thought, "Oh my God, this is horrible." I thought I just might drop out and withdraw, but finally I convinced myself that I would send it to them and see what they thought. And they flipped out over it. John McClay, the few times I've seen him, still says that's his favorite story I've ever done. And that story, along with three or four other events in that period, is what turned my career around and changed my life. It opened the door for stories I'd already written like "By Bizarre Hands" and "The Pit" to be published. It got me the opportunity to finish "On the Far Side of the Cadillac Desert" as well as "Night They Missed the Horror Show."

That, along with the books *The Magic Wagon* and *Dead in the West*, sort of started the trajectory of short stories, small press, and mainstream press, and I realized that to survive, that was a good way to go. And I like telling stories, all kinds of stories, so I felt like a big gate had been opened. Financially, things began to get better, and I also began to edit a few anthologies. So "Tight Little Stitches," along with those other novels, probably were the major doors that opened for me. By 1986, "Tight Little Stitches" was nominated for a World Fantasy award. It didn't win, but it was nominated. People still think it's the one that won, but that story has gone on and on and on and even had a couple of movie options on it. So I'm glad I did it, though at the time I wasn't very sure it was any good.

Slade: I think it's really great. That might have been the first story I ever read of yours, but maybe it was "Dog, Cat, and Baby," which is also really good.

Lansdale: I was writing a lot of those kinds of stories, which I'm proud of. I thought they were really good, but what I think happened with "Tight Little Stitches" is that it shows the more literary side that I had that was there from 1983 on.

Slade: Okay, how about we talk about how you came to write "Perchance to Dream" for *Batman: The Animated Series.*

Lansdale: Okay, yeah, I did like four scripts for them and one *Superman* I contributed to, but a friend of mine, Bob Wayne worked for DC Comics, and I was visiting him in New York. I was at DC Comics and he said, "Let me show you something." He showed me the opening to *Batman: The Animated Series*, and I loved it. Well, he gave my name to someone over at Warner Bros. I had written a couple of Batman pieces that were novellas for some anthology. I had also written a Batman novel. So they called me. I think Michael Reeves may have been the first person I spoke to, and he said, "Would you like to write for the TV series?" I said, "Oh, hell yeah," so I ended up writing "Perchance to Dream" first, and then I went on to do others like "Read My Lips" and "Showdown."

Then later when they changed the series to something more juvenile, I did one called "Critters." I also worked on a Superman, the first Bizarro story they did. Then I went on to do other animation projects after that. That's how it went. I was in the right place at the right time and I had the right amount of experience, so it all came together and it turned out pretty good. "Perchance" and "Read My Lips" are often on the "best of" lists, and even "Showdown" makes it from time to time.

Slade: That's cool. How about we jump to your mysteries? Your bestsellers like *Cold in July*. Where did that come from?

Lansdale: By the end of the eighties I felt burned out on horror and I was writing fewer short stories. I had always loved crime and my first stories were crime stories. My first novel, *Act of Love* was a crime story. Not a great one now, but at the time I thought I did pretty good. I had thought, well, that's where I'm going. Crime writing. But I was interested in horror and there were a lot of markets for it. I was excited by it and I had a lot of people I was beginning to meet who were doing it. I grew up reading all these different genres, so I thought I would write a book like the old Gold Medal crime novels I used to read.

My wife and I were looking at new houses. We were at a point where we thought maybe we could afford one. So we went out and looked at one on Lake Nacogdoches and as we were looking at it with the realtor, I saw a bullet hole in the ceiling. I said, "How'd that get there?" She said, "You know, I don't know." Of course she played that down. We didn't end up buying the house and I don't know if the bullet had anything to do with that, but I went home that night and went to bed and I started dreaming. And that bullet hole actually led to the opening of *Cold in July*, which has to do with the guy who comes in and tries to rob the place and he's killed, more by accident by the homeowner, who becomes the lead in the story. But when I went home that night, I dreamed that it was me and it was our house combined with a house we'd been in. All that just kind of mutated and I woke up from that dream several times that night, but when I would go back to bed, it would pick up where it left off, like pausing a movie. When I would wake up during the night, and it was several times, I would get up and wash the sweat off my face because it was that intense. Strangely, it didn't occur to me it was a novel. It was just an intense dream. Next morning I got up and told my wife the dream I had, and she said that sounds like a book, and I thought, damn, she's right, and it was pretty much blow for blow the story I wrote. The characters were all there: Jim Bob, all of them. I never got into that deeper dream state where it all goes so deep you lose it, or at least don't remember it as clearly, but that night my mind worked out that entire story. I had a couple books out by then, and a lot of short stories, and I was working on a big nonfiction book for Bantam that didn't get published by them, and I told an editor who was visiting me about my dream, and he said, "That sounds good. I think I'd go for that." So I started writing it.

I wrote part of it in the third person, and I thought, this story is just rushing at me, but I don't like the way it feels. Then I talked to a writer friend, Ardath Mayhar, and she said, "Maybe you should do it in the first person. You do better in first person, I think." So I switched to first person. It took off. I wrote it in about two and a half months, right after I'd done *The Drive-In*. And then I was a crime writer and I had a two-book contract. On the second one I wanted to do another Gold Medal, so I wrote *Savage Season*. In that, I took a lot of my real life—it's very much like me, at least at that time—and I turned it into a suspenseful crime novel. I dealt with a lot of things of the sixties, of which I was happily a sixties guy. When people say the sixties, they usually mean from late fifties until after '74, '75, and that's when all of this sort of stuff was going on, like the alternative lifestyles, Civil Rights protests, anti-Vietnam war, and so on.

I was so disappointed in the way Bantam handled the novels, I turned to comics and screenplays a bit, wrote the Batman books, the adult one and the young adult one. I think for two or three years there I didn't write any more novels that were entirely my own. When I eventually wrote *Mucho Mojo*, I had no idea it was going to be a sequel until I started writing it. The series just took off from there. I just kept writing more about these characters. I'd take breaks from them now and again . . . I'd say one break took eight years once, four years another time, and then I returned to them. Right now I've been doing a lot of Hap and Leonard because I really enjoy those guys.

Slade: Now it's going to be a TV show. How did that happen?

Lansdale: Jim Mickle and Nick Dimici approached me about doing the *Cold in July* film. I had optioned it many, many years earlier, and I wrote several drafts of the screenplay. The worst part about it is the only draft that I know of in existence is the draft I don't like. The first two were my best drafts, and they're probably somewhere in my files at one of the universities that keep my stuff. That was with John Irving, who had made *Dogs of War* and *Ghost Story*. I think we worked on the film for like seven years, but then it went fallow.

Then Jim and Nick approached me at a film festival and they were talking to me about it. The first film they had made—Jim had directed and Nick had written and starred in—was called *Mulberry Street*. It was a real-low budget film, kind of like the old Roger Cormans. But it was really well done and I could see potential there, so I said, "Yeah guys, let's see what you've got." It took about seven years, and they made two or three movies in between that. They just couldn't seem to get to *Cold in July*. They couldn't get it financed because the book's kind of quirky and people didn't agree; it was either too fast or too slow. Jim and Nick stayed with it until they made a film out of it, and it was a very good film. Then they thought they wanted to do Hap and Leonard.

The first season comes out March seventh, I think. We're hoping for at least a couple more seasons, which would be wonderful.

Slade: I don't know if you are a fan of *The Rockford Files*, but I can see a little bit of that in *Hap and Leonard*. Especially the way they communicate.

Lansdale: As a matter of fact, you're right. You're absolutely right. I was a big fan of *The Rockford Files* and *Harry O*, which were big shows back when I was young and in my twenties. I really liked those shows, and you know, the private eye stuff really became important to me in the seventies. Chandler was a big influence, Hammett was a big influence, a lot of the TV shows back then, the good ones like *Rockford*, they certainly did influence me. That was the voice I had grown up with, meaning the wisecracks and kind of metaphorical speaking, although it had a southern accent.

Slade: When I read *Cold in July*, I really imagined James Garner as the main character.

Lansdale: That's cool. I can see that. You know, I always said that the one thing I would have really loved to hear was to James Garner doing some of the lines from the Hap and Leonard stuff and, for that matter *Cold in July*. I didn't see Garner in it at the time, maybe as the old guy, or if he were a little younger, Jim Bob, but Garner is one of my favorite actors of all time and I actually met him once. He did a movie here called *The Long Summer of George Adams*, and I was invited to the movie set. It was just a handshake, "How are you doing," him asking me a couple of perfunctory questions and me answering. He's a favorite of mine, but when I was doing *Cold in July*, I always thought of the old guy as Robert Mitchum. As time went on, of course, he aged out and I thought Nick Nolte would be good. They couldn't get him, and it eventually became Sam Shepard. I have no complaints with what they managed. I'm really happy with it. I'm very fortunate.

Slade: And Don Johnson was really good in that.

Lansdale: Oh, he was outstanding. I think it was one of those things that revitalized his career a little bit there.

Slade: So you've been happy with the way your projects have been adapted?

Lansdale Between *Bubba Ho-Tep* and *Cold in July* and *Hap and Leonard* and the "Incident On and Off a Mountain Road" episode of *Masters of Horror*, I've been very fortunate. I'm sure the bad ones are coming if others come. I hope to direct one myself, based on a story of mine that my son did the screenplay for. I've come close to having the money a couple of times then a few things went south. I'm also trying to produce and coproduce a number of other projects with other people. We'll see what happens.

Slade: I've also read you were working with Bill Paxton on *The Bottoms*.

Lansdale: Oh God, yeah. I love Bill. Bill and I worked on that for eight years and we got to be real good friends. But Bill was the kind of guy who, if you knew him for five minutes, you thought he was your best friend. He was that kind of guy, and I loved him dearly. You know, he called me a couple of weeks before he went to the hospital and told me that he had to go in and he was scared. He was worried about it, and I told him, "Bill, they do this all the time. You're gonna be fine." And I truly believed that. We made jokes about splitting up his goods and stuff like that. He went in on Valentine's Day and I emailed and texted him after a few days, didn't hear anything, so I finally found out through a friend who knew the family, that he was struggling, and the next day he died. But you know, he came here to Nacogdoches. We also talked on the phone and emailed each other frequently. I haven't been able to bring myself to discard his texts or emails, and I can't see anything with him in it. And I love the films with him in them, but I'm just not ready.

His death sort of left *The Bottoms* hanging.

Slade: Was he going to star in it as well or just direct?

Lansdale: No, I tried to talk to talk him into doing that, but he didn't think he had enough heat for that, which I'm not sure is true. But nonetheless he was going to direct it. Brett Hanley, who wrote the screenplay for it, we used to joke, and part of it was joking and part of it was real, but we used to joke that we would be riding along with Bill and after a little bit Bill would be telling us about the script. And he would go into great detail about how it would be shot, and he would go into such great detail, and get on a roll, and one of us would kind of go, "Bill, let's talk about the weather, man." He had it down. He knew exactly what he wanted to do.

He was an amazing person. He was a craftsman with wood. He loved art. He was an artist, you know. And of course he was an actor, and he was a great director. He actually wanted to become mostly a director at that point in his life. He was probably sixty, sixty-one when he died. I was four years older, but he was ready to make that turn. I don't know that he was necessarily thinking, "I'll never act again," but I think he was really wanting to become primarily a director. I just feel like the world got cheated. I know I got cheated, and I know there were people close to him and his family, who obviously were cheated. I did meet his son at a photography exhibit where some of the photography was taken of Bill when he was working on his video with James Cameron. James Cameron was there. A lot of people were there, and we all talked a little about Bill and watched the video and all that. And I got to meet James, who is a really nice kid. I've seen a little bit of him in films. He's got talent. I think the kid's going someplace with acting if he pursues it.

Slade: I guess it got passed down in the genes. Bill was really good in the movie *A Simple Plan*, which people have forgotten about.

Lansdale: *Frailty* was also very good. He was good. He directed and starred in that and it was just amazing. Brent Hanley wrote it. I think his best role as an actor was *One False Murder*, directed by Carl Franklin. That is a film that nobody really knows well, but he is absolutely astonishing in that. I think *Frailty* is second, *Simple Plan* third. Bill was one of those guys that there was just something about him. He was a leading man character actor, you know? He started out doing character roles and he kind of went into leading man with *Twister* and *Congo*, things like that. But there was just something about him like he was the guy, everybody's friend, everybody's brother. So when he played evil parts, you still went, "Wow, I still like this guy." And he had a way of connecting with people, even people who don't know his work.

You know, he got confused for Bill Pullman sometimes. I've got this story, and I believe it's true, that one time he was asked to do an interview by somebody in a restaurant where he was eating. He says, "You know I'm eating," and the guy kept really asking him, and Bill finally agreed. So the guy started interviewing him, and Bill realized that this guy thought he was Bill Pullman. He was talking about Bill Pullman movies, so he's joking with him saying, "Oh God, that was terrible, that was awful, those people are ter-rible." Then at the end he said, "Hey, I'm just kidding you. I'm Bill Paxton. You thought you were doing Bill Pullman." And the guy was relieved be-cause he realized it was a joke. Then Bill gave him an interview as Bill Pax-ton. I want to believe that story. That's the kind of guy he was. He was kind. He was good to my kids and my family and I admired him a lot. He was like a younger brother.

Slade: Are there any upcoming projects you can talk about or promote?

Lansdale: Well, you know, I have *Jackrabbit Smile*, the new Hap and Leonard novel, which comes out towards the end of March. I'll be on a book tour for that. I've also got a lot of short stories coming out. I have a collec-tion from Subterranean Press called *Driving to Geronimo's Grave*, which is several long stories. It's got "Wrestling Jesus" in it, which is not a religious story. It's about an old wrestler named Jesus, and it's kind of a coming-of-age story. "The Projectionist," which is the one that I hope to direct, is also in there. "Rapid Robo," which is kind of a science fantasy story. I've got some other stuff that's coming—a few random things here and there.

Bubba Ho-Tep 15th Anniversary with Don Coscarelli and Joe R. Lansdale

Mick Garris / 2018

Aired on *Post Mortem with Mick Garris*, September 26, 2018. Appears by permission of the author.

MICK GARRIS: All right guys, let's talk about the beginning of this collaboration. How did you two first meet?

DON COSCARELLI: I'll take that. I used to go book shopping at a store called Dangerous Visions in Sherman Oaks.

GARRIS: Very well known. Named after a Harlan Ellison collection.

COSCARELLI: Long since gone, unfortunately. They had a lot of cool stuff, and I used to just browse the shelves and try to find something that maybe would spark my fantasy to make a movie. And I went up to the guy who ran the place and I said, "So, what's new and cutting edge in horror?" And he said, "Follow me." [Laughs.] He took me over to the L aisle and goes, "Joe Lansdale. He always has a high body count!"

[Everyone laughs.]

COSCARELLI: Which I later found to not be so true. But it intrigued me, and I grabbed a couple books. I think it was *The Nightrunners* and *The Drive-In*. Went home, and luckily a friend of mine, Jeff Connor, had this business called Scream Press. He was in the publishing world and somehow dug up a phone number for Joe. I think that was maybe before email.

JOE R. LANSDALE: It was definitely before.

COSCARELLI: So I called him up, we started talking. I loved reading *Nightrunners* and *The Drive-In*. Great books. I thought maybe one of them would make a great movie, especially *The Drive-In*. And I called Joe and *The Drive-In*, I think, had just been optioned.

LANSDALE: *Dead in the West* may have come up also. I don't remember.

COSCARELLI: Yeah, I'm not sure I'd seen that one yet. But Joe invited me to come down to Texas and visit, so I went down for the weekend in Nacogdoches.

LANSDALE: Came for a long weekend, yeah.

COSCARELLI: It was really nice.

LANSDALE: We had a lot of fun and we talked about stuff, but we couldn't really get anything going yet because, as he said, *The Drive-In* was optioned and I probably didn't have as much material as that. And then, along came a little time after Don left, and you know, we hit it off immediately. We were friends immediately. When he called me up, he said, "This is Don Coscarelli and . . ." I think you tried to explain who you were. I said, "I know who you are!"

[Everyone laughs.]

LANSDALE: I said, "*Phantasm!*" But he came and we talked, and then when he left, a little while later he came across *Bubba Ho-Tep*. And he called me, I said, "Don, you can't film *Bubba Ho-Tep*! That won't film!" And he said, "Nah." He was pretty persistent. I said, "I don't wanna take your money for that. It won't film." But he made a deal with my agent, and I think a year passed and nothing happened. I think you renewed it, and I think I said, "Okay, if you were foolish enough to get it the first time, you can go ahead and get it the second time." I said, "It's not gonna happen." And he asked me to do the screenplay, and I thought, "That's a hard one to do," and I probably wanted more money. But it was a hard one to do was the real reason. I said, "I don't think it can be done." So then he sent me a screenplay and I read it. I said, "I'll be damned, it can be done."

GARRIS: And Don, you adapted it yourself.

COSCARELLI: Yeah, I did. You know, by the way, Mick, just as a, you know, for aspiring filmmakers . . . I never intended to be a writer by any means.

[Everyone laughs.]

COSCARELLI: I wanted to make a movie! And frequently in the low-budget world, you know, writing is a part of it. You have to do all of it is what it's—

GARRIS: The more you know about every part of it—

COSCARELLI: But before we go further, we've gotta talk about that first meeting down in Nacogdoches, because Joe invited me kindly, and . . . [h]e had this office downstairs with a bed down there. And he told me about all the luminaries that had slept in that bed.

LANSDALE: [Laughs.]

COSCARELLI: David Schow had just been there, I think. Richard Christian Matheson, a great writer.

LANSDALE: A lot of editors. A lot of different people.

GARRIS: A lot of our buddies.

COSCARELLI: And of course there was the creek bed next door, and he said, "Watch out for the water moccasins! They come out at night!"

[Everyone laughs.]

COSCARELLI: So every night I was gonna—

GARRIS: Inspiration slithered by!

LANSDALE: It was not connected to the house. You had to go outside to go around to go up the stairs to the rest of the house.

But you know, you said something in your introduction . . . . And I'm always a little bit bitchy about this. And of course it depends, you know, who is talking about adaptations. The best and most literal adaptation I've ever had, Don did it. If you see that movie, it's 90 percent . . . [m]aybe even higher than that. What he did, he did another thing, and I really appreciated this, is he took some of the, I guess you would call it the prose, and turned it into dialogue.

GARRIS: Yes. One of the things I was going to say was how very faithful to the language the movie is. And people—

COSCARELLI: That's the genius of Joe. His use of language is so amazing. I don't know that anyone can write like him. . . . You know when you're adapting a screenplay, you know, all you can really use is the dialogue. And then the settings and the scenario and the plot. But all of the description—you know, the third-person description, usually just has to be jettisoned. You know, I wish I could say I knew exactly I was doing, because when I first started, I had a narrator. And I took all that stuff—

LANSDALE: Yeah, I remember that.

COSCARELLI: And I took all that narrator—

LANSDALE: Yeah, you actually had me narrate a little piece.

COSCARELLI: And do a test for that. Then the problem was that Joe's story had the construct in there of having Elvis doing narrations. So then you had what you're looking at, and then you've got Elvis's narration, and layered on top of it was a third-party narrator.

GARRIS: Okay, as we get deeper into this, for anybody who has not read the novella or seen the film, Joe, maybe you ought to give a rundown of what the plot is.

LANSDALE: Well, the plot is really pretty simple.

GARRIS: It is simple.

LANSDALE: I think it's the characters and the way they interact. The idea was, and this was kind of a thing then, you'd see it in the magazines all the time—"Elvis didn't die, he's out there livin' in Las Vegas, you know, and he's a truck driver," or whatever. The story was always variable, but he was supposedly alive. And that was the big takeaway from so many of those little cheap magazines and papers that came out. And also, when I was growin' up, I of course, we knew about the Kennedy assassination. I was a kid then. I was probably eleven or something, I don't know. I don't remember. But that had a big impact. So the idea of John F. Kennedy and Elvis were in my mind because my brother actually lived in Memphis and tried to record at Sun Records, and his wife that he met there had gone to school with Elvis. They graduated from Humes High at the same time. So there was that little connection. And he had, of course, met and knew Elvis in passing, before he was the big guy.

GARRIS: The king.

LANSDALE: So those things came to together. My mother had had an accident, and she had to be in a rest home for a while because she had to have around the clock, so you know, I spent a lot of time there. So all of those three things, I think were marinating. And I'd once made up a title as a joke called *Bubba Ho-Tep*. I said that would be the redneck version of an Egyptian mummy film.

[Everyone laughs.]

LANSDALE: I always loved those mummy films—all those Universal films—when I was little. And then when I was asked to do it . . . I wanna say it was Paul Salmmon that was the editor—

GARRIS: Yeah, I think if I remember right.

LANSDALE: And it was originally called *Elvis is Dead*? Maybe that's what it eventually became, *Elvis is Dead*. But all of those factors came together. There was also the fact that when you're visiting people in the old folks' home, as they used to call it in Texas, it's not only that she was there for medical reasons, you know, she was aging and you're seeing people that were even older than that. And though I was not an older man then, as I am now—

[Everyone laughs.]

LANSDALE: But I think that affected me about how people deal with age, and that the fact is, no matter what you do in life, no matter how famous you are, no matter how rich you are . . . you get old. If you don't get old, you're dead before then. And then it's like—

GARRIS: If you're lucky you get old.

LANSDALE: The idea of the theme of, what does it really matter . . . how much sex you've had? How much money you've had, etcetera, etcetera? In the end, what's it worth? So I kind of got this thematic idea that it's not about where you end up, it's where you go as you travel. It's the traveling that counts, 'cause we're all gonna end up in the same place.

GARRIS: Yes. Same box.

LANSDALE: Same box.

GARRIS: So, well, for the uninitiated, *Bubba Ho-Tep* is about Elvis Presley actually still being alive and living in an old folks' home in Texas—

LANSDALE: I didn't finish, did I?

GARRIS: Yes.

[Everyone laughs.]

GARRIS: And an elderly Black gentleman who believes he's John F. Kennedy, who is still alive, and his brain has been replaced by sand by the government.

LANSDALE: And the actual brain is in the White House, powered by batteries.

[Everyone laughs.]

LANSDALE: And he gets vibes from that. And I forgot to mention too that there's a mummy.

GARRIS: Yeah, there's a mummy!

[Everyone laughs.]

GARRIS: There's a passing circus with a mummy that crashes off a bridge.

LANSDALE: Tutankhamun's little brother or something.

GARRIS: And comes to life, so when we're talking about a Joe Lansdale horror story, "Joe Lansdale Meets Don Coscarelli" becomes quite a potent mix, because both of you have very distinct voices. And that's something all creatives artists aspire to.

COSCARELLI: I'd like to just interrupt for a second and say that *Bubba Ho-Tep* really came about because Joe has this fearless writing style that will go where other writers won't tread.

GARRIS: In the eighties it was called splatterpunk.

COSCARELLI: Which, for me, was ridiculous because Joe at one time was one of the splatterpunk guys. No, but what Joe's genius is, and what I don't think anyone in this splatterpunk, the other splatterpunkers did is, he has an ability or . . . a *desire* to mash up genres, and he takes something, you know, you've seen a million times before in some other genre . . . and then he fuses them and mixes them. And then he mixes in a few other things and makes something that is just completely unique.

LANSDALE: You know, I think Don and I both like the idea of it being something poignant and having some purpose, and we thought about these guys. I don't remember, I think Don or Bruce, I don't remember who said this, but it was the idea of how you really wanted to see them end up—a heroic moment instead of being shot in the back of a limousine or dying on the toilet straining a stool.

[Everyone laughs.]

LANSDALE: So you wanted something a little more than that, you know? But we also wanted to capture all of the genre vibes and things that we're interested in. And, I mean, I love Don's work. For me, I always felt that *Bubba* was everything that Don did brilliantly. And not just because it's my work, but because he did such a wonderful job. When you'd doing these kinds of movies, Don's pretty much everything on them; you know, producer, director. He did everything but act in it. And he may have did that. He may have been the mummy for all I know!

COSCARELLI: I couldn't fit into that costume. That was pretty thin.

GARRIS: The funny thing is, it's a mummy story and the mummy is the least important part of the story.

LANSDALE: It's representational of that idea of growing old and deaf.

COSCARELLI: I think when reading the short story originally, it brought imagery and feelings into my mind about Elvis. You know, I was not really an Elvis fan, but I knew about him. And there were certain aspects of Elvis that we all sort of know about. He loved his mother; he was very respectful—he'd always say "sir," you know; he was polite. And there were heroic inherent aspects, intrinsic to Elvis and the Elvis legend. Also, especially, with the karate, with the jumpsuits.

LANSDALE: They're modeled after Shazam, by the way.

COSCARELLI: Of course, because he was so popular with that . . . he started dressing in these jumpsuits in a way to almost poke fun at himself. But it kind of wasn't, because he had this ability to make with the curly lip smile and get anything he wanted.

GARRIS: He also wanted to be an undercover operative for President Nixon.

COSCARELLI: Of course, yes.

LANSDALE: He played heroes in movies. Most of the movies he did were, well, I can't say that . . . I'd say about 99.9 percent weren't very good. But he had chops. But he never got to use 'em. By his own fault, by his manager's fault, whatever, it doesn't matter. But the thing was, he played heroes in those movies.

COSCARELLI: And of course Joe had it all in there where, in the story, where Elvis says what he always wanted to be was a hero. And the movie gives Elvis and the legend and legacy of Elvis, and all the Elvis fans out there this moment. And as Joe used to describe it, it's like *Ride the High Country* with a walker and a wheelchair.

LANSDALE: That's right, that's right.

GARRIS: Elvis Presley and John F. Kennedy, the two most iconic heroes of—

COSCARELLI: Don't forget the Lone Ranger—

LANSDALE: Kemosabe!

COSCARELLI: They all died with their boots on, you know? So it had these American heroes . . . .

GARRIS: So it's about heroism.

COSCARELLI: Absolutely.

LANSDALE: The guy who played Kemosabe was probably in better shape than all of us.

COSCARELLI: That is true.

LANSDALE: He was an older guy, and he was like Tarzan . . . . They had to work to make him look old.

COSCARELLI: Larry Pennell was his name. Great actor.

GARRIS: So what was it about the story when you first read it that made you think, "I wanna make this"?

COSCARELLI: Well, first off, it wasn't even the story. It was the log line in the book. On the dust jacket. It just said, "Elvis battles 4,000-year-old mummy," you know? It was just like, "Oh shit, that's a movie right there!"

GARRIS: It's the weirdest log line for this story, yet it's kind of the log line, yet it's such a miniscule part of what this story is.

COSCARELLI: Just that little nugget alone really intrigued me, but I'll tell you what the closer was for me. There's just a wonderful moment in the book, in the novella, and I think in the movie where, as JFK dies, Elvis salutes him as Mr. President. And when I read that story, I got a little tear in my eye and I was thinking, "Jeez, what's going on here?"

LANSDALE: You know, another thing I was glad Don did, and I was afraid we wouldn't be able to do it because we discussed it and he wasn't sure, was having the hieroglyphics come out of his mouth and present themselves on screen. Because in the story when he speaks, the hieroglyphics are there, and a very fine artist friend of mine, Martin Nelson had created those hieroglyphics based on the *Egyptian Book of the Dead*. I think he maybe spoke two or three times in the story, I think he did it twice in the film. I don't remember thinking, "Gosh, if we don't have that we're gonna lose this sort of thing that makes it unique; that's preposterous in one way, but in another way it reaches out and touches something unexpected and you still believe it. And Don was able to do it.

GARRIS: You actually did it. I mean, on a film with a very tight budget.

COSCARELLI: Well, I brought in some collaborators. David Hartman created that tumbling effect, and Michael Smith, a friend of his, helped with the animation of it. These guys came in and did this for like nothing. And this was back before the processing power in the computers was quite what it is today.

GARRIS: At least they could be kind of cartoony and work.

LANSDALE: You know, after I read Don's script, I was optimistic, but I wasn't sold. I'll be honest with you. Not because of him or anyone else, but just because I thought, "This is so difficult to bring to the screen." And at that time, he had not chosen an actor. And my son said to me, he said, "Dad, get Bruce Campbell, he's my favorite actor!" I said, "I don't have any say in this." Don calls me the very same day and says, "What do you think about Bruce Campbell?"

[Everyone laughs.]

LANSDALE: So I got to be a hero to my son. "Yeah, I got that Bruce Cambell for ya!" [Laughs.]

COSCARELLI: All I've got to say is, Keith knows something that we don't, because . . .

GARRIS: And he was what? Ten years old at the time?

COSCARELLI: I mean, Bruce made this terrific success in the *Evil Dead* movies and had a massive fan base of *Evil Dead* fans.

LANSDALE: He's the Elvis of B-movie movies.

COSCARELLI: Yeah, he was. Or he was moving into it. He was growing and getting bigger, but those of us in the genre, we could start to see that kind of thing. 'Cause I was a good six or seven years before that. I went to a *Fangoria* convention, 'cause Reggie Bannister from *Phantasm* was presenting a lifetime achievement award to Angus [Scrimm], so I went to show support. And they did that, and it was very nice and lovely. And then it finished and Bruce Campbell was coming out to do an award. I'd only seen the movies and I'd never really met him. And he was in . . . I'm losing my lucidity to describe this moment. He came out, and I think there might be a video floating around on the web. He walked out and did a stunt right out of *Evil Dead II*! Right in front of the crowd. He put his hand behind his head and did this complete flip and hit. . . . He kind of ended it with a little James Brown flourish, you know on the ground. And it looked like it hurt. He did it and the audience went nuts, and I thought, "Oh, wow. This is a guy who loves his fans and will risk his life to entertain them."

GARRIS: He'll go anywhere.

LANSDALE: He's a physical comedian, really. He's very much . . . He has a great physicality. He sort of reminds me of Buster Keaton in the way he moves.

COSCARELLI: Very much so.

LANSDALE: Very much so. Maybe even Cary Grant had those, you know, they did those type of pratfalls.

GARRIS: With charm, too. The great thing about casting a guy like Bruce Campbell is, he comes prepared. He's already somebody that has a history. That character existed before the opening titles ran. And he brings the good kind of baggage with him. His personality.

LANSDALE: He's got charisma. And he's handsome, but he's uniquely handsome in a way that makes him really approachable. You know, it makes him like a regular guy, but not quite. So when he played Elvis and they put the makeup on him, which took a while—

GARRIS: This was KNB, right?

COSCARELLI: Yeah, KNB.

LANSDALE: He was that guy. And I remember meeting Ossie Davis out there. And I'm not a starstruck kind of guy normally. Writers do it to me. But stars I'm not much moved by. But Ossie Davis? My God, here's a guy that, because of the civil rights movement, he was involved in that greatly, he gave a eulogy at Martin Luther King's funeral. He spoke at Malcolm X's, and he was one of the first Black producers, directors. He wrote plays. He wrote screenplays. He did stage. He did movies. So I was like in awe, and when I came and he said [imitates voice], "Hello, Mr. Lansdale . . ."

[Everyone laughs.]

LANSDALE: [Timid, high-pitched voice]: "Hi, how are you?" [Laughs.]

GARRIS: Well, we have a little story about that, because I had worked with Ossie on *The Stand*. And it was a great honor.

COSCARELLI: Let me tell the story, because I have to give you your proper accolades. Mick sitting here is one of the reasons that *Bubba Ho-Tep* really got made, because—

GARRIS: That's overstating the case.

COSCARELLI: Seriously. You know, Bruce was a magnificent get for us to star in the film. But we need the lynchpin, which was somebody to bring some level of dignity to that role. And tracking down Ossie's agent, trying to tell one of these guys, "Yeah, it's about a 4,000-year-old mummy and—"

LANSDALE: And it was this great actor.

GARRIS: And he plays John F. Kennedy! [Laughs.]

COSCARELLI: It doesn't connect with those guys the way it does with us, especially now that we've made the movie.

GARRIS: And he passed on it.

COSCARELLI: He did pass.

GARRIS: The agent did.

COSCARELLI: The agent passed, and it was just like dead. And I went back like, "What the hell do I do now?" And I remembered that Mick had worked with Ossie, so I called Mick up and I really imposed on him. I said, "Mick, I need you to write him a nice letter and tell him I'm a good guy and work . . . ." He says, "No problem, Don." And I think we Fed-Exed the letter, because this was before email and we wanted to make sure he got it. And a couple days later, Ossie was in. So thank you, Mick! You are an honorable *Bubba Ho-Tep* hero.

LANSDALE: You know, when we were on the set, and I think you—I know I was there and you were too. I believe they were just sittin' on the bench—him, Bruce, and Ossie, and Bruce said, "What are you doing in this movie?"

[Everyone laughs.]

LANSDALE: And Ossie said, "I liked the script." But you know what's weird is, some years later, I had on my *Bubba Ho-Tep* t-shirt and I was in Italy. My daughter Kasey is a singer, and she was performing in Italy with a number of people at a film . . . excuse me, a book and music festival. So I was over there, and our paths crossed, and I said, "Great!" That happens to us every once in a while, so I was there and I got to see her perform. Then I watched Guy Davis perform and then Charlie Musselwhite, I think. It might have been that year or the year after. But anyway, all this stuff and I had my *Bubba Ho-Tep* T-shirt on, and Guy Davis comes over to me and says, "I loved my dad in that." And I went, "*What?*" I realize that's his son. His son was the blues guitarist and he says, "Ooh, I gotta get a picture for Mama!" So he came over and got a picture and I thought . . . And Ruby Dee, like Ossie, was deeply involved in the civil rights movement. So these were kind of heroes of mine.

GARRIS: One of the greatest honors of my life was working with Ossie Davis and Ruby Dee together as . . . they weren't a couple in it. And in fact, I had cast someone else who got sick and died, and we replaced him with Ossie. Because we didn't want to go the obvious route of putting them together, but they were both so magnificent, and they were both so amazing to work with and learn from, and asking for input, and just really, really amazing human beings, as well as great actors you could possibly hope to work with.

LANSDALE: Ossie said to me once, he says, "I was thinking about changing a line." I said, "Well, I didn't write the script. Ask Don." But he went ahead and just told me and I forget what exactly it was . . . something simple. You know, and had I written the script I'd have said, "Do whatever the hell you want," because I knew he knew. But it was one word. And he would also say, "*arsehole!*"

[Everyone laughs.]

COSCARELLI: [Laughs.] Oh, the arsehole! Where he came with that, God knows, but we loved it. He was just an amazing . . . One time he came up to me, and I can't do an impression like Joe does of Ossie, but he said, "You know, I've met a lot of presidents, but I just never thought I'd be asked to play President JFK."

LANSDALE: He knew Elvis too! He had met Elvis, he had met—

COSCARELLI: Wow. I never talked with him about that.

LANSDALE: Yeah, I think that's right. I believe that's what Bruce told me, so I'm going on that.

GARRIS: It would not be surprising.

LANSDALE: Oh, I'm sure he probably did. It wouldn't surprise me at all. But it was a fascinating place where it was shot too, because it was an old veterans' home or something?

COSCARELLI: It was a rehabilitation hospital that was called Rancho Los Amigos.

LANSDALE: It was spooky. And it had the—

GARRIS: Was that shot here?

COSCARELLI: Yeah, down in Downey is where it was.

LANSDALE: But there was a house across from it that was . . . when you see the exterior, you know, the exterior shot it's that, and then the interior was kind of across the street.

COSCARELLI: We had it all, right on this one property.

LANSDALE: And then down the street is Nacogdoches. And the only thing funny about that is when they would show it, they would show show and say "Nacogdoches, East Texas" and there'd be cars driving and a mountain in the background. And everybody would break out laughing. 'Cause obviously that . . . But in a way, it kind of added to this kind of this surreal element that was part of that picture. And what I was scared was that it would not work. And when I got there, you remember, you showed me a daily, something you had shot, and as soon as I saw it I went, "Okay." Because what it is is the actors played it straight. Even though Bruce is funny, he plays it straight, and you really feel for the guy.

GARRIS: There's quite a bit of pathos in this.

LANSDALE: Oh, my God, yes.

GARRIS: And in a lot of your work. There's a lot of confronting life and death in the work.

LANSDALE: Right. And Don got it, the actors got it, and the atmosphere of the set highly contributed to the moodiness. Not just the kind of creepiness that you wanted for the Mummy, for who, as you said, really is the least important part of it. But . . .

GARRIS: He's the McGuffin.

LANSDALE: Exactly.

GARRIS: The MumMuffin!

LANSDALE: It's a reason to have a story. But there's these things like when Elvis picks up the phone and calls Ossie in his room, and Ossie has like a red phone like—

COSCARELLI: The hotline.

GARRIS: Yeah, right.

COSCARELLI: We all grew up with the hotline.

LANSDALE: And "ask not what your rest home can do for you." Bruce says that as Elvis, and Ossie says, "Hey, you're stealing some of my lines!"

[Everyone laughs.]

COSCARELLI: They were so good. They were both so good with comedy.

GARRIS: Don, we don't think of your work as being comedic, particularly, until that time. I mean, there's always humor in what you do . . .

LANSDALE: That's true. I hadn't thought of it in that way.

GARRIS: But outright comedic. This was the first time we'd seen that take shape. Was there any special homework you did to that, or did you just find it in Joe's words?

COSCARELLI: Yeah, the humor was in the story. Of course working with Bruce Campell . . . When you mentioned that notion of Buster Keaton, I'm thinking about the sequence where Elvis dresses up in his bush jacket and goes on his one mission where he's gonna go scout out the creek down behind the rest home, and he's in his walker, and we have this one extended take—I think we could only do it like twice—where he comes down this really steep hill with the walker. If you watch that from beginning to end, just the way Bruce plays the comedy in that . . . . It's not a scene that people ever really talk about, but being in the editing room, and also just technologically . . . I think we were shooting with some short ends in that particular shot. The negative was a bit fried, so in color correction was always trying to get it so on edge. So we'd watch it again and again, and just watching the evolution of that, he had a Keatonesque feel to the way he did it.

LANSDALE: He reminds me of him in that way.

GARRIS: A little broad.

LANSDALE: Of course. You know, Keaton was stone faced. I'm mainly referring to the body control, the movement, and the humor, where it looks like the person has completely lost control, but they haven't. They're really controlling it. They're giving you that impression.

GARRIS: What feelings did you have going into this? You'd been going through things . . . Well, the first time I heard about you as a writer was from *The Drive-In*, which was an iconic novel that Joe had written, early eighties, I guess, and—

LANSDALE: I really wanted Don to make a film of it, but I can't get him off a dime.

GARRIS: Everybody including Paul Sammon was going to produce it.

COSCARELLI: You should tell what the story is of *The Drive-In*, though.

LANSDALE: Well, yeah, it's the idea that there's this small town where people don't have a lot to do, but they go to this drive-in that's one of the biggest in the world. It was based on a real drive-in, but they go there and they have six screens and the screens—on the weekend they show nothing but horror films. So it's called The Orbit Drive-In, and you had this long line of people going in. You can hear all the music from their cars. You may have Sleepy LaBeef, you may have the Blood Farmers, you name it, different kinds of music are rattling about, and they drive inside, and they're all excited, and people were doing barbecue, which they really did, nearly blowing their damn cars up out there! And so then the movies start, and a giant comet appears in the sky. But it gets closer and closer, and then it smiles. It has teeth. Then it goes away. And when it's gone, the drive-in is encased in a sort of black acidic goo, and nobody can leave.

So, we're following all of this through the eyes of one of the main characters, who does this in first person. But, essentially, they start running out of food. And so the concession stand, they start eating the candies and stuff. That's all they got. People are getting hypoglycemic and it's getting strange and people try to go out and the goo eats you. You know, so it's not a good thing. And then, just when you think it couldn't get worse, the two friends—a guy who's a real fan of horror makeup and kind of a motorcycle guy, he's carrying him on his shoulders while they walk up to the concession stand, and they're hit by a weird, freakish piece of lightning that comes out of the sky and welds them. And the guy was wearing a popcorn bucket on his head, and when it did, it fuses it, and what it did is it changes him and he becomes this monster called the Popcorn King, who becomes their religion inside the drive-in.

GARRIS: All hail the Popcorn King!

LANSDALE: And then it gets weird after that.

GARRIS: Oh, after that!

[Everyone laughs.]

GARRIS: But this was talked about so many times, every year, "Oh, they're going to make *The Drive-In*."

LANSDALE: They do it every year now.

GARRIS: Did you develop a sense of cynicism about adaptation?

LANSDALE: I'm always cynical about film.

[Everyone laughs.]

LANSDALE: I mean, I love it, and I've had things made. I've been more fortunate than many. But I'm always cynical about it because it has so many factors to get it made. You can't just say, "I've got this great director, Don Coscarelli. I've got this good story," or you hope. Or you've got this actor. There are so many factors that have nothing at all to do with the film. They've got to do with who's got the money now, who's hot now, who's connected to who, what they want. And you've always got the people who, "I've got my own vision." Well, fuck your vision. I want them to have their own vision that also captures the vision that I have. And I've always thought that the best adaptations were people who actually tried to capture what was written.

GARRIS: What's the point otherwise? I mean, having done a lot of adaptations—

COSCARELLI: Why would you go to the effort and the legal trouble—

LANSDALE: Just write your own! Yeah, you just come up with your own story, you know? So anyway, in film you have that a lot, but that said, I constantly hear people say, "You know, you can't do the book, or you can't do the story," and I . . . They always say that to me like I . . . "You mean you can't literally put it on . . . ?"

[Everyone laughs.]

LANSDALE: I know that, but I do think a lot of times what that is is an excuse to find a way to not have to worry about what was originally written. And Don did two of my pieces, and both of 'em . . . I thought . . . things were added, but I never felt like, "Oh, that's not my story."

GARRIS: Well, let's get into that, because the other time you guys worked together was on my show, *Masters of Horror*, and it was—

LANSDALE: That's back when you were young, Mick.

GARRIS: Yes, way back . . .

LANSDALE: All of us. But it was such a potent combination that we decided to debut the show with that episode. It was out premiere episode. This is "Incident On and Off a Mountain Road." So tell me, Don, what led you to choose that when we came to you and said—

COSCARELLI: Listening to Joe talk about the difficulties in movies, it also brings me around, and I didn't hear your introduction, but I do need to plug my new memoir that's coming out—

GARRIS: Yeah, we're going to get to that.

COSCARELLI: It's called *True Indie.*

GARRIS: *True Indie*, it's a great autobiography.

COSCARELLI: It has a lot of elements about how one gets a movie made, from the nuts and bolts from the indie part of things. But "Incident On and Off a Mountain Road," interesting story was, I don't know if Joe remembers, but when I first optioned *Bubba Ho-Tep* I also optioned his story "Incident" because for me when I read this story, it's a great, very simple story about a woman who's out at night driving in her car, and she's in a little bit of a crash, and then she wakes up and she ends up fighting to the death with this terrible serial killer. And it's a very traditional what used to be called "damsel in distress," which I don't know if we're, with the #MeToo movement, it's going away. But this, ten years ago, or twenty years ago when Joe wrote it, it turns the whole thing on its ear. When I read it, because I came from a family of feminists, my mother and my sister, and I read it and I thought, "Wow, this is a horror feminist story! I gotta see if I can . . . ." Because it's hard to . . . especially in the film genre, the way that the slashers just for years, most of them are so damned misogynistic, and we go and watch 'em and kind of go, "Should we be watching movies like this?"

GARRIS: Eighty-five minutes of titillation and five minutes of—

COSCARELLI: Women have sex and then are bloodily brutalized. But anyway, Joe's story had a twist and was so cool, and so, at the time I read them both and optioned them. But the problem was, I couldn't get anyone to fund that story. And I was casting about: "How can I get this to a major actress to read this thing and see that?" And I'm thinking, Moonface with the steel teeth . . . It's not gonna—

LANSDALE: The problem is, when you tell those log lines, they seem like something you've seen before, but they aren't.

GARRIS: It's all in the handling. It's all in the characters, and it's all in the twists and turns.

COSCARELLI: I think that's why Joe and I like working together, because we're like-minded souls in that way, which is that it's okay to . . . I think that both of us . . . well, Joe's pushed out a little bit of the genre, not so much with me, but the thing is, while working in the genre we're trying to look for ways of making something a little different and a little interesting.

GARRIS: Or a lot.

COSCARELLI: Or a lot. But in any case, so I had made *Bubba Ho-Tep*, I think things had gone great and all of that, and then one day I get this phone call from Mick and he . . . I guess I'd better back it up even further . . . Before— as I was making *Bubba Ho-Tep*, I got a call from Mick and he said, "I'm gonna have a dinner with some of my good friends and they're all directors. Would you like to come?" And I said, "Oh, that'll be great." And he had this dinner, and invited all these horror legends from Stuart Gordon to Larry Cohen to John Carpenter to Tobe Hooper, John Landis . . . Who else am I missing?

GARRIS: Bill Malone, Guillermo del Toro . . .

COSCARELLI: Guillermo del Toro was there, and—

GARRIS: This was our very first *Masters* dinner. There were twelve of us.

COSCARELLI: And it's . . . We casually throw around this *Masters of Horror* and everybody probably thinks, "Oh God, those guys have their heads stuck up their assholes!" It was a joke. It all came out of a joke, because Guillermo was there and everybody was laughing. I'll have to diverge a little. It was a really great evening because you let me meet all these like-minded filmmakers, and the last thing they want to talk about is themselves. All they wanna talk about is your movie! They're all horror fans. And the best part about it is that at the end of the night, we had so much fun, that Mick's counting up the money when everybody contributed, you had like a hundred bucks, everybody kicked in extra money. And then everybody said Mick could get keep it for the next dinner.

GARRIS: I made an extra hundred bucks off of that! [Laughs.] I'm gonna do this more often!

COSCARELLI: The name came from the fact that we were being quite raucous and making a lot of noise, laughing and having a great time, and there was this group of four people that were celebrating a birthday in the restaurant next to us. I don't know if they were enjoying our laughter as much as that, but anyway, the woman's birthday cake arrived and Guillermo del Toro jumps to his feet and he illicitly says, "Please accept our best birthday wishes . . . from the masters of horror!"

[Everyone laughs.]

COSCARELLI: And that's where the name came from. But at any rate, so Mick decided to monetize the masters of horror and he had this plan—

GARRIS: Well, I don't wanna—

COSCARELLI: Well, that's being crass, but in a good way, he had a plan to basically put together a deal to make thirteen one-hour movies for the Showtime network. And so he came around to all of his friends and he came to me and he said, "So, you can do anything you want." Like I'm thinking, hmmm, what I do I have?

LANSDALE: *"I paid for that thing!"*

[Everyone laughs.]

COSCARELLI: No, it had actually gone back to you, and I went, *click!* "Incident On and Off a Mountain Road."

LANSDALE: God, what a nice job you did on that, too. And I know you were frustrated because you were having to work fast and whatever. And Bree Turner, gosh, was so—

COSCARELLI: Yeah, the cast was—

LANSDALE: So good!

COSCARELLI: She and Ethan Embree deserved—

LANSDALE: They were so good.

COSCARELLI: John DeSantis as the bad guy. Angus Scrimm had a nice little role. And we've gotta give some credit to Stephen Romano, who came on and helped me put the screenplay together.

GARRIS: I know this was a tough one for you, because working all your life as an independent, having a union crew and a start and stop and needing to be out on certain hours and things like that.

COSCARELLI: It was a dream on any level. You know, I had a little problem with one crew member, and that was it. But everything else—

LANSDALE: It was a dream now, Don.

[Everyone laughs.]

COSCARELLI: I mean, the Canadian crew's good . . .

LANSDALE: I was on the set watching you. It was fun.

GARRIS: Yeah, but having all their resources available that that kind of operation allowed us to have was pretty astounding because on one stage, you're shooting there, and on the other stage, we're prepping the next show. Or we're out on location, doing location . . . .

COSCARELLI: Which also caused problems for the directors because then Mick, a good executive producer would come in and go, "You know, Dario Argento is filming his episode, and his is *really* bloody. Really, the action's *good*! I'm going . . . I don't wanna be the slacker in the bunch. [Laughs.]

GARRIS: Let me say again, we scheduled your show for the premiere show for a reason. And it was not the first one shot, but it was the first one aired.

LANSDALE: I saw Dario Argento. I had dinner with him in Italy.

GARRIS: Ahhh.

COSCARELLI: You're kidding.

LANSDALE: No.

COSCARELLI: Tell us everything.

LANSDALE: He didn't speak perfect English or anything, but he was funny as hell.

GARRIS: Yes.

LANSDALE: We talked about it, and he remembered your episode. And we talked about the one he had done and all that. But he had had a really good time on *Masters of Horror*.

GARRIS: He did, and he two of them.

LANSDALE: Yes! He said that, and he wanted more of them, you know. I did too, but he was so sweet because I came in and he went, "You are famous!" I went, "Like hell I am. For God's sake!"

[Everyone laughs.]

LANSDALE: Humility is enough. But we had a great, great dinner, me, Karen, my wife, and him . . . a bunch of other people that were . . . and somebody else that was there that had something to do with it. I can't remember. I'm not sure now, it's been so long ago. But what a cool guy. What a nice guy.

COSCARELLI: Another favorite memory of mine was, after we made the show, I got kindly invited to join some of the other directors in Torino, Italy, for the film festival where we screened. And to walk through the streets of Turin at night with Mick, Joe Dante, John Landis . . . but Dario Argento's like a rock star in Italy.

GARRIS: He shoots all of his movies in Torino.

LANSDALE: I love Torino. You know what's weird is that I'm really well known in Italy. I'm like, people recognize me on the street.

GARRIS: For a novelist, that's pretty amazing.

LANSDALE: Yeah, for a writer. But it's so much fun. Torino is this cool city that's very artistic. It's very . . . it's kind of got a moodier feel than a lot of other places in Italy. It's more . . . it's got some influences of France and some different things like that. They have a film festival there every year. I got to be a judge there one year.

GARRIS: We were there two years in a row.

LANSDALE: Yeah. Then they have the great film museum there. I'm really pimpin' for Torino because it's my favorite city in Italy. I go there a lot, and in case any of my Italian friends or fans are listening I want 'em to know how much I appreciate how kind they are.

COSCARELLI: Plus if you go in October, it's truffle season.

LANSDALE: That's true.

COSCARELLI: I developed a taste. And I can't afford them here.

GARRIS: Well, there's kind of been a transition in the direction of your work, Joe. You were first very well known for your horror. And it's kind of transitioned . . . well, Westerns and crime. Hap and Leonard was a series of books and short stories that has been a three-season run on Sundance. Was that an intentional transition, or just a natural thing that happened to you, your interests moved in a different direction?

LANSDALE: I always had interest in that. I mean, the very first things I sold were mysteries. They were mystery stories for *Mike Shayne Mystery Magazine*. They were novellas, or novelettes, as they called them. And I wrote a few things like that. My first novel, *Act of Love*, was a crime novel. It was a police prodedural. Very dated now, but that got me going. *The Nightrunners* was a cross between horror and crime, So I think that was always there, but if you look at most of my work, and I include *Bubba Ho-Tep* in this, they're Westerns.

GARRIS: Interesting.

LANSDALE: *Ride the High Country*, like we said . . .

GARRIS: There's a lot of boots in *Bubba Ho-Tep*.

LANSDALE: Well, yeah, but . . .

[Everyone laughs.]

LANSDALE: But it's the storyline. It has the showdown. It's like a . . . [t]he term "Westerns," for a lot of people they have a bad idea because they don't really know anything about 'em. But there were certain formats that I liked. Hap and Leonard, I think of them kind of as Western characters in a modern sense.

GARRIS: Absolutely.

LANSDALE: So there's a lot of that influence there, so I think I always had the influence. It's just at that time I was doing a lot more horror. But I still write horror. I have stuff coming out now in horror. I think the interests were always multiple, and I think it's why the genre crossing was there so early on, because I was influenced heavily by books and short stories, as well as films and television shows. Of course television now is a unique place to work if you can get it because it's more novelistic. It's more character-driven because it has more room.

GARRIS: Production values have met and exceeded feature films in a lot of cases. And that was not the case before. Digital filmmaking has a lot to do with that.

LANSDALE: Yep.

GARRIS: You did some screenwriting early on doing animation. Doing superheroes and things like that.

LANSDALE: *Batman: The Animated Series* and one *Superman: The Animated Series*. Some of the greatest fun I ever had. And you know what is really nice is I'll meet people that are, I don't know, in their thirties, like my son's age and my daughter, and they'll come up and go, "Did you write that 'Read My Lips'? Oh my God!" And for them, that was their entry into my work a lot of times. Or the comics. I did Jonah Hex comics, I did Conan comics, Lone Ranger, all those different things in which you had comic people come to the work, you had animation fans come to the work. And that's a cross genre there in a way, so I've been very fortunate because I liked all these different genres, so I've been able to be new several different times instead of being new once.

GARRIS: Have you intentionally not pursued the screenwriting aspect we talked about?

LANSDALE: Actually I have. You know, I did a thing called *Son of Batman*, an animated film. And then I wrote a script for *Hap and Leonard*. And I wrote a script for Ridley Scott for *The Big Blow*, and for a while they were gonna shoot that. And as things changed there, it got lost and then they were gonna shoot one by Oren Moverman. And then they came back and they were gonna shoot my script because they had a director that I liked and I thought would be interesting to do it, but they were not able to make a deal. That's why I won't mention his name, because I don't wanna . . . But now they've got the script by Moverman again and they've got a director in line and they've announced they're gonna do it, but they announce they're gonna do it every three years.

GARRIS: Sort of like *The Drive-In.*

LANSDALE: Well, yeah, and one time I remember when they wanted to reoption it and I went crazy about them reoptioning it because they'd had it a long time and my wife and I went to Paris for some reason, some kind of a thing, and so when we came back, I had no more landed than my agent—my agent at that time, it's not my current agent—called and said, "We sold that to Ridley Scott." I said, "I told you I didn't want to option that." He said, "No, no, we *sold* it." And I said, "How much?" And he told me and I went, "*Oooh!* Yeah, that was a good move."

[Everyone laughs.]

LANSDALE: But they had something in the contract after it had been optioned enough . . . because my option didn't go to the back end, it was just free money, and I think one day they looked and said, "You know, we've been doing this a long time." And David Lynch had it before that. I had the same deal with him. So it's still not made, and yet . . .

GARRIS: But you're making good scratch on it.

LANSDALE: At that moment in time it changed things for me, because several other things were comin', but I'm just saying, that's how film is, you think somebody isn't working in it and they are. My son and I have a script out for a television pilot. My daughter and I are trying to . . . are working in film things. So I mean, you do it, and occasionally something happens. [Laughs.] There are people I know who've sold scripts but never had one filmed that are actually quite wealthy.

GARRIS: Living quite well on being paid to write without getting produced. Speaking of writing, for someone who struggles with the writing process, your book, *True Indie*, felt like it just flowed out of you. This is a really great autobiography from someone who's worked in the trenches. Your career, Don, has been almost exclusively independent film. And it's incredibly honest and incredibly inspiring and heartbreaking at the same time. So tell me about the process of deciding to put it all in a book and the process of doing it and getting it out there.

COSCARELLI: Look, it's hard to put my finger on one reason that caused this to happen . . . other than I do know that I've been through a lot of interesting stories, and I'm always, always meeting aspiring filmmakers, you know, looking for their path into the business. And they ask me for advice about things, and I'm always thinking, "I'm the last person to be giving you advice." But you know, it was a—

GARRIS: But who better with this long list of things that you've done entirely on your own?

COSCARELLI: Well, you know, one part of it was nice and, you know, actually, Joe, I recommend it to you, if you ever think about writing a memoir, because it gives you a chance to go back and look at some of the eras that you've passed and . . . sometimes I tend to compartmentalize and put things away and not . . . especially failures. And this forces you to go through and address some of them. You know, one of my biggest failures in my mind was my very first movie. Because I made this film, it started as a student project, and it ended up Universal Studios purchased it.

GARRIS: And you were how old?

COSCARELLI: Well, when they bought it, I was nineteen years old. And my neighborhood friend and I—Craig Mitchell was his name—we codirected this movie. And we had an office on the lot at Universal Pictures, with Universal Studios. And what's more interesting is, as I tell it in the book I'd forgotten . . . what we had was, at that time, we had access to the president of the studio. He was the one who had originally seen the movie and bought it, brought us to the studio.

LANSDALE: What's the name of the movie?

COSCARELLI: Oh, the name of the movie? *Jim, the World's Greatest.* Good luck finding it, because it never came out on video or VHS or DVD. Still lost in the vaults. I think it was a pretty decent movie. It was drama. And it starred Angus Scrimm. Reggie Bannister was in it. So early collaborators.

GARRIS: Was he going by Angus that early?

COSCARELLI: No, he went by Lawrence Scott. He was a man of multiple names. But imagine, Mick, being nineteen years old and we could go up, get in the elevator at what was then called the Black Tower at Universal . . .

GARRIS: I think it's still called the Black Tower.

COSCARELLI: And we could ride up to the fifteenth floor, and the gentleman's name was Sid Sheinberg and go right up to his secretary and go, "Hey, is Sid in? We wanna ask him about something." We would have like a new idea. And you know, he'd wave us in and we'd tell him. It's interesting because there was a culture of fear at the studio there at that time. And we were like these wild card kids that had access to him. Of course, as my career has continued I've never had access like that again. I've never had an office on a studio lot since that time. But going back and looking at it, I saw so many interesting stories about that, and I just started to write it, but I think part of it, interesting as . . . *Bubba Ho-Tep* played a part in this. Not only the fact that I made the movie and I could tell the stories about it, but the editor who really pursued me to do this had made his bones . . . Well, he'd had excellent success publishing Bruce Campbell's autobiography. So that was the connection. He thought, well, I had success with Bruce. And I kept telling him, "Look, I'm not going to sell the numbers that Bruce sells." Because we've both seen the lines that Bruce has. But in any case, I think it was an interesting point of self-reflection, to go through these different phases in my life and tell . . . basically telling the story of my various film exploits. And at the same time try to make it a handbook on indie film filmmaking, distribution, you know, how to . . . working, struggling to find funding to get your films made, dealing with actors, writing. There are so many different aspects of it. I think that, if nowhere else, somebody who is twenty years old and wants to get in the movie business, it would be an interesting book for them to read.

GARRIS: When's this coming out?

COSCARELLI: October second.

LANSDALE: And the title?

COSCARELLI: *True Indie: Life and Death in Filmmaking.*

GARRIS: Well, and that's something that should be said about *Bubba Ho-Tep*—it could only have been an independent film. The ideas are so wild and imaginative, and yet it's set on such solid ground and with these human performances, but it's totally independent. Because it's also really fucking weird.

COSCARELLI: Nobody would have made it, but I think that probably to both to Joe and my everlasting gratitude, was the real breakthrough in my mind and success was the fact that the movie worked with younger audiences. Because when I was going out to try to get funding, people would say, "Oh, well who's gonna wanna sit for two hours with old codgers in a rest home? Come on, you gotta put a—"

LANSDALE: There are long scenes in bed.

COSCARELLI: Exactly. "Can you put a hunky guy in there, like his orderly?" And I'm thinking, no, there's no role for them. And the thing was, from our very first screenings, there would be the Joe Lansdale fans, the black T-shirt *Evil Dead* and *Phantasm* fans, age sixteen to thirty.

LANSDALE: You hit a sweet spot.

COSCARELLI: But they *got* the storyline about our culture's treatment of the elderly. You know, about how we warehouse people, and all these people who had such meaningful rich lives we just dismiss. And this worked with young people, and what it proved was, I think, and this is no great surprise, but the powers that be who make the movies tend to underestimate their audiences.

LANSDALE: Well, yeah, and you know, the other thing too is that I think Bruce's performance is the best he ever gave, and I think that that was really an award-winning performance, and I wished he had got more attention for that. But the other thing I was gonna say, although you often hear it's called a "cult movie" or a B-movie, it's made a transition in the last few years to being something else.

GARRIS: Respectable.

LANSDALE: Respectable. Who would have ever thought that?

COSCARELLI: I'll take that word, you know?

GARRIS: But it's true, and it really probably got you more good reviews than you'd had up until that time in your career.

COSCARELLI: It was generally well-reviewed, no question about it.

LANSDALE: And I've also talked to people who saw it when they were younger that *didn't* get it. Because it wasn't a kick-ass Bruce Campbell, in the way that they thought of it. Then some of them said, "You know, I saw that thing again and I missed the boat." I said, "No, you were just too young." Because when they saw it the next time . . . and Don and I were younger obviously then, but we were starting to have people we knew and were starting to think about this is the future you have to look at, because it's very likely.

COSCARELLI: And it's a real horror story. I mean, you wanna talk about ending your days in one of those old folks' homes, just neglected. And you know, all in that original short story, that scene where Elvis is laying there, you know, feeling sorry for himself, everything is so bad, and then this young woman comes in and she's going through . . . his roommate had died and she's going through his things, there's his Purple Heart medal, and she's just throwing it in the trash. Photos of him as a young man . . . just tossing it in the trash. Just so touching and powerful.

LANSDALE: Yeah, it's powerful because I had seen something somewhat like that when I was there, you know, with my mother. Because I would go and sit and then my brother would go, and she did get better, but she never left that home. And you start looking around, and it's the sort of thing that makes you go, "Yeah." It doesn't matter how famous you are or how much money you've got . . . Nothing matters. Then in the end you need people there that matter to you.

GARRIS: Exactly. Well, we can't wrap this up without addressing *Bubba Nosferatu*, and the possibility—

LANSDALE: It doesn't look good.

GARRIS: It does not look promising?

COSCARELLI: Not from a film point of view, but yeah, just to fill everybody in, for a couple of years there, and I'm gonna have to say it for the first time here—the reason I never took you up on your kind offer on season two of *Masters of Horror* was because I thought I was gonna make *Bubba*

Nosferatu, and it didn't happen. There was a lot of good stuff there. It could have been, I think, a wonderful movie in some respects.

GARRIS: Had either of you worked on ideas for that?

COSCARELLI: Not so much.

LANSDALE: You know, I did write a prequel to it called *Bubba and the Cosmic Bloodusckers* as a novel and then as a comic book series right now.

COSCARELLI: Yeah, Joe has carried the torch . . . continued the torch with a whole line of new . . . with a novel and then a comic book series with a lot of interesting, really transgressively strange vampires in that.

GARRIS: [Laughs.] *Really*? With Joe Lansdale?

LANSDALE: And you know, the thing is it got to the point that we were talking about a prequel at one point. It got to the point where I don't think Bruce could play the younger Elvis anymore, convincingly.

COSCARELLI: I'd never tell him that, but if you want to . . .

LANSDALE: When we first started talking about it, it was perfect, but I mean now, I'm talking about now . . . I think it would be very, very hard for him to go back and play a guy who's in his late thirties or forties or so on. It would be difficult for anybody, because Bruce is older, that's it. But we could have continued with the older Elvis quite easily, because Bruce said nobody could tell him he doesn't look like the older Elvis.

LANSDALE: Who knows? So, was that tag at the end of *Bubba Ho-Tep* a joke, or a promise?

COSCARELLI: Well, when I first put it down in the script, it was . . . I had loved the way that the 007 movies always ended with a promise of the next 007. And the movie was so down with what happened to Elvis, you know, by the creek bed, and you know, all is well and the tears are welling. And I thought, well, we've got to leave the audience with a little hope, you know, so I decided to put that in at the end. And then I remember standing there with Joe and Bruce at Cinevegas at the very first screening, and they'd brought us up to the front and we were ready to go on as the credits were running. That came up and the whole audience was just going "*Aaagggghhh!*"

LANSDALE: I thought it was a joke, but people responded to it.

COSCARELLI: You could see that they really wanted it. But hey, you'll have to read *True Indie* for the whole story.

LANSDALE: One thing I really liked about that film, I love that it had this big opening, like it was gonna be *Ben Hur*.

[Everyone laughs.]

LANSDALE: I just loved that, you know? I think it kind of ended that way.

GARRIS: It ain't *Ben Hur*!

LANSDALE: It ain't *Ben Hur*. And we had that archival footage of the German archaeology, which I saw recently on an archaeological show I was . . .

COSCARELLI: They probably . . .

GARRIS: They used the same stuff.

LANSDALE: It was the real deal, and it was there, and I just thought that was so . . . [y]ou know, there's this giant *Ben Hur*, then that, then the rest home.

GARRIS: Well, Joe Lansdale, Don Coscarelli, thank you so much for joining us to celebrate this wonderful movie that deserves celebration for many years to come. Thanks for joining us.

COSCARELLI: Our pleasure. Thanks for having us.

The Evolution of Joe R. Lansdale's Hap and Leonard

Scott Montgomery / 2018

Published in *Crime Reads*, September 18, 2020. Reprinted by the author.

With his latest novel, *Jackrabbit Smile*, Joe Lansdale continues with the mis-adventures of Hap and Leonard, an East Texas redneck liberal and his lethal Black gay Republican pal. This time the two have to go back to Hap's home-town in search of a missing girl and go up against a religion lead by a man known as "The Professor," who's buying up land for a white utopia. It fits into the themes of race, religion, and politics Lansdale often dives into with no fear and a ton of humor. I recently spoke with the writer about the book and these issues that drive his work.

Scott Montgomery: It seems like in the last couple of *Hap and Leon-ards*, you've been using the two to express your political views more.

Joe R. Lansdale: I think it's always been that way from the start. *Savage Season* looked at the aftermath of the Vietnam War and the shift in social climate to the eighties. *Mucho Mojo* and *Two Bear Mambo* deal with racial issues. *Bad Chili* deals with how gays were treated, mugged, killed, and what have you. *Rumble Tumble* may have been more of a romp than *Captains Outrageous*. Some are stronger than others with the commentary; *Vanilla Ride* is pretty critical of religion. I think it's always been there, brother.

Montgomery: Maybe it just seems like the times lately have been ampli-fied enough to catch up to the series; like when *Rusty Puppy* came out, we were dealing with a lot of police shootings.

Lansdale: Something like *Rusty Puppy* has been going on for years; it's just that people weren't paying attention. Part of that is because people want to believe in law and order. And I'm one of them. I think it works most of the time, and I'm glad those guys are out there. Now, people are capturing things on their cell phones. All of us that grew up in the South and the big cities, and well, all over the country, we know about that. Black people knew it was happening.

Also, the far right has opened up a gate for people to be racist, narrow-minded, and thoughtless with this belief that the white person is being pushed down. Which is ridiculous. Being white has never hurt me any, but I know it has hurt for Black and brown people. I believe in the American dream, but it's an opportunity, not a promise and being Black or brown can get in the way of that opportunity.

When we were doing table reads and getting ready for the new season of *Hap and Leonard*, based on *Two Bear Mambo*, one of the actors asked if we could do The Klan as bad guys, wondering if they were a joke now. Then Charlottesville happened the second week of shooting. So it's not that far away. That's what I've been trying to say.

Some of the things that are broad or ridiculous are exactly on the money. Now don't think I'm trying to say every one is a social commentary. I think they are crime novels, adventure novels, they're exciting, but to answer the initial question, they are definitely a part of the books even if they sometimes take a back seat to the adventure aspects.

Montgomery: Do you think when you look at a subject in a genre novel it allows you to do it differently?

Lansdale: With genre you have that hard-driving engine of a story to move those ideas forward. Literary fiction often tackles those subjects and genre rarely does it, but that is mainly because the idea of what genre fiction is. In the eighties, I was in a group of writers that mixed the two. A large percentage of what I write is driven by social issues.

Montgomery: What makes Hap and Leonard a good vehicle to go through these issues?

Lansdale: The characters seem simple, but they're not. Both Michael K. Williams and James Purefoy find more layers when they're playing them. They're not always absolutely consistent. They're these everyday working-class guys, like I was, and I still think of myself as a blue-collar writer at least from a class perspective. They prove that all southerners don't fit the stereotype and are contradictory in a lot of ways. One is Black and one's white, one is Black and gay. Hap, I don't know if he was really a hippie, works against those ideals to get justice. I don't think they really completely succeed. They keep trying to do the right thing and it often leads to Hap questioning his morals. And both of them have killed people and so it's a very interesting contrast. You read about some horrible person and you think that's someone for the devil: then you read about their circumstances: then you think maybe they're not for the devil. So they're dealing with all that and trying to pay the bills.

Montgomery: I think what's made them even more interesting is they've become more aware of their flaws.

Lansdale: I think that's absolutely correct. Like all of us in life, we begin to recognize our faults as we get older, and as time goes on we discover those flaws, you know. I look back at where I was at twenty, and when I was thirty, and forty, and in many ways I remain consistent, but I'm more aware of what's wrong with me.

Montgomery: In *Jackrabbit Smile*, you tackle religion again. You've been public about being an atheist. What is your biggest problem with religion?

Lansdale: It's really the hypocrisy, the fact that it is all based on contradictory material. I'm of the school that I have nothing against religion as long as it isn't in politics or you don't beat me over the head with it. I always believe you have the right to your religion, but I have the right not to be persecuted by it and I mean that with a small "p," although it can be with a big "P." I think that right now, our guy in office is the least Christian I've ever seen and they're saying that's okay because he's for what we're for, but they don't forgive the other side if they've done something wrong.

Montgomery: During the election, you wrote a piece for the *Texas Observer* about Trump and the Trump voter. After a year with him as president, do you find it difficult to write what you do with a satirical bent, when you turn on the news and it seems like it's satire but it's real?

Lansdale: The main point of that article was that it just wasn't stupid rednecks that were voting for him, even though that was part of it, but it was more about taking a side. Now, I've pretty much been a Democrat coming out of the civil rights movement, but what it comes down to, unfortunately, more than issues, is what side you're on. I hope we reach a point where we actually realize we have to move back from that. Right now, it's like a *Saturday Night Live* skit or even more like something from National Lampoon articles I used to read, it's gotten so ridiculous.

Montgomery: It does seem like the right has made ignorance a virtue.

Lansdale: I was excited by life as a child of the fifties and sixties because science was taking us so many places. It was considered sacred, mainly because we dropped the bomb, and it fueled belief as well. You even look at the comics of the time like *The Flash* and *The Hulk*, and they had science as part of their origin. You had John F. Kennedy pushing advancement in science and education, and there was an excitement about learning. Sadly, I think that started to change in the Reagan era. And here is one of my other major problems with religion: it is static. Now you have science being questioned, when science questions itself. It embraces change. Religion told us everything: the sun and the planets revolved around the Earth. To slide back after so many years of advancement, religion has become a hole many have crawled into.

Montgomery: You've cited Flannery O'Connor, someone who was a believer, as an influence. How do you look at her work and take it in your direction?

Lansdale: I think she was addressing the narrow-mindedness of people and that look at the South. She had views of Pentecostal and Baptist beliefs that reflected her Catholic upbringing. I don't think she was ever trying to beat you over the head with her beliefs; she was trying to tell a story of growing up in the South with those religions. When I was a kid, I wanted to be a preacher, until I read the Bible all the way through and thought this was more like mythology, but it did show me the structure of story.

Montgomery: You have books like *Paradise Sky*, which I wouldn't say is religious, but it does have a biblical feel to it.

Lansdale: When I was growing up in the South, everyone had a King James Bible. That's what the preacher preached from and it also influenced the music, the rhythms from the choir and all. The King James Bible still seems closer to our speech and slang, being a landlocked culture.

Montgomery: You're big in Italy, which is a very Catholic country. When you delve into religion, do they relate or see it as something exotic?

Lansdale: I have a lot of fans and readers who are Christian, and they have no problem and even see a different view from my writing. Many are what I'd refer to as cultural Christians, for whom it was part of their upbringing and now in their social life, but would admit their more agnostic in private. I found Italy to be a lot like that.

Montgomery: Do you still offend people with your books, or do they know what they're getting by now?

Lansdale: I still get a few people who don't understand context. If you use the word *shit*, they take it like it's coming out of my mouth and not how I may be trying to turn that word on its ear. Or people who don't get what I'm saying about race and religion. They don't get I'm speaking through the characters.

Montgomery: You have fun with that at times when Hap talks about how he uses the term *"Black."*

Lansdale: When I was growing up, I used to hear *"colored,"* and now people think that's terrible, but was common usage. The National Association for the Advancement of Colored People, then it became black or Afro-American and now it's African American, but I still use the term Black and a lot of Black people use the term black and that's young and old. "*African American*" feels forced. It's like I don't refer to my Italian friends as Italian Americans or all the Irish as Irish Americans. The only reason we say "*Black Americans*" is because we have to address the situation they are currently experiencing. Anyway, the biggest problem is that we have to identify at all, but it's impossible to get away from that because it's part of the context of the story you're trying to write.

Joe R. Lansdale on Atheism, God, and Trump

Andrew J. Rausch / 2019

Published in Andrew J. Rausch, *Godless Heathens: Conversations with Atheists* (Troy: Clash Books, 2019). Reprinted by permission of the author.

Popular author Joe R. Lansdale has written more than forty novels and thirty short story collections in a variety of genres, including Western, horror, suspense, crime, and science fiction. He has also written chapbooks, comic book adaptations, and worked on *Batman: The Animated Series* (1992). Lansdale is perhaps best-known for his offbeat Bram Stoker Award–nominated novella *Bubba Ho-Tep* (1994). The novella, which depicts Elvis Presley and John F. Kennedy battling an undead mummy in a nursing home, was later adapted into a successful film by Don Coscarelli of *Phantasm* (1979) fame.

He is also the author of the bestselling Hap and Leonard series, which (to date) includes nine novels, three novellas, and three short story collections. The crime series, which focuses on the exploits of best friends and private investigators Hap Collins and Leonard Pine, has also been adapted into the popular Sundance television series starring James Purefoy and Michael K. Williams.

Lansdale has won an impressive ten Bram Stoker Awards and has been nominated for another nine. He has also received the American Mystery Award, the Horror Critics Award, and the "Shot in the Dark" International Crime Writers Award. In 2011, he received the Bram Stoker Award for Lifetime Achievement, and in 2012 he was inducted into the Texas Literary Hall of Fame. He has been nominated for the World Fantasy Award eleven times.

Lansdale continues to churn out books at the speed of light. In addition to his usual output of novels and short stories, he published the memoir *Miracles Ain't What They Used to Be* (2016). In the book's titular essay,

Lansdale discusses his atheism and the many reasons he doesn't believe in gods. He calls God "the adult Santa Claus" and goes to work dissecting popular Christian apologist arguments. After reading this illuminating essay, I sought him out to talk with him about his beliefs.

Andrew J. Rausch: In your interview with Terry Bison, "That's How You Kill a Squirrel," you said, "I actually am not against religion itself, but when people use it to justify bad behavior, or when they show how hypocritical they are, I always wonder if they've read the Bible they love to quote and shake." You've also said reading the Bible "cured me of Christianity." Isn't it strange how many Christians don't even know what's in the Bible? I find it both telling and funny that most atheists I know are far more knowledgeable about the Bible than Christians are.

Jon R. Lansdale: I think that's fairly common, because I think that's a lot of why we become nonbelievers. Actually reading it and seeing how similar it is to other mythology, and I think also that it's such a cultural element to our country that you would think people would be aware of it in the same way they are aware of *Huckleberry Finn* or something of that nature. That's what cured me. The more you read the more you see the obvious human failings in the construction and the inconsistencies and hypocrisy. I think what amazes me most is how many people I've met who claim to be Christians and haven't read the Bible, or they're misquoting it, or they're saying, "I know this because this is what my preacher tells me and he's called by God." As if I can accept that any more than accepting that my pit bull was called by God.

Rausch: When people find out you're an atheist, a lot of them will say, "You just need to read the Bible. Have you read the Bible?" When you tell them that you are knowledgeable of the Bible, it makes them uncomfortable and it kind of pisses them off.

Lansdale: It does. It's a step beyond that, too. It isn't just that a lot of atheists are well-read in the Bible, but they're often well-read in religion in general. I think a lot of times if you grow up in that and you have questions, you may even go to the Bible to reinforce what you think to be true, and then realize that it's not true. Then you begin to reinforce the other viewpoint of it being just part of mythology. I always thought that the fact that I grew up reading Greek and Roman and Norse mythology and seeing those similarities sort of put me on that track and made me skeptical at first. Then by the time I was in high school I was a nonbeliever.

Rausch: At what age did you let people know you were a nonbeliever, and what was the reaction to that?

Lansdale: It usually just came from asking questions. It wasn't so much saying, "I'm a nonbeliever," as it was saying, "If that is true, then why . . . ?" And then you keep getting answers like: "He moves in mysterious ways," like a bowel movement. I just thought, "Well, that's not fulfilling." I never thought about calling myself an atheist or not an atheist, but it certainly was not a common viewpoint where I grew up. But I don't remember ever being afraid to say it, but I think I was about eighteen when I was like, "You know what? I'm an atheist." [Laughs.] It was there before, but I think that's when I realized it in a concrete kind of way.

Rausch: I think I tried to deny it for a long time. I tried to push those thoughts away. You're basically taught that to question these things is a sin in itself.

Lansdale: Oh, yeah. I did the same thing when I was younger. You know what I think is a unique point of view here is that when I was about eleven, I started out saying, "I'm gonna be a preacher." My mother was religious, but she was a skeptical religious person. And I don't think my father cared about it one way or the other. He told me, "Once you die, you're meat for the worms." But I don't think he would have ever thought of himself as an atheist; he just thought, "This doesn't make any sense to me."

I said, "If I'm going to be a preacher, I've got to know this Bible frontwards and forwards." Then I read it and I went, hmmm. So I started having questions, and then I started trying to make excuses for it, loopholes and denying this and that, but just as time went on . . . . As I got older and started getting interested in anthropology, archaeology, and like, I said I was already reading mythological text or stories about Greek, Roman, and Norse mythology, and then later that expanded to others, then finally that's when I couldn't make any excuses for it anymore.

Rausch: I'm not trying to be a dick, but I always thought it was funny that Christians would talk about other people's religions and mock them for being silly, but they don't seem to realize that their religion does a lot of those exact same things and handles things in the same manner as the ones they think are silly.

Lansdale: It's because they are culturally bonded. It's like when you grow up you can look at wherever you are born or raised, you can have some fairly accurate belief as to what that person's religious beliefs are gonna be. Not always, but . . . if you were born in a Muslim country, then you are very likely to be that religious ilk. Just like if you are born in certain areas you are more likely to be a Christian or a Jew or a Hindu or a Buddhist. That unto itself was one of my early suspicions that location had a lot to do with what you believed. That's what I think of and call "cultural bonding." You bond with it to such an extent that you don't question it. I even saw something on TV the other day where they were listing these important historical events. "King David did this, and so and so did this . . ." But no one ever thinks to say, "That isn't history." But it's so built into our consciousness that we believe these people did these things. Sometimes you can't even find evidence that they exist. Of course even if you did find evidence that they exist, that doesn't make them part of a divine plan. Nor is there anything there that proves religion. But the starting point there is that they can't even find evidence that the Old Testament people existed, and for that matter Jesus is kind of a questionable thing too. He's mentioned maybe once in Josephus, and that's a suspicious mention, and I think he's mentioned like twice in some volumes that even the Christians doubt. You can't find mention of this incredible teacher anywhere else other than in the Bible or in this mention in Josephus which many people feel was sort of added in. And even then, he's just mentioned in passing—he's not like this great guy. Then you start reading about Apolonius and Simon the Magician and you see how all those things have been conflated.

Rausch: One of the things you bring up in your essay, "Miracles Ain't What They Used to Be," is the Apocrypha, which most Christians don't even know exist. Why do you think so many Christians don't know about these deleted books of the Bible, and if they did know about them, do you think they'd care?

Lansdale: It must make a difference to some since a lot of us started out in that religion as believers. The Apocrypha was one of the things that was also part of the dismantling of this cultural bonding. But I think for most people it wouldn't make a difference because they have made a commitment to a belief and they have built their entire lives around it. They have friends that go to church, they go to church, a lot of their life is involved with church. Even though a lot of people won't admit it, a lot of people that are heavy church-going people are more social Christians than they are theological Christians. That's often the case. I think they say there are about twenty percent they know of who are atheists, but that's just the twenty percent who are saying they are. There's probably a larger percentage in there that are atheist or agnostic and just aren't saying it.

Rausch: I had a minister tell me one time, "Fake it till you make it. If you don't believe it, just pretend." I always thought that was really weird. That's common, but the Bible says God knows what's in your heart if he exists. So if you were faking it, it wouldn't get you anywhere. I always thought that was really bizarre.

Lansdale: I had a discussion not long ago. I forget how it came up. I don't go around pulling people's coat sleeves. But somebody brought it up to me. I don't care if you believe those things. I think you have the perfect right to. But somebody said, "You have to respect my belief." I said, "I respect your right to believe it. I don't respect your belief, or I would believe it." But the thing is, he said, "I just go ahead and decide to believe it because what if you're wrong?" I said, "Well, here's the problem with that," and it's the same thing you said. Biblically this powerful being is supposed to know what you are thinking and what you're believing, so that's just a false belief.

Rausch: It does amaze me the degree to which people who are otherwise very intelligent and very discerning will just reject things that are common sense or just reject science out of hand and point at religion as being their reason why. I find that scary.

Lansdale: Yeah, I do too. When I was growing up in the fifties and the sixties, there was heavy-ingrained religion and anti-Darwinism and all of that sort of stuff, but there was also a larger group of people who were willing to say "science is science" and religion was left to the church. There weren't these things that you put in school where they had religious doubts where they could come in and say, "Well, maybe Creationism exists." There was none of that. A lot of that had to do with John Kennedy when he came in and became president because he was very education and science-oriented, as was his wife. It promoted that heavily. After World War II and the atomic bomb, that led people to become more aware of things that science knew and that science could do. Even comic books that I read—DC characters like Green Lantern and the Flash—promoted that. Prior to that, most of the characters had their powers through magic. But after World War II, they began to have powers through science because that was the big thing.

What I'm seeing now, you had those anti-Darwin and antiscience people in the fifties and sixties, and we're now seeing a growth of those people. They're ignorant and they're proud of it. It's the scariest damn thing, because when I was growing up, there were people who thought we didn't go to the moon. Even my father, who was not an educated man and was in fact illiterate for all practical purposes, didn't believe we went to the moon. There was no convincing them. I'm thinking, "So we spent millions of dollars to go out in the desert and fake it so they can tell us they did this." And the Russians are in on it, too. It just becomes such a ludicrous thing. But if people can believe that, then they're gonna believe some guy died and came back and went to heaven and is waiting for you there. I was talking to someone and I said, "If God's all powerful, why didn't he just make everybody perfect to begin with?" They always say, "Perfection would become boring." I always say, "The actual definition of perfection is that it's perfect; therefore, it could not become boring because it's perfect." I say, "Why are you trying to get to heaven? Is heaven perfect?" They say, "Of course." "So you believe perfection when it's time to, but you don't believe in perfection when it clashes with your basic mythology."

Rausch: In your "miracles" essay you bring up what has always been my favorite question about God, which is his apparent inability to cause severed limbs to grow back. This argument is usually a conversation stopper, as Christians have no real explanation for why their all-powerful God either cannot or chooses not to heal these people. Why, in the history of the world, did they never ever not even once grow back?

Lansdale: But at least in the Bible, if you're reading it, the people are cured of blindness immediately, and it's not like they have to go to the doctor and have medicine and recovery time. Somebody will say "Well, I died on the operating table." And I'll say, "Well, your body quit functioning for a while, but you obviously didn't die. You came back." They say, "It was a miracle." "Well, how about all of those other people who died? What's so special about you?" Why is this happening? And if that is a miracle, why can't they grow back arms, and legs, and missing eyes? If their head gets blown off, why can't they just sew it back on there and pray and then they can get up and walk back home? Those are fucking miracles, and I don't want to hear about some goddamn birds singing in the tree being a miracle. It's miraculous in the broad term. We can all use that word, but it doesn't have to be theological; it can just mean amazing, or that it's surprising. Every day I think about the earth or the universe, and the things they keep discovering, and to me, that is miraculous in one sense, but not what they mean in terms of God's miracles. In fact, if they go through those things immediately, they find they dug a hole too deep to get out, and by saying "Gee, there's all this miraculous wonderful stuff in the universe," it doesn't prove that there's a God in the universe. It proves a certain uniqueness and a wonder, and in a broader sense of nature and the cosmos, yeah, that's miraculous. But that has nothing to do with God.

People say, "Well, how can you believe that just happened?" And I say, "Well, I don't know how that's happened." But to ask me to believe in a science that I can't explain, these things that go on, doesn't really enforce the idea that there's a God, because in another way, you're asking me to believe, on some level, the same kind of thing—that there's a God always here, that there are these forces affecting nature and the cosmos. Now which one sounds the most logical? Some invented, supernatural deity who's been hanging around? They didn't have the better sense than to have to go on Zoloft at some point and to become more kind, and to decide that they're going to be Christians? Talk about a convoluted message and a convoluted way of doing it. The more that you look at it straight-eyed, the more ridiculous it seems. And that there's the one God, and you have all of this rigamarole. And from the beginning of time, you had a different plan, and yet, he's supposed to have an idea of how this all works. And what happened to all of these people before Jesus, if that's supposed to be the Christian's answer. What was their faith if they didn't know a Jesus because Jesus had not come down? You can just keep compounding these questions. And the answers are usually nonexistent.

What'll happen nearly every time, if you keep asking these questions, is you'll feel them getting backed into a corner, and they'll say you have to take it on faith. And my take on that is and has always been that there are people in the world who have faith that the world is flat even in this day and age. There are people all over who have absolute faith in all kinds of other religions and ideas, so I don't have to take it on faith, and to me, that's just a "Get Out of Jail Free" card. That doesn't work for me. It's not an ultimate religion if it can't be obvious. If it's supposed to be an ultimate answer, why isn't it obvious?

Rausch: In that essay you brought up a point that I've been making for years, and a lot of us have, that there's the situation with a guy in a trailer park who survives a tornado and fifty other people die but he claims he was saved by God. And then there's another example where there's a Bible—just the book—survives a fire or an auto accident, in which human lives are taken, and then the saving of the Bible is said to be a miracle. I find that humorous and also sick that someone would think that a loving deity would place more importance on a book than on a human life.

Lansdale: They find His image in a cheese sandwich. "I can't explain babies with AIDS, but I'm gonna place Jesus's face in a fucking cheese sandwich, because that's really important." You know, if you believe in God, explain babies with AIDS. I hear some people say that they're being punished for what their parents did, and I say, "Your god punishes innocent children for something someone else did?" That makes no sense, at least in the way you're trying to tell me that your god is all-loving. You just have to accept that God's like what Twain said, that he's a maligned thug or a malicious thug. Because that's exactly what you're telling me, but yet in the next breath, you're telling me that God is love and that all of these things are wonderful and what we need is more prayer. And every asshole who's got a mouth has been praying from the beginning of this religion for these things that never happen. If they want something and they get it, He answered their prayers. But God can't seem to figure out how to end wars, get rid of terrible diseases, abused children, abused animals; none of that stuff seems to be a priority for Him. It's more like if you pray for a car, and you get it, that's your prayer answered. And if you don't get it, it's God's will, meaning that He's never wrong. Prayer doesn't matter, because it just fits whatever you want to decide. It was either answered or it was God's will. It makes no sense. It's just conflicting testimony.

Rausch: Nobody seems to take into account that prayer works approximately 50 percent of the time. It works in the same way that everything else works. Some shit happens and some shit doesn't. And they still say, "Oh, it was the prayer." It's odd to me.

Lansdale: It's just another branch of things like numerology, astrology—they're actually all connected in some way. Even if a person does numerology or astrology, which is not religious, it's this idea that there's some organized purpose in the cosmos. I've had people tell me, "Well, my number is nine, and the person I married is number nine, and the date I got married is a nine . . . ." And I say "Well, you know, if there's one true ten, counting the zero, you've got a lot of chances that that number is going to come up. What if they don't come up? What does that mean? What it means is you're not identifying the times it doesn't come up. You're identifying the moments it does come up. And you're picking the moments it does come up that matter to you. But you can find a lot of moments where it did come up, but the moments didn't matter to you." It just doesn't mean anything.

Rausch: You obviously say a lot of incendiary things about religion in your essay. When you sat down to write that, were you at all concerned about the likelihood that it might cost you some fans?

Lansdale: No. I can't live life like that. If people read my books, I think that it's pretty obvious that those elements are in my books. And I've often had Christians who were good people and other people say, "Why are the Christians always the bad people?" And I say, "If you read my work that close, you'll see that there are some good ones in there." A lot of my friends are Christians. And a lot of them live by the basic tenets like Jesus in the beatitudes. And if you live like that, I'm cool. But when you start using it as reasoning for hating gays or people of different religions, then I'm out. In the last ten to fifteen years of my life, I've actually lost a number of friends.

Not because I'm an atheist, but because they're hypocrites, and they've grown to be stronger and stronger hypocrites, suddenly embracing ideas that they didn't embrace when they were younger. I don't know what's happened, but it's like there's a nut hole open, and all of these nuts are flowing through it. And it's not just religion. There have been a lot of people who are religious that I admire and respect. Jimmy Carter is one of my favorite Christians because he actually tries to do that stuff. And there are other people who try to do that stuff. And there are a lot of people who are social Christians who may not even think about the complications of it. But they go to church because it's part of their lives. I have some friends who say, "To tell you the truth, I don't think there's any afterlife, but I go to church because I really believe in those basic ideas of Jesus." And I get it. That's fine. The problem is that a lot of people in your group have a lot of different views on how to interpret those things. And my belief is that I can try to do those things and be a good person and a kind person without having to accept some mythical zombie.

Rausch: In the essay you write, "Truth is, the gun-toting, tough-talking, warmongering Christians I know do not consider Jesus their hero so much as John Wayne. They don't want to turn the other cheek, they want to kill something. If it can't be a human, there's always a deer." I share those same views a lot of the time, and often find myself extremely leery of overly religious people from the very start. If someone you've just met reveals themselves to be a Christian, do you find yourself guilty of immediate skepticism?

Lansdale: I'm skeptical in the same way that when I tell them I'm atheist, they're skeptical. But on the other hand, that doesn't mean that some of those people don't become good friends of mine. They have at least as associates or friends. But I'm always skeptical because religion is one of those things that always lets me down. With my good friends, they bring the better aspects of it. But you have people who start talking about Christianity and the next thing out of their mouth is something hideous about gays or Black people or Hispanic people or you name it. And that's not to say that atheists can't be racist or be assholes, because they certainly can be. I know some people who are atheist that I wouldn't piss on them if they were on fire. I'm not trying to make this point that being an atheist makes you good. It doesn't, but it doesn't make you evil either. And some people have this idea that being an atheist is like being a Satan worshipper. They don't even know what it means, but they can't embrace it.

Rausch: I don't often tell people I'm an atheist because I don't want to get into an argument about it, and they'll never change their minds.

Lansdale: But sometimes they do. I've seen some people in my life who change their minds because of discussions that we've had. I wasn't out to change their minds. They were people who just start thinking about it and they say, "You know what? Yeah, where's the answer in this?"

Rausch: At first, my next question is going to sound like it's unrelated, but it's not. It's actually very closely related. As an atheist progressive living in a red state, what are your thoughts on Donald Trump?

Lansdale: I loathe him. I can't stand the guy. And one of the reasons why I can't is the embracing of Christianity and that the Christians who voted for him are putting him on a pedestal and have decided that he can do no wrong, and they say they can forgive, but they can't forgive Hillary Clinton or whoever else they don't like. They can forgive the person who is a racist jackass and who is an antiwoman leader. I just don't get it; I don't understand it. I don't understand why they can't see their own hypocrisy. It's sort of like the water's up to their neck, and they think they're still on dry land. They just can't get that because most of the Christians I know, and I'm not saying this is all of them, are sadly in that camp. They're willing to let him do what he wants, be who he wants—they're willing to accept pussy-grabbing; they're willing to accept all of these things that he's done; they're willing to accept that he won't stand up for a woman; that he mocks people who are Muslim who have lost a son in our military; and so on and so on. The list is endless. I just can't figure it. I don't know what to think. I'm surprised he's lasted this long.

I knew he was going to be elected, though. Before the election, a couple of weeks out, I thought, "Oh my god. He's going to win." Not because most people are going to vote for him, but because *enough* people are going to vote for him. I knew they were going to vote in areas where Democrats had decided not to really put their resources. And I remember when they were making fun of him for flying out to all of these little places at the last minute, and I thought that's where they were screwing up. Because it makes them seem elitist, first of all. Second of all, these are vital areas to the electoral college. And they ignored them. I said I thought he was gonna win, and I had friends who were progressives who said I was crazy. They said, "Look at the polls." I'd say, "Yeah, look at them. They go up and down everyday, constantly. That means that there are a lot of people that just won't change; there are a lot of people who are lying when they won't admit they're voting for the pussy-grabber-in-chief. That was exactly what happened. So when it did, I wasn't surprised. I was shocked, even though I was right, but I wasn't surprised.

I do think a reckoning should be coming. I was pretty sure it was, but I've gotten to where I don't know anymore, because there's not a thing he can do that seems to have an impact on that hardcore thirty, thirty-five percent. And I hate to say this, but a lot of those people are just plain dedicated to trying to reproduce this America of the fifties and sixties that never really existed. What they mean is "white." I was talking to a friend of mine who voted for Trump, and I said, "How many people on the Democratic side belong to the KKK or belong to the Aryan Nation or belong to these Hitler-like organizations and came out in support of Clinton?" None. "But they do come out in support of you guys." He said, "He can't help who votes for him." I said, "Why do you think they voted for him? Why do you think he got their support and the other one didn't or there wasn't some kind of split support?" It's obvious what it's about.

Some of the people I know that I never really thought of as racist actually are, because they're telling me about how the white people are losing their power. I thought, you know what? Being white has never hurt me a bit, and I come from the poorest backgrounds, and I have known people who have come from equal or worse backgrounds, and I got opportunities they didn't get. I guarantee you it was their skin color. I just get tired of the horse shit. I remember one time my wife and I—this was in the nineties—were in a restaurant and we heard some people talking. He said about Affirmative Action, "I wouldn't hire any of those you-know-whats if I didn't have to." That's when I thought, people keep telling me things are getting better, and they tell me Affirmative Action isn't needed, and then I hear people talking like that . . . . And now we're seeing the results of all that. These guys are coming in and saying, "We don't want to give any special privileges to those people." I certainly believe as soon as we get to the point where people are hired on the basis of their character and their skills and not their color, we can get rid of that. And maybe we're closer to that than we once were, but man, what Trump did, and actually what Obama did as far as people reacting to him being a Black president, it's all revealed this nasty, deep divide, where people are showing what they really believe. It's scary and it's sad.

Rausch: I think it's frightening that polls repeatedly show that Americans would rather have a pedophile be President than an atheist.

Lansdale: It's crazy. I've had this happen numerous times when people found out I was an atheist. "God, I thought you were a Christian." I say, "Why did you think that?" They say, "Because of the way you act and the way you treat people." I thought, in other words, I'm not doing it for a reward—I don't get to go to heaven and play a harp like I want to—but I'm doing it because I think it's the right thing to do. I'm setting a positive example and being a positive force in the universe. If you want to do something that is a force, it's your actions and how they're passed on. Don't get me wrong, I'm not trying to paint myself as some perfect person. I am not. But I've done the best I can, and certainly I've made the right and proper effort.

Champion Joe on Screen: Joe R. Lansdale Discusses *Love, Death & Robots, Creepshow, Hap and Leonard*, and the Possibility He'll Direct

Andrew J. Rausch / 2019

Published in *Diabolique*, May 7, 2019. Reprinted by permission of the author.

Joe R. Lansdale has been doing big things for a lot of years now (he published his first novel, *Act of Love*, way back in 1981), and yet somehow it seems like he's doing even bigger things now. The prolific author, best known for novels like *Cold in July*, *The Bottoms*, the novella *Bubba Ho-Tep*, and his popular Hap and Leonard series (the basis for the Sundance Channel TV show), has been writing professionally and publishing since the 1970s. He has written nearly fifty novels and thirty short story collections. He's always been popular, but he didn't burst out of the gates with a major success like Stephen King. He just kept plugging away, year after year, writing and publishing, steadily developing a massive cult following. And now he, like Elmore Leonard (of whom he's a fan), has finally broken through and become a prominent mainstream success after having written for five decades.

Despite having found success in virtually every aspect of writing, from scripts to short stories to novels to comic books, and having won a significant number of prestigious awards, Lansdale remains the same "aw shucks" down-to-earth guy he's always been. He makes time for fans at signings, continues to occasionally write for the occasional small publication or publisher, and is known for sharing his hard-earned wisdom with less-experienced writers. The reason for all of this is simple: Lansdale spent so many years toiling in the literary trenches that he still sees himself as one of the common folk. If you ask him about his success, he shrugs off comparisons to the "big name" authors. He never wanted to be a celebrity. Ask him about this and he will share the tried-and-true sentiment of his late friend Bill Paxton, saying all he ever wanted was "a place at the table." Lansdale has money, but he isn't J. K. Rowling rich. And that suits him just fine. He gets paid well to do the thing he enjoys most. He's already achieved more than he ever believed he would, and for that he remains grateful.

Today there seem to be new opportunities around every corner. Among them are having two episodes of the new David Fincher/Tim Miller Netflix series *Love, Death & Robots*, adapted from his stories "Fish Night" and "The Dump," having an episode of Greg Nicotero's forthcoming *Creepshow* series adapted from another, "The Companion," and several potential film projects, one of which he hopes to direct. And then there are those pesky questions regarding the future of the *Hap and Leonard* television series . . .

Andrew J. Rausch: Were you a fan of the original George Romero *Creepshow* film?

Joe R. Lansdale: Yeah, I liked that. At the time, I thought it was grim, so I enjoyed that. My favorite vignettes were "The Crate" and "Father's Day." I liked that one quite a bit. Those were my two favorites.

Rausch: What was your initial reaction when you first learned that they were making the series?

Lansdale: The way I found out about it, if I remember correctly, is I saw Greg Nicotero in Burbank at one of my signings. He may have mentioned it there, or it may have been his manager who told me. Anyway, one of them told me about it and mentioned they might want me to do a script for it. That was the original plan, but that changed. I had a friend named Matt Venne who had, many years ago, tried to adapt the story "The Companion." That's a story I wrote with my kids, Keith and Kasey. I don't remember the details of why it didn't happen, but that deal didn't occur. As much as I thought I'd love to do a script, when Matt said, "Hey man, what do you think about me doing this?" I thought, well, this way if they're interested my family gets in and one of my friends gets in, too. And that's what happened. I'm very pleased with Matt's script. I haven't seen the episode yet, but Matt went to the set and was able to see it, and he says high things about it, so I'm hoping for the best. And I love Greg. I've known him for a long time; long before he was doing *Walking Dead*. I'm happy for him and all the success he's had.

Rausch: The other writers announced for season one to include Stephen King, Joe Hill, and Josh Malerman, who's hot right now. You're in good company.

Lansdale: I love it! I've been around a long time. I have an extremely varied career, so I'm not just known for one thing. I always love it when any one of those branches identifies me. I never feel like I'm a horror writer or a mystery writer or a crime writer. I'm all of those things, but I'm not exclusively those things. To be lumped in with such great talent is wonderful.

Rausch: As you mentioned, you cowrote the story with your children. That story first appeared in the anthology *Great Writers and Kids Write Spooky Stories*. What do you remember about that experience?

Lansdale: The people doing the anthology came to me and asked, "Do you think your kids will want to do that?" I said, "Let me check." I asked them and they were ecstatic about it. I said, "Look, here's a basic idea I've got, and you guys can write it. I can help polish it. My son at the time was twelve. My daughter was eight. My son already had a pretty good way of handling words, so he kind of put the story together. Then Kasey would say, "No, we need this to happen and this to happen . . . ." I just stood there like a hockey goalie, and I'd knock them back into play when they got too far out. And then when they got finished, I typed it up for them. I helped with some of the logic problems. Then when we were done, Kasey put some stuff in there that she really liked. We sent it in and they wrote back, "We love this, but some of these things are too intense for younger readers." They were some of the scenes Kasey did. In one of them, someone was hanged in the scene. I went to her and said, "They feel like because they're kids they're going to have to take the scene out." I could tell she was a little dejected. She hung her head. "Well, shit, it's just not the same!" [Laughs.] I've never forgotten that. She'd probably learned it from me! But they didn't use that scene. The story came out well. It's the kind of story that strikes me as something perfect for *Creepshow*. I'm interested to see the adaptation myself.

Rausch: Does having worked on the story with Kasey and Keith make this adaptation more special for you?

Lansdale: Yes, it does. Keith, Kasey, and I have gone on to do other things together. We've sold screenplays and articles and fictions and things like that. We've done that. But to have what was essentially their first story at ages eight and twelve be adapted is pretty special. People always ask, "How much of it did they do?" They did a lot! They're kind of precocious children, to be honest. I know everybody thinks that, but mine really are. We all got this opportunity where we got to make something together, and now we get to see it made into a television show. And not only that, but a show based on an old movie that I liked. It was something the kids saw when they were young, too.

Rausch: And you wrote two episodes for the new Netflix series *Love, Death & Robots.*

Lansdale: I did. I wrote "Fish Night" and "The Dump."

Rausch: What has that experience been like?

Lansdale: Tim Miller contacted my agent. He was interested in those two stories. I was out in Los Angeles at the time, and Kasey and I went over to visit him at Blur Studios. He's a really nice guy! Just an incredibly nice guy. Well-read in the science fiction and fantasy/horror field. He was not just a guy saying he's gonna make this up. He's a guy that really is a fan and is very well-versed. We had a great time talking about writers and stories. He showed Kasey and I some of the animation they were doing, and I knew I wanted to be part of that. So we made the deal. I've been very, very pleased. He's been a great guy, keeping me in the loop. I'm excited about it! I've seen 'em, and I love 'em both. They're very good.

Writers always ask, "What do you think about these things?" If I really like something, I'll tell you. As a writer, you always think, well, I wish they had done this or I wish they had done that . . . because there are certain things you feel get lost in translation. I'm really pleased with these two episodes. I have probably, so far, had the most unique career regarding that. All the adaptations that have been done in a major way. I've been very pleased with! *Bubba Ho-Tep*, *Cold in July*, "Incident On and Off a Mountain Road" from the *Masters of Horror* series, these two stories that were done for *Love, Death & Robots*, as well as the *Batman* animated scripts I wrote . . . They've all been handled well. I'm really a fortunate guy as far as adaptations go! I always say the next thing that's going to happen is the big shoe is going to drop and then: "God, I hate this one." But so far, so good.

Rausch: The series was created by Tim Miller and produced by David Fincher. Those are big names to be next to. What is it like to have your work recognized by talents such as those?

Lansdale: It's pleasing. You love doing that. I've been doing it so long that I'm rarely starstruck, I think. But I am talent struck, which is a different thing. Tim is just an amazing talent, and Blur Studios is absolutely unique. It's the best! I love that guy and I love all of his animators and what everybody who works there is doing. It's impressive. It feels good, you know? Fincher, I never met, so I don't really have any actual relationship with him. He's somebody that's talented in the business, and it's great seeing him get behind a project like this.

Rausch: Is there any talk of further collaborations if the series moves forward?

Lansdale: I think if they're renewed, they might consider something else. I really don't know. That's going to be entirely up to them when they're ready to move forward. I kind of hope they do. That'd be fun.

Rausch: Speaking of Netflix, a lot of fans have been hoping Hap and Leonard might be revived by them or another outlet. Do you see any hope for that?

Lansdale: I really don't, mostly because it hasn't been renewed at this point. I don't think it looks good. The other thing, James Purefoy and Michael Kenneth Williams, the main characters, on top of the periphery characters, as well as peripheral characters, have gone on to get other jobs and move on. James loved his character and would have loved to keep doing it. I don't know everybody else. I think if they had renewed it at the time, yeah, we would've had those seasons. If somebody wants to come in now and it can be arranged, I'd be all for it. James Purefoy and I wrote each other the day we knew it was cancelled, and we both said we're not sad; we were happy we had three great seasons. I've got that, and I can go to my grave with three great seasons of probably my most famous characters.

Rausch: They both did such great jobs in those roles.

Lansdale: You never know. When people first named them, I thought, well, these are two great actors! I was a big fan of both of them already. I was excited about that. Then Christina Hendricks was in the first season, and I'm getting all these great character actors. Neil Sandilands and Jeff Pope. It just went on and on. Everybody there. All of those people were just unique talents. I felt very, very pleased that they came in.

The thing is, you don't know until they do it. When I started seeing them play the parts, I saw the transformations. I saw how hard James worked to get an accent that was going to sell. I was very, very pleased with how they inhabited the characters. James just became Hap Collins. I think because we have a lot in common, and the character was based on me. We were both country boys. He's a British country boy, but we're both country boys. We both grew up in small towns. We knew a lot of the kinds of people that appeared in the Hap and Leonard series. I'm not talking about the murderous and dark side, but the kind of everyday people that make up rural life. He came into it with that. He was willed to try to look at those kinds of characters and the area where they existed. I was just so pleased. Mike, too! But I knew James a little bit better. We communicated a little more frequently. I'm very, very pleased with it, and if they were to renew it tomorrow, I'd love to see those guys come back. Who knows in the future? Maybe it'll be renewed with totally different actors and a different network and so on.

Rausch: I read that the first novel, *Savage Season*, was optioned for film. Is that correct?

Lansdale: It was. The script was done. I loved it! The original version, that is. It was optioned by John Badham. The script was by a guy named Steve Katz. There's more than one guy who works in the field with that name. This guy, I think he quit writing screenplays, but he sold it to John and it looked great! It was just like a novel. And then what happened, as time went on, they started getting cold feet; they started changing it to be more like every damn thing else that was out there. Then I was glad it died. Later on, I wrote a script for *Two Bear Mambo* that was lost through the ages. It was over at Propaganda Films, which fell apart, so the whole deal fell apart. I don't even know if that script is in existence. Later on, they optioned *Savage Season* again and this time I wrote the script. I thought I did a very good script on it, but they weren't able to get traction as a film. My friend, Lowell Northrop, who was one of the people, had a partner who had optioned that particular novel and started pushing it as a TV show. He's one of the guys that gets pushed out of the talk, but there would be no *Hap and Leonard* show without Lowell Northrop. He's listed as a coexecutive producer, as I am, which is accurate. He really is the main guy, because in a way, if he hadn't done that, then Jim and Nick would not have had that connection. Although, they were interested in it independently. All of that works together, and I've always thought Lowell deserved more credit than he got.

Rausch: Do you have any other film or TV adaptations coming up?

Lansdale: I have some things I can't talk about, but I will say there's a lot of interest in TV shows as well as some films. One that I can talk about is *The Thicket*, which was optioned by Peter Dinklage. He's had that for several years now. Ever since it came out, pretty much. Now there's a director named Elliott Lester attached. We're hopeful that that'll go before the camera. We'll see.

Edge of Dark Water is still optioned. And "The Projectionist," which I wrote for Lawrence Block's anthology *In Sunlight or in Shadow* is under option. My son wrote the screenplay for that, and I'm supposed to direct it if it gets made. That would be a different thing for me to do. People always say, "Oh my god, you're going to become a director now?" No. I'm a writer first. But I also like films and I'm interested in that aspect of it, that side of it, or have become so since the eighties. I'd like to give that a spin. I wouldn't say it so cavalier if I had not thought about it, studied it, and been ready to do it.

Rausch: That would be fascinating. And who in their right mind would pass on that? Your success has provided you with opportunities to do other things, so why not go for them?

Lansdale: I don't know yet that I will get that opportunity, but I'm hopeful. I've had a great schooling. I had Don Coscerelli with *Bubba Ho-Tep*. I got to be on set, watch him, listen to him. And then you learn from actors. I've learned a lot just from Bruce Campbell, just in an offhand way. Not just observing, but in things he's said. He gave me a piece of directing advice, and I laughed when I heard it, but he's essentially correct. He said, "Always make sure everybody's in the same movie." I thought, "Ah! That is good advice." Jim Mickle, who wrote the script for *Cold in July*, told me, "If you've gotta shoot something, you have to be able to get to the other end comfortably and then shoot it from the other angle." Meaning, if you have a couch against a wall and you want to shoot that shot, you might not be able to get that shot you want. Or at least not easily. I understood the general advice he gave me. Then Bill Paxton and I were friends, and Bill was supposed to direct *The Bottoms*. Unfortunately, he died. I learned a tremendous amount from him. Seeing *Frailty* and in listening to him talk to me about directing and what his plans were for *The Bottoms*, I learned a lot.

Then there was a little movie done here called *Christmas with the Dead*, based on a short story of mine. A real small budget. My friend always hates when I say it, but I think it's a Roger Corman-style film that Terrill Lee Lankford directed. I probably learned more from him than anybody, because he knew a little bit about all the aspects of film. And because I was helping produce it, I was there and was privy to a lot of conversations about it. I did a little on editing and different things like that. I had to be a minor jack-of-all-trades, although I didn't do much in comparison to what others did. But by being there with them and watching them, and by doing the little bits that I did do, I think I probably learned more about film from that little low-budget basement film than I did from anybody else.

Two Hands Flowing

James Grady / 2020

Interview conducted expressly for this book and appears here for the first time. Published by permission of the author.

Joe Lansdale is a rarity, a person who excels in two different art forms—in his case, prose fiction and martial arts.

Sure, hordes of brilliant creative cultural stars are known for their excellences in two different categories of cultural accomplishment, but usually those wonderful creators expand their efforts from the base of their core craft: Nobel Prize winner Bob Dylan has published wonderful prose, but the core of that effort and his more formidable and famous efforts as a songwriter/singer are both *wordplays*, the spinning of linguistic images, visions, ideas and abstractions into alphabet-based, communicated effects. Our world is graced by thousands of such "multi-talented" artists who stretch their gift in often unexpected ways—poets who shine as fiction authors (Gertrude Stein), performing artists like classical cellists who shine as thespians (Lori Singer), film virtuosos who command the camera from both sides (Charlie Chaplin).

But people who excel in two "*seemingly*" different arts are hard to find.

Lansdale, with his classic American name, is far from "your average Joe."

Let other critiques of Joe deal with his wordsmith triumphs, what we examine here is his second major creative realization as one of the world's recognized foremost practitioners and pioneers of martial arts.

To quote big gun Clint Eastwood: "I know what you're thinking."

Those "martial arts" activities most global citizens experience as entertainment via movies, TV, books or even (falsely) in twentieth century+ sweaty arenas of dollars and egos seem too . . . street ugly to be compared to Picasso swirling blue wonders on white canvas.

But Joe's and thousands of (but not all) other practitioners' approach to martial arts epitomizes its definition as more than skilled violence.

It depends, says Joe, on if you have a philosophy about what you do.

And his real-world, down-to-earth analytical approach and accomplishments should break your skepticism about martial studies as an art form as surely as he can snap your right arm at its elbow.

Go back to Joe's beginnings, East Texas, USA. Long after 1900's Boxer Rebellion in colonized China slammed stationed American soldiers with the awareness of a stylized hand-to-hand combat different from the European brutal pugilism and wrestling that flourished in places like Brooklyn and my Montana; after America's victory in WWII exposed hundreds of thousands of Americans to "Japanese wrestling" called Judo; go back to Gladewater, a Fabulous Fifties small town and Joe's thoughtful father who introduced his eleven-year-old son to boxing and wrestling. He did so in part because of pragmatism. Gladewater then—like more than a few small Western outposts of civilization—was a tough town.

"He told me [that] if you get used to letting people walk on you, it becomes a habit. I didn't want that habit," says Joe, who was a "Huck Finn" kind of kid who "ran the creeks and woods all the time."

The explosion of media in that era also introduced Joe to martial arts.

Comic books, oh wonderful comic books, nickel-and-dime cultural delivery devices most (but economically not all) American kids could easily hold in their hands. Batman used Judo to defeat the bad guys. By age four, Joe was writing comic books.

And soon he found books, novels, and some like the early James Bond tales featured martial arts as part of a Double O license to kill. Trips to the public library were the first portal to other worlds for many seekers and dreamers.

Then came seminal movies like Frank Sinatra's *The Manchurian Candidate*, and on TV, an episode of the Western samurai series "Have Gun, Will Travel" featured a show-stopping, one-episode "Asian" warrior throwing bullies out of a saloon with martial arts explained to both hero gunslinger Paladin and his watching fans.

Between his father's coaching and his culture's revelations, when Joe was fourteen, he was ready and eager to sign up for a YMCA Judo class: Walking on to that (Judo) mat, I knew I was in my element," says Joe. "There was something about the formality, at first. . . . it made me feel a part of something unique. It was empowering in a psychological way before it was empowering in a physical way, and finally empowering in a philosophical way.

Thus did a journey into Joe's second artistic career formally begin.

A journey that, like all explorations, was defined by the intent of the traveler and the opportunities time, geography, hard work and luck provide.

Joe rightly categorizes boxing and wrestling as martial arts—but with a caveat that what became known as "pro wrestling" is not. That televised spectacle watched by millions since President Eisenhower's days of Gorgeous George is without any philosophical foundation or experience of a "true" martial art and is most often fixed as "reality TV" entertainment based on dollars and egos, complete with absurd "fighting" antics, big hair, braggadocio, and glowering looks.

Similarly, the twenty-first century rise of "mixed martial arts" as a sport and a pastime steps off the mats of classic martial arts, even though its combat events are close to "the real thing." MMA is a sport, a contest, an enterprise that even with its legitimacy of actions by its dangerous and skilled "players" has as its goal money and ego. Plus, while MMA uses techniques and skills from several classic martial arts—notably wrestling, Ju-jitsu (a Japanese art now often taught with a Brazilian beat), kickboxing, and Muay Thai (a style of kickboxing from Bangkok culture, not the Savate of Paris)—there are rules in MMA. One of Joe's students won an MMA bout with a finger lock but had his victory disqualified as not allowed. The differences between martial arts techniques and rules of engagement in a sport are clarified in back alleys of rape and murder and in the meditativelike presence found in a quiet practice in the park.

Joe's journey of martial arts discovery led him through studies of boxing and wrestling, through arts varied in national origins, including Judo and Ju-jitsu, Hapkido and Kenpo karate. Korean Tae Kwon Do before it significantly evolved from a self-defense system to an Olympic sport. Diato Ryu, Aikido, various styles of Chinese *gung fu* and *wushu*. He studied and practiced in Texas, San Francisco, Berkley, and ports of call like London, whenever he'd get a chance—including a friendly sharing experience of knowledge where with a surgically precise nerve strike to the ribs, Joe dropped this author quivering to the floor of an Italian hotel room.

And *yes*, along the way Joe earned black belts and masters' certificates from various systems, and while he uses a belt system when he teaches as an educational benchmark students can relate to, such rankings are beside the point and only as significant as the entirety of what a student acquires.

The philosophy(ies) associated with the classic martial arts Joe journeys through are often shoved into textbook fields like Zen or Taoism, but such academic constraints—often misunderstood and misapplied in and of themselves—are labels that do not reveal the whole of what Joe's philosophical expressions realized through swirling bodies and blinding fists.

"It's meditation in motion, in practice," says Joe. "It settles you. It doesn't work for everyone. It's the philosophy you have that has to go with it. And the more you can express the philosophy, the less you really understand it. It becomes a part of you and to explain how you've reached the feeling you have requires too much obvious awareness. I can explain it in the way I have, the way I explained writing, but beyond that, it's a personal revelation . . . . It isn't all about physical conduct, it's about personal conduct in other ways, too. The martial art spirit has guided me through life. Even should I get to where I can't do it physically anymore, I'll still be a martial artist in mind and philosophy."

That awareness of activity, aesthetics, intent, and effect is what makes the practice of mindful violence by Joe an art, one akin to a ballet star like Rudolf Nureyev on stage, waving his arms and legs and spinning around in practiced-to-perfection swirls effecting other dancers.

The reality of how Joe's work as a writer fits with his dedication as a martial practitioner shows a linkage that defines both those endeavors as arts and him as an artist.

"They are intertwined for me," says Joe. "Dedication. Focus. Economy of motion. Confidence in self. Learning to write relaxed, mind of no mind. I work from the subconscious . . . . It's doing all the plotting and planning without me knowing it. Martial arts teaches you this. Especially as you have more and more experience. Muscle memory and the subconscious are the same. You do it without thought of doing it."

Joe's approach to both his arts is at its core practical. You learn from reading and other creative activities, schedule and do the work of your own writing. You practice what you've learned in dank basement rooms and sunlit second story schools and parks while other people bicycle past. You create and evolve physical responses for existing realities with mindful, moral choices.

That evolutionary learning attitude in about 1996 led Joe to develop his own style of martial arts: Shen Chuan—"Spirit Fist," an educational system now taught primarily in Nacogdoches, Texas, where Joe lives, a process that won recognition from the United Martial Arts Hall of Fame.

Beyond such recognition for that art, plus the awards for his fiction arts, Joe deserves recognition for being what used to be called "a good man," praise with an intent beyond gender qualification. He's essentially a homebody, a family man who takes care of and cares for his children and his wife, his life in Nacogdoches, all true to his East Texas roots.

As his Italian translator journalist/musician/author Seba Pezzani puts it, Joe is: "A fabulous human being, witty and generous, with a virtually boundless imagination and a wide pop culture. A true modern time American classic."

One who can open your mind with his wondrous fiction.

Or drop you to the floor with a surgical strike.

That's artistry.

Comic Book Catch Up with Writer Joe R. Lansdale

Manuel Gomez / 2020

Published in *Monkeys Fighting Robots*, April 21, 2020. Reprinted by permission of *Monkeys Fighting Robots*.

Joe R. Lansdale is one of the most prolific writers in any genre. He's written everything from horror to crime fiction, historical fiction, and even some nonfiction. He's also written a bunch of comics (like the excellent *Jonah Hex* series for DC/Vertigo) and is a die-hard comics fan. With that in mind, we at *Monkeys Fighting Robots* tapped Champion Joe (as his fans call him) for a chat about what else but comics! Read on and enjoy.

Monkeys Fighting Robots: Joe, first of all, thanks for taking the time to talk to us during this national crisis. How are you and yours holding up? As a writer has social distancing changed your day-to-day life?

Joe R. Lansdale: We are holding up very well. I hate it for others, but for us, it's really no different than when there isn't a pandemic. We're home as usual, and I write in the mornings as usual. I always read, but I might be reading a hair more, and we watch films. I exercise at home. Only thing missing is my martial arts class that I teach. I only teach private lessons these days, but I miss that. I do travel from time to time for fun or for business, so we're not doing that, of course. Otherwise, nothing is really different for us. I'm one of those peculiar people who likes being with people, but I like being home with my wife and a routine as well. When the virus passes, I will be glad to go to the bookstore and visit with people, and we have a couple of trips we'd like to make, but again, for us, it really isn't bad. We have food stocks anyway, just because we tend to do that, and of course, we have the essential, toilet paper. Special items our son picks up for us and delivers. He goes early in the morning, dressed in his mask, looking like a bandit, and he buys us anything we might need once or twice a week, but we don't need much. Thanks for asking. I hope you are well.

MFR: I'm holding on strong, thanks for asking! So apart from being an acclaimed novelist, short-story writer and screenwriter, you have also written many comics. What was your very first comic book writing?

JRL: My first comic gig was *Blood and Shadows*. It was an original comic I wrote and Mark Nelson illustrated. Only problem was, Mark was slow. So by the time he finished I had written and seen published *Two-Gun Mojo*, the Jonah Hex comic. That did great. *Blood and Shadows* finally came out, but by then the wind had blown out of its sails and it never got the attention it deserves. It's creator-owned, so someday it may see the light of day again.

MFR: How do you approach writing a comic book as compared to a short story, or prose piece?

JRL: I show up. It used to seem very different for each concern, but less so now. I do have to spend a day or two becoming comfortable with the comic or screenplay format, but then it's about telling the story in that form, and story is the thing. I also try to write scripts that do more than tell you what happens next but are fun to read. Prose is always natural for me, as I do a lot more of it, but comics and screenplays after that initial readjustment to form, are pretty much the same. Scripts have the time-limit factor, or in the case of comics, the page-limit factor. Tim Truman and I did a Hex series where we started out doing five comics, but they cut it to four, so I always felt it was truncated more than I liked. So there are limitations like that. Requested short stories can have a limit, but mostly they don't have a drop-dead number. Comics do have that as far as page count goes, so that's something to keep in mind and the thing I have the hardest time with.

MFR: Were comics a huge influence for you growing up? How about as an adult?

JRL: I started reading comics in the fifties, and they are to this day the most important thing, along with parental encouragement, that led me to my career, and for that I am deeply grateful. Like most kids, it was the superhero stuff that excited me. I read the kid comics, the ones with talking animals, *Casper the Ghost, Hot Stuff*, and so on, but it was Superman who moved me first, and then I found Batman, and that was a sure-fire fit for me. I read all the DC comics heroes. Loved The Flash, Wonder Woman, and I read comics and collected them right on up until I was sixteen. And during that time I also read Classics Illustrated, which are the flip side of comics. They led me to reading a lot of the books they were based on. They have been revived, and they are reprinting and adding new comics to their line, and I buy them. I read them religiously as a kid. They led me to so many books, and since I never graduated at the university, they were a great source of my education. Without them there are so many novels and stories I wouldn't have discovered. There are other influences, early television shows, all the reruns they did of *Hopalong Cassidy*, as well as new shows they made for TV. The *Superman* TV show, *Lone Ranger*, showing old serials like Flash Gordon and Buck Rogers. And the Tarzan movies were a big influence. But that's getting off the comic subject a bit. Bottom line, they are what made me want to be a writer. I was trying to write and draw my own comics when I was four years old. My mother stapled them for me after I finished.

As an adult, I read fewer comics. Like a lot of teenagers, I was dating and learning about myself. I was reading still, but comics were less and less a part of it. I would now and again buy a batch, as everything wasn't continued. The stretched-out stories that went issues and crossed over to other comics, sort of sucked the wind out of it for me in the nineties. But before that I would read them in patches, so to speak. Friends would suggest a run of comics, and then I would buy the whole run, so as not to wait for each issue. I could read a comic in fifteen to twenty minutes, so I preferred to have the whole storyline to sit down with. But I wasn't reading them nearly as much by the time I was sixteen, and only begin to pick them up on a regular basis at the end of the eighties and into the nineties, and then, as I said, the multiple crossovers burned me out. I read a number of comics that weren't superhero comics during the nineties, and then I dried up on the new ones for a while, even though I was writing comics.

In the last ten years, I've gone back to reading a few new superhero comics, but the stuff I've really enjoyed, are comics like *Capote in Kansas*, and the *To Kill a Mockingbird* adaptation, Richard Stark Parker novel adaptations—there weren't many, as it's a long series. *Savage Season* based on a novel by me was adapted but printed way too dark, but I enjoyed reading the artist's interpretation. It was almost exactly the novel. *Mucho Mojo* has been done, and it'll be out in the wild eventually. What I really enjoy reading these days is rereading the DC archives, the ones before I was reading comics, the ones during my time growing up, the Silver Age, as well as gatherings of later periods.

I buy nearly DC exclusively. Marvel was better in the sixties, but DC caught up, and though I like Marvel, it was always the DC characters that thrilled me. I buy a lot of old comics I used to read that have been collected. Stuff like Brothers of the Spear, Tarzan, Korak, anything to do with John

Carter of Mars, and I'm once again buying the *Classics Illustrated*. I order a few every few months, and they are a treat.

MFR: Do you have a favorite comic creative team? A favorite writer or artist?

JRL: If Tim Truman is involved in a comic, with anyone, I try and read those. I loved a lot of different comics, so I don't know if I had a favorite team. Gardner Fox was always a name I looked for when I started seeing his name on comics. The Julie Schwartz-edited comics with so many different creators were really important to me when I was young. I got to know Julie and we became friendly. It was quite an honor for me. The comics he edited were important to my childhood and the making of my career.

MFR: Do you have a favorite comic book character?

JRL: Batman. Duh.

MFR: Did you have a favorite title?

JRL: I still love Batman, though I don't read the comics regularly. I watch animated films with Batman in them, and I wrote for *Batman: The Animated Series*, as well as wrote the script for *Son of Batman*. The animated series is a highlight of my career. It was like being a kid again, but with adult sensibilities. That is my favorite version of Batman, comics, film, or otherwise. I also wrote a plot outline, or that's how I was credited, for a *Superman* episode. I wrote a stand-alone, unnamed Jonah Hex short, that was on the Blu-ray of *Under the Red Hood* and was in a DVD collection of short animated films about a variety of DC characters. I love writing for animation and would like to do more of it.

MFR: I actually discovered you through comics, in a backdoor kind of way. I first read *Preacher* in trade and the edition of volume one I had contained a foreword by you. I was so taken by how you wrote about the comic that I looked up the rest of your work and read the first Hap & Leonard, *Savage Season*, novel shortly after. How did you end up writing that foreword to *Preacher*?

JRL: Garth was a fan of my Jonah Hex comics, and he and DC thought I'd be the right person to write it since I was a reader of the comics. It was a lot of fun, and interestingly enough, a lot of readers tell me they came to my work through that introduction, or through the comics I wrote.

MFR: You mentioned Tim Truman a few times. I wanted to get into your relationship with Tim, whom I think is one of the best artists in the industry. How did you first get linked up with Tim? Were you a fan of his work like *Grim Jack* or *Scout*?

JRL: I love Tim. He's a brother. DC comics put us together. I think Tim had read something of mine and suggested it. I'm not certain, to be honest, but it is always great fun to work with Tim. There are a lot of great artists out there, but Tim is a great one with a unique style that really knows how to tell a story through his art. They aren't just pictures in panels, they manage to tell the story by the way they are constructed. He's my favorite artist to work with, and my favorite comic book artist, period.

MFR: How did the development of *Jonah Hex: Two Gun Mojo* come about?

JRL: That was Tim and DC, I think. They teamed us up because as someone said: "He draws like you write."

MFR: What led to the sequel, *Riders of The Worm and Such*?

JRL: Popularity of the first series of Hex comics, Two-Gun Mojo. Success breeds sequels. I like all of the ones we did, but the first, Two-Gun Mojo is my favorite, hands down. Each time we did a Hex series we tried to do something different with it.

MFR: Now you guys also worked on Topps' *Lone Ranger & Tonto* series in the nineties. What was like that? Was it working on Hex that led to that gig?

JRL: Topps was trying out comics, and Hex led us to that gig. I actually wrote two scripts for the Lone Ranger, but by the second Tim had to move on as he had another gig, the artist who worked with me on the second was great, Ted Naifeh. It hit right when Topps decided it was cutting back on comics, perhaps cutting them out altogether, I don't remember exactly. Anyway, that one, which was a Kung-fu Western in San Francisco China-town, was never published.

MFR: One of my personal favorite comics of yours is Dark Horse Comics' *Dead in the West* adaptation, which was illustrated by Jack (Jaxon) Johnson, who has a history that goes back to underground comics, as well drawing historical and war comics. Did you have a choice in him as an artist? Were you aware of his work?

JRL: I always liked Jack's stylized work. I knew Jack a little, and my friend Neal Barrett Jr. did the adaptation. It was cool. Would love to see a new version of it done. I did have a choice, and I was aware of his underground work. I read a few underground comics here and there and thought it would be an interesting idea. It was.

MFR: Avatar has also adapted some of your work in the past, what was it like working with them?

JRL: We made a deal. They did the comics. Pretty much it. I liked the comics, though the artwork, good as it was, sort of got monotonous on *The Drive-In*. Good stuff, but being more suggestive than specific, the white space began to feel like a brain wound after a bit. Again, that's not the artist, it's just that the sort of art wears without color over long spaces. I like black and white a lot, but most comics need color. That's one of the tools that makes them comics. Film black and white is a different matter, and certainly, specific comics in black and white are great, but if there was a comic that needed to be in moody colors, it was *The Drive-In*.

MFR: How involved are you in those comic adaptations of your work?

JRL: I was very involved in some, less in others. By Bizarre Hands was a comic series based on my stories, first done by Dark Horse, later by Avatar, which I think added a few stories. Anyway, I like the idea of that and would love to see it as a TV series.

MFR: Do you have a favorite comic adaptation of your work?

JRL: I'm pretty damn fond of several. *On the Far Side of the Cadillac Desert with Dead Folks* that Tim did for Avatar was a favorite. There have been some Italian adaptations I really love. Western material of mine and horror/sci-fi adaptations

MFR: What are you working on now, comic or noncomic related? Anything you want to talk about?

JRL: There's a possible comic that isn't quite up to bat, yet, but is waiting in the dugout. We'll see. I'm writing another novel for Little Brown/Mulholland. I don't normally talk about something unless I'm finished with it, so nothing to say yet. I do have novels and short story collections coming out. *Jane Goes North* is out from Subterranean, and a short story collection of Hap and Leonard stories, about their youth, is forthcoming, as well as the stand-alone novel in July, *More Better Deals* from Mulholland Books. And then a collection from Subterranean Press titled *Fishing for Dinosaurs*.

Additional Resources

Interviews/Profiles

Cooper, Thomas M. "A Talk with Joe R. Lansdale," *Castle Rock: The Stephen King Newsletter* (August 1989): 1–3.

Iglesias, Gabino. "Joe R. Lansdale Interview," HorrorDNA, January 6, 2012, HorrorDNA.com.

Kinney, Don. "Joe Lansdale's East Texas Tones," *Horror Magazine*, no. 9 (1997): 3–10.

Leighton, Susan. "Holding Court with the Popcorn King," *Fansided* (2019).

Montgomery, Scott. "Above the Influence: An Interview with Joe R. Lansdale," *MysteryPeople*, September 14, 2020.

Rausch, Andrew J. "All Hail the Popcorn King: A Film About Joe R. Lansdale," *Diabolique*, October 10, 2019.

Salov, Marc "Interview with Joe R. Lansdale," *Austin Chronicle*, August 20, 1997.

Slater, Maggie "Interview with Joe R. Lansdale," *Apex Magazine*, May 7, 2013.

Books

Lansdale, Joe R. *Miracles Ain't What They Used to Be*. Oakland: PM Press, 2016.

Leonard, Frances, and Cearley, Ramona. *Conversations with Texas Writers*. Austin: University Press of Texas, 2005. 203–25.

Mynhardt, Joe, and Johnson, Eugene. *It's Alive: Bringing Your Nightmares to Life*. Pittsburgh: Crystal Lake Publishing, 2018.

Mynhardt, Joe, and Johnson, Eugene. *Where Nightmares Come From: The Art of Storytelling in the Horror Genre*. Pittsburgh: Crystal Lake Publishing, 2017.

Rausch, Andrew J. *Methods of Madness: 100 Writers Discuss Their Craft*. BearManor Media, 2019.

Podcasts

Davies, Dave. "*Hap and Leonard* Creator Needed to *Burn Bridges* to Make It as a Writer," *NPR's Fresh Air*, February 24, 2016, https://www.npr.org/2016/02/24/467946095 /hap-and-leonard-creator-needed-to-burn-bridges-to-make-it-as-a-writer.

"Joe R. Lansdale on Do the Work," *The Prolific Writer*, June 8, 2018, https://thepro lificwriter.libsyn.com/the-prolific-writer-065-joe-r-lansdale-on-do-the-work.

"Horror Author Joe R. Lansdale," *Deadman's Tome*, September 5, 2019, https://deadmanstome.net/2019/09/05/horror-author-joe-r-lansdale/.

"Nisi Shawl, Joe R. Lansdale, and Tim Shockey," *The Author's Voice Podcast*, August 2, 2020, https://tunein.com/podcasts/Arts--Culture-Podcasts/The-Authors-Voice -p1329616/.

"Joe R. Lansdale," *The Movie Crypt*, September 7, 2020, https://moviecrypt.libsyn.com /ep-379-joe-r-lansdale.

Documentaries

Oppenheimer, Hansi, *All Hail the Popcorn King* (Austin, Texas: Squee Projects, 2019), film.

Blum, Brian, *Making of "Bubba Ho-Tep"* (Hard Boiled Films, 2004), video.

Index

About the Editors

Andrew J. Rausch is a film journalist and the author of nearly fifty books, including *The Films of Martin Scorsese and Robert De Niro, The Cinematic Misadventures of Ed Wood,* and *Perspectives on Stephen King.* He is an online editor at *Diabolique* magazine and writes a recurring column for *Screem* magazine.

Mark Slade's work has appeared in several publications. He is the author of *Yardbird: A Scratch Williams Mystery,* coauthor of *Screaming Eye Press Presents* and the Barry London novels. He has written audiodramas and recently created the publishing company Screaming Eye Press. He lives in Williamsburg, Virginia, with his wife and daughter.